The Pictorial History of
WORLD WAR II

The Pictorial History of
WORLD WAR II
Charles Messenger

Colour
Library
Direct

Published by
Saturn Book Ltd.
Kiln House
210 New Kings Rd.
London SW6 4NZ

CLD 20443
This edition published
in 1997 for colour
Library Direct, Godalming
Business centre,
Woolsack Way,
Godalming, Surrey GU71XW

ISBN 1 85833 789 5

Printed in China

PAGE 1: *A US flamethrower operator
moves forward to deal with a Japanese
strong-point on a Pacific Island.*

PAGES 2-3: *Typical German
infantrymen in action in Norway in
spring 1940. The front man carries an
MG34 in the light machine-gun role.
Note also his cylindrical gasmask
canister.*

THIS PAGE: *RAF Spitfire pilots. It
was men like these who fought so
gallantly during the Battle of Britain
in late summer 1940 and whom
Winston Churchill dubbed 'The Few'.
Note the different styles of dress.*

Contents

Introduction

World War II was the most widespread and costly war that the world has ever known. There were few people alive at the time around the world whose lives were not directly or indirectly affected by it. While World War I had been widely believed to be the war to end all war, the legacy of it would be the cause of its successor. In some ways, too, 1939-45 paralleled 1914-18, especially in that both began as European conflicts, which then eventually drew in a generally unwilling United States of America. The main weapons with which World War II was fought – the aircraft, submarine, aircraft carrier and tank – were used in World War I. The difference was that 20 years of rapidly developing technology had made them much more efficient by 1939.

Another major difference was that World War II was very much more global in character, especially from December 1941 when the vast Pacific theater came into play. Fighting took place in many more parts of the world, and many more nations became actively involved.

World War II was also very much more total in character. True, civilians had found themselves in the firing line during World War I, as a result of bombing and the sinking of passenger ships at sea, but during 1939-45 they were even more so. The destruction of cities through air attack became common practice, culminating in the dropping of the atomic bombs on Japan in August 1945. Apart, perhaps, from the Turkish treatment of the Armenians, there was no policy of mass genocide in World War I, but Hitler's determination to eradicate the Jewish race in Europe was the darkest shadow cast over the Second World War.

Apart from civilians in Europe and elsewhere being more physically exposed to the war, they were also kept very much more closely in touch with the war by radio which the previous generation did not have. Combat reporters could bring the sounds of battle into their living rooms as, a generation later, television would bring not only the sounds, but the sights of Vietnam to the family fireside. Yet movie newsreels could also give them visual contact with the war. It was thus very much more difficult, for those who wanted to, to pretend that the war was not taking place or keep it at a distance.

As for those who did the fighting, the higher level of technology meant that supporting services became very much larger in proportion to the combat arms, and by war's end, for every GI in the frontline, there were 10 men or women supporting him along the lines of communication. Many of the senior commanders had experienced at first hand the bloody deadlock of trench warfare during 1914-18 and were determined that it should not be repeated. Apart from the Japanese, and, in some circumstances, the Russians, they were generally more careful to avoid unnecessary casualties, and the military losses were usually not as high. Again, technology played a large part in making the war more mobile than it was 20 years before.

Those who actively participated in World War II are now grand-parents. This book serves to remind them, their children and grand-children of what they went through.

CHARLES MESSENGER
London, 1987

ABOVE: *Refugees in Europe. Sights like this were common throughout the war. Many people lost their homes and others even their countries. This upheaval was to remain one of the scars of the war long after 1945.*
LEFT: *The first victim of nuclear war, the Japanese city of Hiroshima photographed late in 1945. Its shadow and that of its fellow victim, Nagasaki, continue to haunt the world to this day.*

RIGHT: *'Day of Infamy.' American warships burn after the Japanese attack on Pearl Harbor on 7 December 1941. Although this attack forced the United States into the war, it was, as in 1917, inevitable that the USA would become embroiled.*

1939-1941

The Axis Triumphant

Chronology 1919-1941

1919	Treaty of Versailles
1922	Mussolini seizes power in Italy
1923	Hitler attempts a putsch in Munich, Germany
1924	Lenin dies and is succeeded by Stalin
1929	Wall Street Crash
1931	Japan invades Manchuria
1932	Roosevelt elected US president
1933	Hitler becomes Chancellor of Germany
1935	Italy invades Abyssinia
1936	Hitler reoccupies the Rhineland
1936-39	Spanish Civil War
1936	Rome-Berlin Axis agreement signed
1938	Nazi takeover in Austria
1938	Munich agreement signed
1939	German annexation of Czechoslovakia completed
1939	German-Soviet Non-Aggression Pact signed
September 1	Hitler invades Poland
September 3	Britain and France declare war on Germany
September 17	Russia invades Poland
November 30	Russia invades Finland
1940	
March 12	Russia and Finland sign peace treaty
April 9	Germany invades Denmark and Norway
May 10	Germany invades France and Low Countries
	Churchill becomes British Prime Minister
May 15	Holland surrenders
May 27	Evacuation from Dunkirk begins
May 28	Belgium surrenders
June 10	Italy declares war and invades Southern France
June 22	France signs armistice with Germany
July 16	Hitler issues orders for invasion of Britain
September 13	Italian troops invade Libya from Egypt
September 15	Climax of Battle of Britain
October 28	Italy attacks Greece through Albania
November 20	Hungary, then Rumania, join the Axis
December 9	British begin to drive the Italians from Egypt
1941	
January 19	British invade Eritrea, East Africa
February 8	Bulgaria joins Axis
March 11	US Lend-Lease Bill becomes law
March 16	British enter Abyssinia
March 24	Rommel launches an offensive in Libya
April 6	Germany invades Yugoslavia, then Greece
April 13	Russia and Japan sign 5-year non-aggression pact
April 29	Pro-Fascist revolt in Iraq, put down by British
May 20	German airborne assault on Crete
June 8	British invade Vichy French Syria

'Action: The German Navy.'
Although Hitler's rapid surface
shipbuilding program in the 1930s
gave the German Navy prestige, it was
the U-boat which became its most
dangerous weapon.

The Causes

When, after over four years' ceaseless thundering, the guns were finally stilled on 11 November 1918, most people believed that the war to end all wars had been fought. Little did they imagine that in just over 20 years they would witness the outbreak of another global conflict in many ways more terrible than World War I. Yet many of the causes of World War II had their roots in the immediate aftermath of 1914-18.

It was United States President Wilson who had put forward a plan for preventing war in the future. This was the League of Nations, which all states, apart from the defeated, were invited to join. Member nations pledged themselves to renounce war as a means of solving problems and any state that broke this pledge would have economic sanctions and other penalties imposed on it. Unfortunately the American people refused to support their president; they believed that Europe was the cause of most of the world's problems and wanted to turn their backs on it. The United States therefore entered a period of self-imposed isolation and did not join the League. Thus, when the 1930s brought outbreaks of aggression in parts of the world the League found itself virtually incapable of stopping or preventing them without American support.

The Treaty of Versailles, which formally brought World War I to an end, imposed harsh terms on the defeated nations, especially Germany. She was forced to pay enormous financial reparations to the victors, especially Belgium and France. She lost her overseas colonies and, worse, part of her territory at home. This was especially so in the east where a large tract of land was given up to the recreated state of Poland, with the result that East Prussia became isolated from the rest

LEFT: *War reparation payments caused galloping inflation in Germany in 1923. The currency values fell from 18,000 marks to the US dollar at the beginning of the year to 4 billion in November.*
BOTTOM LEFT: *There was revolution in Berlin even before the armistice was signed in November 1918. Armed supporters of the Leftist Workers' and Soldiers' Council are seen here in the Unter den Linden, a famous Berlin street.*
RIGHT: *The first National Socialist Party Day, Munich, 28 January 1923. Most of those present were curious bystanders rather than supporters. Munich remained Hitler's headquarters until he came to power.*
BELOW: *Austrian students demonstrate in Vienna at the time of Anschluss in 1938. There was sufficient support for Hitler in the country to enable a bloodless takeover.*

of Germany. Her armaments industry was stripped and severe limitations were placed on the size of her armed forces. Many Germans refused to accept that their army had been defeated and blamed the surrender on the politicians. Others believed that the time had come to follow the example of the Russians and embrace the creed of communism. The result was civil war between left and right. The Kaiser had abdicated just before the end of the war and the government of the newly created republic was for a time powerless to control matters and only did so because the right was prepared to support it against the left. The government, however, remained unpopular with the right because of its acceptance of the Versailles terms. This atmosphere proved a fertile breeding ground for Nazism.

The battle between left and right was not just confined to Germany. Italy did not achieve the territorial gains from Versailles that she had hoped for and her system of democratic government proved weak. Communist agitation led to unrest both in the urban and rural areas and rightwing groups were formed to counter this. Benito Mussolini, a former journalist, soon became the leading rightwing figure and raised his own private army, the Blackshirts. At the end of October 1922, he marched on Rome and the King of Italy invited him to form a government, which he soon turned into an absolute dictatorship. This inspired Hitler, his German counterpart, who attempted a coup in Munich in November 1923. This failed and Hitler was imprisoned, albeit for a short period. Germany was not yet ready for the Nazis.

In the meantime, in Russia, civil war between the Reds and Whites raged on for two years after the end of the war, devastating much of the country. Nevertheless Lenin hoped to be able to export communism abroad and created the Communist International or Comintern for this purpose. In 1920 he attempted an invasion of Poland, but his forces were flung back at the gates of Warsaw. This and the ravages within Russia curbed his designs and he now turned inward in order to consolidate the revolution.

The western European democracies were, although victorious, almost as exhausted, especially economically, as their late enemies. Indeed, their economies never regained their pre-1914 levels. Matters were aggravated by the 1929 Wall Street Crash, whose effects were felt throughout the industrialized world and which brought about the great Depression, which hit Americans and Europeans alike. In the meantime, they made strenuous efforts to reduce the risks of war through negotiations on arms reductions and by strengthening the laws of war in the shape of the Geneva Convention, conferences on international law at The Hague, and various international treaties.

The first rent in the fabric of peace took place in 1931, but not in Europe. The Japanese were increasingly determined to become the dominant power in the Far East and were turning their eyes toward China, which since 1927 had been wracked by civil war between the government of Chiang Kai-shek and the communists under Mao Tsetung. The key lay in the industrialized region of Manchuria which the Japanese Army occupied in the fall of 1931. Since the two nations with major influence in the Far East were the United States of America and the Soviet Union, neither of whom were members of the League of Nations, all the League could do was to make a verbal condemnation, which resulted in Japan leaving the League in 1933 and continuing her efforts to subjugate China.

ABOVE: *Benito Mussolini (1883-1945). Like Hitler in Germany, he exercised an extraordinary charisma over the Italian people. While he did much to make the country run more efficiently, his pride and vanity were to be his downfall.*

RIGHT: *Adolf Hitler (1889-1945). Hitler, unlike many dictators, never awarded himself any decorations, but proudly wore his Iron Cross and wound badge from World War I as these showed that he had been a front soldat. Nazi art, of which this is a good example, considered anything avant-garde as degenerate.*

LEFT: *'In the end Victory stands!' The swastika is a very ancient symbol, used by many religions, and stands for prosperity and creativity. The Nazis mistakenly thought it purely Aryan.*

Am Ende fteht der Sieg!

The Depression did much to help Hitler's cause. In the 1930 German elections he dramatically increased his representation in the Reichstag by almost tenfold. After further elections the German president, the venerable Field Marshal von Hindenburg, invited him, in January 1933, to form a government. Like Mussolini before him, he soon turned Germany into a one-party state and his dictatorship became total with the death of von Hindenburg in August 1934. His first step now was to break the terms of Versailles by setting in motion a major rearmament program, and his plan was to expand and develop the program as the years went by.

Yet it was not Hitler but his fellow dictator Mussolini who initiated the first act of naked aggression when, determined to enlarge his African empire, he invaded Abyssinia in October 1935. Apart from halfhearted economic sanctions, the League of Nations could do nothing. Hitler took advantage of the League's preoccupation with Abyssinia to reoccupy the Rhineland, which had been demilitarized under the terms of Versailles, in March 1936. The League accepted this as a *fait accompli*. This was followed by Hitler's announcement that he was fortifying his western border with France with the Siegfried Line, as a counter to the French Maginot Line. Then, in November 1936, he and Mussolini formed the Rome-Berlin Axis, which later became the Anti-Comintern Pact when Japan joined them. In this same year the Spanish Civil War broke out. Russia sided with the left-leaning Republican Government, while Germany and Italy gave active support to the Nationalist rebels under General Franco, who were, by 1939, firmly in control of the country. Britain and France, neither in a

LEFT: *Republican militiamen fighting Franco's Nationalist rebel troops in Toledo, south of Madrid, in August 1936. German and Italian troops fought on Franco's side, while the Russians fought against them. They all used Spain to test their new weapons, while the western democracies remained as bystanders.*

position to go to war, stood on the sidelines, although there were a number of individual volunteers, including some from the United States, who did go out there to fight, mainly on the Republican side.

Encouraged by the seeming impotence of the western European democracies, Hitler now embarked on the next step of his grand design, union with German-speaking Austria, or *Anschluss*. This he achieved through peaceful invasion in March 1938. He now turned to Czechoslovakia, one of the Versailles creations, which had a sizeable German minority in the Sudetenland region. The Czechs, however, had a well-equipped army and were not prepared to surrender the Sudetenland without a fight. Throughout the summer of 1938 the tension grew. France and Russia sided with the Czechs and general war seemed ever more likely. That it was averted, albeit only temporarily, was thanks to the efforts of British Prime Minister Chamberlain. He negotiated with Hitler in the belief that this was the last of Hitler's territorial ambitions and the result was that Sudetenland was handed over without a fight.

Chamberlain's hopes that war could be avoided were soon dispelled. In March 1939 Hitler forced the Czechs to become a German protectorate and the following month he forced Lithuania to cede Memel to him. In May he and Mussolini reaffirmed their support for one another, signing the Pact of Steel which committed them to assist each other in the event of war. In the meantime Mussolini had invaded and occupied Albania. Hitler now turned to Poland, from which he wanted territory to gain access to East Prussia. The British and French had signed a treaty committing Britain to the defense of Poland in case of German attack. Such support was, however, worthless without the Russians who, in August, signed a neutrality pact with Hitler. At much the same time they signed a similar pact with Japan after repulsing a Japanese incursion into Soviet Mongolia. The Poles remained adamant and Hitler now believed that force was the only way to obtain his objective.

In the early hours of 1 September 1939 Hitler's forces crossed the border into Poland. World War II had begun.

LEFT: *The United States, 1929. Men plead desperately for jobs as the full force of the Depression bites home. The suffering would continue until President Roosevelt launched his New Deal.*

RIGHT: *Japanese troops enter Nanking, December 1937. Unlike in 1931, when the Japanese fabricated an incident in order to invade Manchuria, in 1937 the fighting in North China was started by the Chinese. However, the treatment of the inhabitants of Nanking, reported around the the world as the 'Rape of Nanking,' showed the world how bestial the Japanese could be.*

BELOW: *British Prime Minister Neville Chamberlain returned from Munich in September 1938 believing he had averted war in Europe. Most of Britain agreed with him. Some accused him of appeasement, but he gained his country a year's valuable breathing space in which to rearm.*

Outline of Events 1939-1941

Although fighting eventually took place in many arenas outside the continent of Europe, until December 1941 World War II remained entirely a European conflict. British and French ultimatums to Hitler to withdraw his troops from Poland fell on deaf ears and on 3 September both countries declared war on Germany. Italy, however, remained on the sidelines for the time being and the United States made a public declaration of neutrality on 5 September – the American people were not prepared to sacrifice their new-found prosperity in what they saw as a purely European squabble.

If the Poles hoped that Britain and France would take the pressure off them, they were mistaken. France had long pinned her hopes on the Maginot Line and was not prepared to sacrifice her security by advancing into Germany. As it was, though the Poles fought gallantly, they were outmatched, both in terms of equipment and tactics, by the Germans and by 16 September their capital Warsaw had been surrounded. Next day the Russians invaded from the east and by the end of the month Poland had been totally vanquished. The two victors then split the country between them.

As in 1914, the British sent an expeditionary force across to France and the Allies set about defensive preparations for the German attack westward, which now seemed inevitable. At sea, Hitler's small fleet of U-boats had a number of early successes against British shipping, both naval and commercial. In the air, on the other hand, little happened. No attempt was made to bomb Germany for fear of retaliation and only leaflet raids and ineffectual attacks on shipping were carried out. Indeed, the marked lack of military activity in the west resulted in this period of the conflict being dubbed the Phony War or Sitzkrieg.

In November 1939 attention became focused on Scandinavia. Russian attempts to negotiate an exchange of territory with the Finns so as to obtain additional ports in the northern waters failed and, at the end of the month, Stalin's troops invaded the country. The stubbornness of the Finnish defense surprised both the Russians, whose army was suffering from the effects of Stalin's purges of the late 1930s, and onlookers alike. France and Britain resolved to give help to the embattled Finns, but the refusal of neutral Norway and Sweden to allow troops and supplies to cross their territory put paid to this. Eventually the Finns were forced to give way to Russian superiority in numbers and in March 1940 sought an armistice.

Hitler had wanted to turn on France as soon as possible after his victory over Poland, but was thwarted, firstly by his generals, who

RIGHT: *The rate of Hitler's territorial annexations increased as the 1930s wore on. In the end Britain and France were forced to act.*

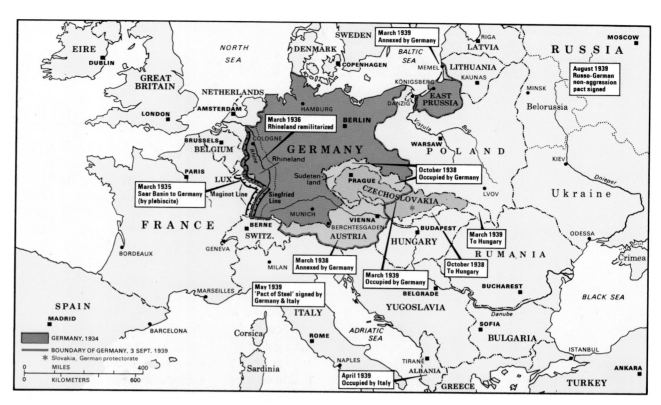

wanted time to implement vital lessons learned in Poland, then by the capture of his attack plans in January 1940, and finally because of debates over how the attack should be mounted. Early in 1940 Allied attention once more turned to Scandinavia, where there was concern that the Germans would seize Norway's ports and secure access to Sweden's valuable iron ore deposits and plans were drawn up to mine Norwegian waters to prevent this. The Germans got wind of this and on 9 April suddenly struck, overrunning neutral Denmark in one day and simultaneously landing troops in Norway. The Allies responded by sending forces to Norway, but they were too ill-equipped and uncoordinated. By early June, this country, too, was in German hands.

In the meantime the long awaited main blow in the west came on 10 May 1940 when the German armies crossed the borders of Belgium, Holland and Luxembourg, thus outflanking the Maginot Line to the south. Holland was quickly overrun, as was Belgium, and the Franco-British armies were soon split by a German armored thrust across the Meuse. After two weeks' fighting the British found themselves pinned with their backs to the English Channel and evacuation was the only answer. Thus followed the so-called Miracle of Dunkirk. The French

fought on, but the situation became increasingly hopeless and on 22 June they signed an armistice. Just before this, Mussolini finally entered the war, invading the south of France.

Britain now stood alone. Hitler hoped that she would give in, but her new prime minister, Winston Churchill, made it clear that he would fight on. Hitler now saw invasion as the only option, but for this to succeed he had to have air supremacy over the English Channel and southern England. Throughout the last part of July, August and the first half of September the Luftwaffe and RAF were locked in battle, but the RAF turned out to be the victor. Hitler was forced to postpone his invasion plans and instead launched the Blitz – bombing attacks by night on Britain's cities. The RAF replied in kind.

While the American people continued to turn their backs on what was happening in Europe, their president, Franklin D Roosevelt, became increasingly sympathetic to Britain. In September 1940, in exchange for the lease of British bases which were in the Caribbean, he gave Churchill 50 old destroyers. These were mainly to help in the Battle of the Atlantic, which, now that the U-boats were able to operate from the French Atlantic ports, had entered a new and omi-

RIGHT: *France had since the late 1920s pinned her hopes on her Maginot Line, named for the minister of war who began building it, as a war deterrent. Troops manning it take their ease.*

LEFT: *The experience of 1917-18 convinced the British that the U-boat was no real threat, provided that convoying was used and escort vessels had Asdic submarine detection equipment (now known as Sonar). At the outbreak of war, however, escorts were too few and anti-U-boat tactics wrong.*

RIGHT: *While the Poles fought gallantly, the German blitzkrieg tactics proved too much for them. German motorcycle troops were an integral part of the Panzer Divisions.*

BELOW: *Men of the British Expeditionary Force (BEF) on their way back from Dunkirk. Although defeated, they were surprised to find that the British people welcomed them like heroes.*

nous phase. Roosevelt realized, however, the threat to the world at large of a triumphant Nazi Germany. At the end of 1940 he declared that the United States must make herself the 'arsenal of democracy' and in March 1941 succeeded in steering the Lend-Lease Bill through Congress, which gave him clearance to supply Britain and China, for her fight against Japan, with war materials. Recipients of Lend-Lease were supposedly to pay for supplies after the war but in the event these debts were largely written off.

As far as the war on land was concerned, the focus switched in late summer 1940 to North Africa. Here the British in Egypt and Palestine

and, indeed, that vital communication link, the Suez Canal, came under threat from large forces in the Italian colonies in East Africa, Abyssinia, and Libya. In August, British Somaliland was quickly overrun and incursions made into the Sudan. Next month the large Italian army in Libya crossed the border with Egypt, advanced 60 miles and halted. In early December, the British, encouraged by Italian inaction, attacked them, drove them back into Libya, and by early February 1941 stood masters of the Libyan province of Cyrenaica. Hitler realized that he would have to bale out his ally and sent a German contingent to Libya under General Erwin Rommel. By this time, though, Mussolini was in trouble elsewhere.

At the end of October 1940 Hitler decided that he must occupy the Rumanian oilfields which were vital to the German war effort. Mussolini considered that these lay in the Italian sphere of influence and, almost in a fit of pique, launched an invasion of Greece from Albania. The Greeks not only resisted the Italians but threw them back into Albania which they virtually overran.

In early April 1941, the Germans invaded first Yugoslavia, which had just undergone a successful pro-Allied coup, and then Greece. In the meantime the British had sent troops from North Africa to help their new ally. It was to no avail and in just two weeks the Greeks had surrendered and the British troops had to be evacuated. Worse, the weakening of the British forces in Libya enabled Rommel to launch an attack, which, by early May, had driven the British back into Egypt.

RIGHT: *The signing of the Nazi-Soviet Pact, 23 August 1939. German Foreign Minister Joachim von Ribbentrop signs while Josef Stalin and Soviet Foreign Minister Vyacheslav Molotov look on.*

BELOW: *Bren gun in the anti-aircraft role near the Egyptian-Libyan border, summer 1940. The numerically very inferior Western Desert Force could do little else but wait for the Italians to invade from Libya.*

ABOVE: *Hitler meets Marshal Henri Pétain, who was to lead the Vichy French Government during 1940-44. His seeming compliance with the Germans led to a conviction for treachery after the war.*

RIGHT: *Winston Churchill became Prime Minister on the day Germany invaded France. His bulldog tenacity and stirring speeches inspired not only the British people, but all those in the Free World and Occupied Europe.*

Crete in the eastern Mediterranean also fell to an audacious German airborne assault. Only in East Africa did the British enjoy any success at this time, recapturing their lost territories, clearing the Italians from Eritrea and restoring the Emperor of Abyssinia to his throne. They also succeeded in putting down a pro-Axis revolt in Iraq and in over-running Vichy French Syria.

In mid-1941 the overall picture was a grim one for the British. They still stood alone against the Axis powers and in spite of President Roosevelt's personal sympathy for their plight and the arms with which he was now supplying them, there still seemed little prospect of America entering the war. Reverses far outnumbered successes and the main question was how long the British could hold on without help.

BELOW: *President Franklin D Roosevelt takes the Oath of Office for his third presidential term, 20 January 1941. He realized that his country was duty-bound to resist Nazi oppression.*

RIGHT: *The* Kreigswinterhilfswerk *or War Winter Relief Fund was a charity which Hitler used to raise more money from the German people for the war effort.*

2. KRIEGSWINTERHILFSWERK 1940/4

Dankt ihnen!
AM TAG DER
Wehrmacht
SONNTAG, DEN 23. MÄRZ 41

Poland

The German invasion of Poland was the first practical demonstration of a new form of warfare, blitzkrieg or 'lightning war.' Its origins lay in the efforts to break the deadlock of trench warfare during 1914-18 and it was evolved through the efforts of a number of military theorists, foremost among whom were the Britons Major General J F C Fuller and Captain Basil Liddell Hart. The Germans took their ideas to heart and, since, because of Versailles, they had to carry out their rearmament virtually from scratch, they were less hidebound than the armies of other nations. The driving force behind the implementation of blitzkrieg was a comparatively junior officer, Heinz Guderian, and, in essence, the concept was directed toward the dislocation of the enemy's forces rather than just their wholesale destruction. This called for fast-moving armored columns, supported by ground-attack aircraft, especially the Ju87 Stuka divebomber, which were used as aerial artillery. It must, however, be stressed that lack of raw materials meant that at no time during the war were the armored or Panzer divisions any more than a fraction of the German Army, the bulk of which would continue to rely primarily on its own feet and on its horsedrawn transport.

Having obtained Russian assurances that they would remain neutral, Hitler had mobilized his forces in mid-August 1939, as he planned to invade Poland on 26 August. Eleventh hour attempts by France and Britain to find a peaceful solution and unwillingness by Mussolini to go to war, caused a last-minute postponement, but one or two sabotage units did not get the order in time, which put the Poles on their guard. These units had the task of faking frontier incidents in order to give Hitler the pretext to invade and, after Hitler had given his final confirmatory orders, they carried out their tasks on the night of 31 August/1 September. Next morning, preceded by Luftwaffe attacks on communications targets and airfields, German ground forces then crossed the frontier in several places.

The German thrusts were led by the Panzer divisions which quickly cut deep into the Polish defenses, creating huge pockets which were reduced by the follow-up foot-marching infantry divisions. The Poles

resisted with desperate bravery, but the sheer speed and pace of the German attack proved too much. By the 8th the German Panzers had already reached the outskirts of Warsaw and soon the bulk of the Polish forces were entrapped by two huge pincers. Warsaw, however, refused to surrender, and so the Germans bombarded it from the air and ground. On the 17th, Stalin, taken by surprise over the speed of the German advance and not wanting Hitler's troops sitting on his borders, invaded Poland from the east. By the end of the month the fighting in Poland was all over.

Hitler and Stalin divided the country between them along the line of the River Bug. At the same time, the Russians also occupied the Baltic

ABOVE: *Polish 6-ton Vickers tanks with twin machine-gun turrets. Poland had some 660 tanks at the outbreak of war, but most were too light and they were too dispersed to have much effect on the Germans. The helmets are an indication of the French influence on the Polish Army.* LEFT: *1 September 1939. German troops break down a Polish border barrier, which is adorned by the Polish eagle. Because of border incidents a week earlier, the Poles knew an attack was coming.*

RIGHT: *Polish prisoners of war being moved to a camp. The anxiety and bewilderment can be clearly seen on their faces. Many Poles were captured in the pockets created by the German Panzer Divisions.*

BELOW: *Warsaw as it looked in 1945. Some of the damage was caused by German bombs and artillery fire in September 1939. By war's end this could have been almost any city in Europe.*

states of Estonia, Latvia and Lithuania. Both dictators, determined that Poland should never rise again as an independent state, now embarked on a systematic purging of the country's upper classes and intelligentsia. Some, though, did manage to escape and joined the banner of the Polish Government-in-Exile, which was set up by General Wladyslaw Sikorski in Paris. Apart from providing a haven after defeat, the Western Allies had not been able to offer material support or do anything to aid the Poles.

The Russo-Finnish War

The next bout of fighting on land was very different in character to what had happened in Poland and was to give the Russians a severe shock. The origins of the conflict lay in the Russian desire to improve their defenses against a feared attack from the west. At the beginning of October 1939 they demanded from the Finns a lease on the island of Hango, which guards the Gulf of Finland and thus the approach to Leningrad; the western part of the Rybachi Peninsula, which likewise covers the port of Murmansk in the Barents Sea; and territory on the Karelian Isthmus north of Leningrad. The Finns refused to accept this and on 30 November the Russians attacked on a wide front.

BELOW: *Josef Stalin (1879-1953) in typical pose. He never trusted Hitler nor his own people and his purges of the latter in the late 1930s meant that his army had a difficult time in Finland.*
BELOW RIGHT: *Field Marshal Baron Carl von Mannerheim (1867-1951) inspired his countrymen in the defense against the Russian onslaught. Later, as President of Finland, he would make final peace with Russia.*

Since the Russians could deploy one million men and the Finns only 175,000 the result should have been a foregone conclusion, but it was not. For a start, the Russian forces were suffering from low morale caused by Stalin's purges, which had stripped them of almost all their talent. The Finns, on the other hand were fighting on territory and in conditions that they knew well. Thus, during the early weeks of the fighting, the Russians were thrown back or halted all along the long border. This was especially so in the south, where their efforts to break through the Mannerheim Line, named after the Finnish commander, met with heavy casualties and no progress. In particular, the Finnish ski troops had notable successes against the slow-moving enemy masses.

The epic David-versus-Goliath contest caught the imagination of the free world, both in Western Europe and in the United States. Americans volunteered to go to Finland, and the British and French, conscious of the lack of material support which they had given Poland, began to organize forces and supplies to be sent. The problem was that neutral Norway and Sweden would not allow the passage of men and supplies across their territory and there was no suitable Finnish port where troops could be landed, one of the few Russian successes

having been the capture of the port of Petsamo in the Barents Sea. Before these problems could be overcome or the earmarked forces trained for the type of winter warfare being waged, Russian superiority in numbers eventually told. They now concentrated their efforts on the Karelian Isthmus and in early March 1940 were able to outflank it by crossing the icebound Viipuri Bay.

On 12 March 1940 hostilities formally came to an end. By the Treaty of Moscow the Finns were forced to give in to all the original Russian demands and also surrender Viipuri as well. This did not mean, though, that they were prepared to accept this redrawn map as any more than a very temporary state of affairs. In little over a year they would be at war once more with their giant neighbor.

ABOVE: *Quick-moving Finnish ski troops, here wearing gasmasks, proved a constant thorn in the Russian flesh.*
LEFT: *A shocked Russian prisoner. The incompetence of his commanders caused the death of many of his fellows.*

BELOW: *Finnish women volunteers support their menfolk. In the end patriotism was not enough to prevent the Russian Bear from achieving his object.*

The War at Sea

The outbreak of the war at sea was not marked by any mighty clash of battle fleets. Hitler, although he had as a result of German rearmament some impressive surface warships, had too much respect for the power of the Royal Navy to want to risk them in this way. Rather, he correctly saw how dependent Britain was on her mercantile trade and it was this that he concentrated on. But, once again because of shortage of resources, his main weapon, the U-boat fleet, was comparatively small, with little more than 50 boats at the outbreak of war. Yet they would quickly make their presence felt.

On 3 September 1939, the day that Britain declared war, a U-boat, albeit in error, sunk the passenger liner *Athenia* off the coast of southern Ireland. The British immediately instituted the convoy system which had proved so successful during 1917-18, but their weakness lay in lack of escort ships and the correct tactics for hunting and destroying the U-boats. Initially they sent out anti-U-boat task forces built round an aircraft carrier, but gave this up within three weeks after the carrier *Ark Royal* had had a near miss from a torpedo, and another, *Courageous*, had been sunk. Worse was to follow in October when the U-boat ace Günther Prien penetrated the Home Fleet anchorage at Scapa Flow off the north of Scotland and sank the battleship *Royal Oak*. The Germans also employed surface raiders, which caused havoc not just in the Atlantic, but elsewhere as well. One of the few British naval successes of this period of the war came in December, when three British warships managed to corner the pocket battleship *Graf Spee* by the River Plate in South America and force her captain to scuttle her. Yet convoying did manage to contain losses in ships.

The Norwegian campaign did see some dramatic destroyer-versus-destroyer actions, with losses on both sides, but the Allies would have suffered more if the U-boats present had not had trouble with their torpedoes. The fall of France, however, saw a dramatic swing in favor of the U-boats since they could now use the French Atlantic ports. During the winter of 1940-41 shipping losses rose dramatically and the U-boat captains called it their 'first happy time.'

ABOVE: *The first German U-boat ace of World War II, Günther Prien, whose U.47 sank the British battleship* Royal Oak *in Scapa Flow. Even Churchill called him 'the redoubtable Prien.' He and his crew were killed on 8 March 1941 when his U.47 was sunk by HMS* Wolverine, *but his death was kept secret from his countrymen for many months.*
LEFT: *Trapped in Montevideo harbor, the Captain of the* Graf Spee *chose to scuttle her rather than allow her to be sunk by the British. He himself committed suicide.*

The surface threat remained, however. In May 1941, the Germans decided to concentrate some of their capital ships in a squadron based on Brest. This meant bringing the *Bismarck*, Germany's only true battleship, and the heavy cruiser *Prinz Eugen* round from the Baltic. British air reconnaissance spotted them and a Royal Navy squadron containing some of Britain's finest ships was sent to intercept. In the battle that followed the battlecruiser *Hood* was sunk, but the *Bismarck* was damaged. Harried by British ships, she was sunk on 27 May. The *Prinz Eugen* escaped, however, and joined the *Scharnhorst* and *Gneisenau* in Brest, where the three continued to remain a serious threat to Allied convoys.

Gradually the necessary technical aids were developed to combat the U-boats, but it was only slowly realized that crucial to winning the Battle of the Atlantic was long-range air cover and, until this could be provided, shipping in mid-Atlantic, the so-called Black Gap, would remain especially vulnerable. For the British an encouraging sign, as 1941 wore on, was that the Americans showed increasing willingness to assist in convoy escort, at least on their side of the Atlantic.

ABOVE: *One of the epics of the early months of the war at sea. The British destroyer HMS* Glowworm, *outgunned by the German cruiser* Hipper, *in her death throes off Norway, 8 April 1940. Her captain was awarded a posthumous Victoria Cross.*
LEFT: *Allied submarines also had their successes. The Free Norwegian* Ula *after a successful cruise. Her impovised flag represents 11 ships and one U-boat sunk, and two raids on shore.*

Denmark and Norway

After the devastating victory over Poland there was, as far as the Germans were concerned, a lull in the fighting. True, as we shall see in the next section, Hitler wanted to turn against the western Allies immediately, but various factors prevented this. The Germans, like Britain and France, were mere bystanders during the Russo-Finnish war, but after its conclusion Scandinavia continued to remain a focus of attention for both sides.

Norway was important to both Germany and the Allies, because much of the vital Swedish iron-ore deposits passed through the country to the port of Narvik. Norway, too, as was to be later proved, was like an aircraft carrier which could dominate the sea west of Greenland. The Norwegians, however, had no intention of being drawn into the war, and when they were, it was because of circumstances over which they had no control. Denmark was in the same position.

The first contact with the war that Norway had, apart from her refusal to allow troops going to Finland's assistance to cross her territory, came in February 1940, when a British destroyer seized a German merchant vessel, housing captured sailors from British merchant vessels in a Norwegian fjord. It was this that prompted Hitler to finalize plans for the capture of both Norway and Denmark, which together not only provided a natural stepping stone but also occupied an important position in the Baltic. The seizure of Norway would also safeguard Germany's vital iron ore supplies from Sweden. France and Britain were only too aware of this and drew up plans to mine Norwegian waters, and also gathered together troops with a view to occupying the country should the Germans try to invade.

On 7 April both sides finally put their respective plans into operation, but the Allies had no idea what the Germans had up their sleeves. That day British aircraft tried without success to bomb the German ships sailing for Norway, but on the 8th the British destroyer *Glowworm* rammed the cruiser *Hipper*, causing her some damage and sinking in the process, and a German transport was sunk. Next day, with the Luftwaffe hovering ominously above, three transports sailed into the harbor of Copenhagen where troops landed and by the end of the day the Germans had secured the whole of Denmark without a shot being fired. At the same time, amphibious landings were made at Oslo, Kristiansand, Bergen, Trondheim and Narvik, while the air base at Stavanger was seized by parachute troops. Norwegian coastal batteries managed, however, to sink the brand-new heavy cruiser *Blücher* and to inflict damage on two other vessels.

BELOW LEFT: *Norway marked the first operational use of paratroops by the Germans. Their main task, to seize the Norwegian airfields at Fornebu, outside Oslo, and Sola, outside Stavanger, was quickly achieved.*
BELOW RIGHT: *Once this had occurred Ju 52 transport aircraft with reinforcements and supplies could begin using the airfields.*

Norway, which had not been at war since 1814, was caught totally unprepared, but her larger size compared to Denmark, did give her time and space in which to organize some resistance and one of the first steps was to ask for British and French aid. Troops, which had been standing by, therefore set sail. In the meantime there were fierce destroyer actions off Narvik in which the British came off best, sinking 10 German ships for the loss of two of their own.

The main German land thrust was launched from the Oslo area, the idea being that it should link up with the landings farther north. Having seized airfields on the first day, the Germans could and did enjoy air supremacy throughout the campaign. Another major advantage they had was that their troops were far better organized, trained and equipped than the *ad hoc* forces that the French and British had been able to scrape together. Furthermore, the Allies suffered from a cumbersome and disjointed command structure, which meant that there was a distinct lack of coordination among the troops involved in the various landings.

The first Allied landing was by British troops at Harstad, which faced Narvik, on the Lofoten Islands, on 15 April. Indeed, this force would also be the last to leave Norway, but their efforts to reduce the German forces holding Narvik were to be in vain. Next day, another force was landed well to the south at Namsos and, farther south still, additional troops were put ashore at Andalsnes. The idea was that these forces would move inland and, in combination with Norwegian troops, halt the German drive north and also reduce the German force near Trondheim. Unfortunately, such was German air supremacy that it proved impossible to land essential heavier equipment and this, combined with lack of experience of the Norwegian winter, meant that the move inland was much too slow. In particular, the Namsos force became quickly unstuck when the Germans managed to slip through two destroyers filled with troops, who were able to carry out a successful outflanking movement. By the end of the month both forces found themselves bypassed and with their backs to the sea. There was no option but to evacuate them.

Til vakt ved Nordens grense mot øst!
SS-SKIJEGERBATALJON NORGE

ABOVE: *Norway's best troops, as with the Finns, were her ski troops and the Germans later recruited some for service on the Eastern Front with the Waffen-SS.*
LEFT: *Likewise, the Germans found that the only way to patrol the Norwegian countryside effectively in winter was on skis.*

ABOVE: *British troops with a French sailor in Norway. Many of the British troops were only partly trained Territorials and ill-equipped for fighting in the snowbound Norwegian terrain. The French, who sent two brigades of Chasseurs Alpins and a Foreign Legion battalion, fared better.*
RIGHT: *The harbor at Narvik, scene of desperate battles between opposing destroyers at the beginning of the campaign. One of the few Allied successes was the capture of Narvik by French and Norwegian troops on 28 May 1940.*

This left merely the Allied lodgment in the Narvik area, although scattered forces, Norwegian and British, did do their best to hold up the main German drive north. The fighting around Narvik continued as late as 8 June when the last Allied troops left, and the Norwegians had no option but to surrender.

Two more countries now lay under Hitler's thrall and both set up governments-in-exile in London. Whereas King Haakon of Norway believed that he could better inspire his people by fighting on from outside, his fellow monarch, Christian of Denmark, felt that his duty lay in keeping up the morale of his people by remaining in Copenhagen. In both cases, however, strong resistance movements were soon set up in order to harry the occupying forces as much as possible. For the British and French, there was no time to digest the lessons of Norway. Hitler had already struck a devastating blow elsewhere.

ABOVE: *German infantry behind a PzKw Mk II tank. Although the Germans used few tanks in Norway, the Allies, who had none of their own and few antitank weapons, were virtually powerless against them.*
RIGHT: *Vidkun Quisling (seated) at his trial for treachery in September 1945. He collaborated with the Germans over the invasion of his country and then became their puppet prime minister. So infamous was he that his name entered the English language. He was executed in November 1945.*

Hitler Turns West

Hitler, having hoped that the Western Allies might, as a result of Poland, change their minds about war against Germany, issued orders in early October 1939 for an attack on France and the Low Countries. He wanted it launched as soon as possible and envisaged a repeat of 1914, the only difference being that Holland was now to be included in the large enveloping movement. The fact that Belgium and Holland were neutral states made, as in 1914, no difference.

At the end of October Hitler told his generals that he wanted the attack launched on 12 November. They, however, did not consider that they would be ready before the end of the year. The Western Allies were a very much more formidable enemy than Poland had been and one of the main lessons to come out of that campaign had been the need for more Panzer divisions, which could not be raised overnight. It had been also recognized that the lighter makes of German tank were ineffective, except for reconnaissance, and more medium tanks were needed. This was partially solved by using Czech tanks, with which the new Panzer divisions were mainly equipped. Transferring the troops from the east would also take time. The German forces were to be organized into three army groups, A, B and C. Originally von Bock's Army Group B was given the leading role of attacking through the Low Countries and then swinging south into France and thrusting west of Paris in order to get round the back of the bulk of the Allied line. For this von Bock was given all the available armor. Army Group A under Gerd von Rundstedt was to guard von Bock's southern flank and von Leeb's Army Group C, the weakest of the three, would make feints against the Maginot Line. Von Rundstedt believed, though, that a more effective main thrust could be mounted through the wooded and hilly Ardennes area in southern Belgium. As well as masking forward movement, this approach could also produce surprise because the Ardennes was generally regarded as being unsuitable for tanks. It was von Rundstedt's chief of staff, von Manstein, who had originally conceived this plan and gradually Hitler began to give more weight to Army Group A, and eventually agreed that the attack should be postponed until late January.

ABOVE: *Another typical example of German art employed as propaganda. Shown, right to left, are a Hitler Youth member, an SA man and a Panzer soldier.*
RIGHT: *Hitler with some of his inner military circle at the end of 1940. From the right: Wilhelm Keitel (Chief of Staff of the Armed Forces throughout the war), Hitler and Walther von Brauchitsch (Commander-in-Chief of the Army, 1938-41). The tall figure in the background is Friedrich Paulus, then Deputy Chief of Staff but later the defender of Stalingrad.*

LEFT: *The German equivalent of the Maginot Line was the Siegfried Line. The dragon's teeth shown here make a formidable tank obstacle.*

RIGHT: *This scene of British troops in France during the winter 1939-40 could have been the Western Front 1915-17 apart from minor details. The rum ration is being issued; usually it was taken in tea.*

35

LEFT: *Dutch artillery. Dutch guns were obsolete even by 1914 standards and it is hardly surprising that the Dutch troops were unable to stand up to the German invasion and caved in very quickly.*
BELOW: *Hitler with heroes of the German glider assault on the Belgian fortress of Eben Emael. To prepare for the operation an exact replica was built. The majority of these men have just been decorated with the Knight's Cross.*

On 10 January 1940, a light aircraft carrying a German staff officer with the plan was forced down by bad weather on to Belgian soil. He partially burned the plan before capture, but the risk that the Allies now knew his intentions was too great and Hitler began to pay serious attention to von Manstein's idea. The result was a new plan dated 24 February. Von Bock would still overrun Holland and northern Belgium, while von Rundstedt, now given the bulk of the armor, would make the decisive thrust through the center. Norway, however, prevented the plan from being put into immediate effect.

The Allies had been expecting the Germans to repeat their 1914 plan and believed that the decisive battles would take place in the north. Accordingly they positioned their best troops, including the British, here. In order to give themselves more room to maneuver they decided that as soon as the Germans attacked they would move these northern forces into Belgium and take up a position along the River Dyle. The problem with this was that the Belgians refused to allow their neutrality to be jeopardized and would not permit any reconnaissance on their territory. It was also clear that both the British and French had not understood the lessons of Poland and had little appreciation of the sheer pace of the blitzkrieg style of warfare. As the winter of 1939-40 wore on, there was little attempt to train for maneuver warfare and most activity concentrated on digging anti-tank defenses. The French, in particular, having believed for such a long time in the invincibility of the Maginot Line, had become wholly

LEFT: *Rotterdam, seen from the docks, burns after the tragic air raid which took place on 14 May 1940. A large area of the city was devastated and there were many civilian casualties.*
BELOW: *French refugees flee in the face of the German attack. Few had anywhere definite to go to and they created a large problem for the Allied forces by blocking the roads. Attacks on them by German aircraft created panic and compounded the problem.*

defensive-minded. Worse, the nation was gripped by an increasing malaise. As the months rolled by and nothing seemed to happen, the war became boring and morale dropped.

Both in terms of numbers and quality of weapons, the Allies were not at a disadvantage. Indeed, they had significantly more tanks, but, unlike their enemy, they were scattered rather than concentrated, and their armored formations were generally not sufficiently trained. The command structure, too, was unnecessarily complicated and hardly tailored to the high-speed campaign that was about to be fought.

As winter turned to spring a German attack seemed increasingly more likely, but many people had a wistful belief that perhaps Hitler would not attack after all. On 9 May 1940, however, Hitler passed the codeward 'Danzig' to his troops. Plan Yellow, as the operation was called, was to be mounted the next day.

The Fall of France

Preceded by Luftwaffe attacks on Allied airfields, the German Army thrust across the borders of Holland, Belgium and Luxembourg at dawn on 10 May 1940. The Allies countered by deploying their northern armies to the River Dyle. The Belgian forward defenses were quickly penetrated thanks to dramatic airborne *coups de main* on the supposedly impregnable fortress of Eben Emael south of Maastricht and on two vital bridges over the Albert Canal, with the result that soon the Belgians were scurrying back toward the Dyle. The Dutch, like the Danes and Norwegians before them, had not fought a war for well over a century, and were bemused from the start. By the 14th the Germans were at the outskirts of Rotterdam and demanding its surrender. This was slow in coming and when it did, bombers were already en route for the city. Messages ordering them to abort their attack did not get through and the result was the devastation of much of Rotterdam. It was a portent, like Warsaw, of things to come. As it was, the immediate result was that the Dutch caved in. In the meantime the Allies stood firm on the Dyle, still convinced that the German main effort was in the north.

Army Group A, led by its seven Panzer divisions, had succeeded in getting through the Ardennes with little trouble and by the evening of the 12th were closing up to the River Meuse. Here the French were well positioned, but continuous attacks by Stukas enabled the Germans to establish toeholds on the far bank by late on the following day. Too slow in organizing counterattacks, the French allowed the Germans to get their tanks across and by first light on the 15th these were ready to break out of their bridgeheads. In the meantime the Allies mounted gallant but costly and unsuccessful attempts by aircraft to slow down the German momentum by attacking key bridges on their main lines of communication.

Yet there was some nervousness among the German high command. If the armor was allowed to get too far ahead of the main body it would be cut off. This, in fact, was what the Allies tried to do, but their reactions were too slow. In spite of a temporary halt order, Guderian, commanding XIX Panzer Corps, did manage to obtain a 24-hour reprieve and by the end of the 16th had penetrated 25 miles, throwing the French forces opposing him into utter confusion.

On the 15th the Allies finally woke up to the threat in the south and began to pull back in the north to the River Escaut. Within three days

ABOVE: *The Allied Commander-in-Chief, General Maurice Gamelin, and Viscount Gort, commanding the BEF. Gamelin was dismissed from his command on 19 May 1940 and replaced by General Maxime Weygand.*

BELOW: *Compared with the Dutch field gun shown on page 36, the British 25-pounder proved to be one of the outstanding field pieces of the war. Here it is seen in action in France in May 1940.*

ABOVE: *The Ju 87 Stuka divebomber was largely used by the Germans as aerial artillery in support of the swiftly moving mechanized columns on the ground. A Stuka attack was a terrifying experience and this effect was increased by the fitting of sirens on the Stuka's wings. The noise made as a Stuka dived was often enough to make troops break.*

RIGHT: *This map shows how the German armies swept through France after the BEF had been evacuated from Dunkirk. It should be noted that the Italians only invaded on the eve of the armistice and were largely held up by the French defenses.*

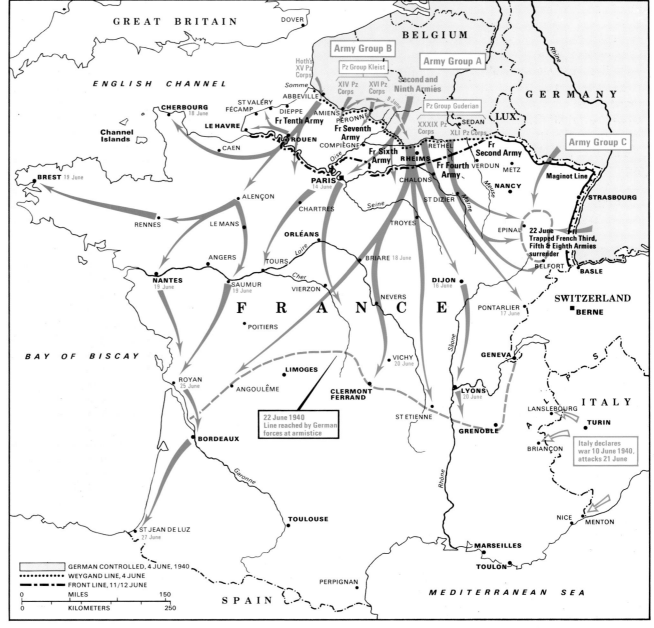

the Germans had opened up a gap in the Allied line between Douai and the River Somme, and, with orders to advance once more, no less than five Panzer divisions headed for this gap. The British now organized a counterattack, using their one tank brigade in France, and this was launched against 7th Panzer Division, commanded by Erwin Rommel, at Arras on 21 May. For a few hours the Germans were caught off balance, but the British forces were too weak to make this more than a very temporary setback.

The British commander, Lord Gort, now realized that his army was in very real danger of being cut off with its back to the sea. If Britain was to be able to fight on her army must be kept in being and hence Churchill agreed that the army should be evacuated back to Britain. Accordingly the British Expeditionary Force (BEF) withdrew to the area of Dunkirk while a motley collection of ships, everything from warships to pleasure craft, was organized to bring troops back across the Channel. At this moment, rather than allow the victorious Panzer divisions to drive the BEF into the sea, Hitler gave the task to Hermann Göring's Luftwaffe on the grounds that after its drive across France, the armor would be in urgent need of maintenance before it could overrun the rest of the country. This, and the courage of the crews of the evacuation ships, probably saved the BEF. Although it had to leave all of its heavy equipment behind, no less than 225,000 British and 103,000 Allied troops were successfully evacuated during the period 27 May–4 June

LEFT: *General Heinz Guderian, driving force behind the German Panzer arm. He believed that an armor commander should be close behind his leading troops. Here he is in his command vehicle, with an Enigma cipher machine in the foreground.*

BELOW: *German troops cross the Meuse on 13 May 1940. An early forcing of this river, crucial to the German plan, was achieved by close harmonization between Guderian's XIX Panzer Corps and the Stukas of II and VIII Air Corps.*

Through an inferno of bombs and shells the B.E.F. is crossing the Channel from Dunkirk—in history's strangest armada

Gracie goes to America

TENS OF THOUSANDS SAFELY HOME ALREADY

Many more coming by day and night

SHIPS OF ALL SIZES DARE THE GERMAN GUNS

UNDER THE GUNS OF THE BRITISH FLEET, UNDER THE WINGS OF THE ROYAL AIR FORCE, A LARGE PROPORTION OF THE B.E.F. WHO FOR THREE DAYS HAD BEEN FIGHTING THEIR WAY BACK TO THE FLANDERS COAST, HAVE NOW BEEN BROUGHT SAFELY TO ENGLAND FROM DUNKIRK.

Tired, dirty, hungry they came back —unbeatable

THREE DESTROYERS LOST
As Navy helps B.E.F.

Signposts to be removed

STOP PRESS

ABOVE AND INSET: *The newspaper headlines appear in almost stark contrast to the columns of seemingly dejected British troops waiting on the sands outside Dunkirk for the ships to take them home.*
RIGHT: *Hitler in Paris in June 1940 at his hour of greatest triumph. He changed his mind over having a victory parade in Paris, believing this would inflame the French and discourage the British from making peace.*

For a few days there were thoughts of sending a second expeditionary force to France and, indeed, many of the French troops who had been evacuated did return, but the situation quickly became worse. The Germans now turned south, thrusting on a broad front across the whole of France. Paris, which had been declared an open city, was entered on 14 June, Dijon on the 16th and Lyons on the 20th. The final straw came on 10 June, when Mussolini, seeing that there were easy pickings to be had, entered the war and invaded the French Riviera on 20 June. The French were now forced to sue for an armistice and this was signed with Hitler himself present on the 22nd in – to add insult to injury – the very same railway carriage that had been used to sign that of November 1918.

France was now split in two, the northern half occupied by the Germans and the southern, which was allowed to rule itself. This became known as Vichy France after the town which held the new government under that aged hero of World War I, Marshal Pétain. All the French garrisons abroad were also expected to be subservient to Vichy and most were. Yet, there were Frenchmen who could not accept this defeat and were determined to fight on. Under General Charles de Gaulle, who was under-secretary for war in the last French government, they hoisted the Free French banner in London, where they joined the growing number of governments-in-exile.

Britain was now alone and it seemed that nothing could save her from the darkness which covered the continent of Europe.

The Battle of Britain

After the fall of France Hitler hoped that Britain could be persuaded to abandon the struggle, but Churchill made it clear that she would fight on to the end. There now seemed to be no option open to the Germans other than a cross-Channel invasion.

On 16 July 1940 the details of Operation Sealion, as it was called, were issued. In order to secure the Channel the German and Italian navies were to tie down the Royal Navy in the North Sea and Mediterranean, and the Channel was to be sealed with mines at both ends. The German Navy was to scour the waterways of Europe for suitable troop-carrying craft, while the troops earmarked for the invasion were to carry out extensive training in amphibious landings. By far the most vital role was that given to the Luftwaffe. No invasion would be possible without first establishing air supremacy and this was what Göring had to achieve.

While the Luftwaffe had a major advantage in numbers of aircraft and could now operate from bases in northern France, it did not have things all its own way at the outset. For a start, the main German fighter, the Me109, was well matched by the Spitfire, and the British Hurricane outclassed the other German fighter, the twin-engined Me110. The German bombers had limited range and payload and the fuel capacity of the fighters meant that they could not stay over England for more than a very limited time. Most important of all was the chain of radar stations around the British coasts, which could give sufficient warning of approaching enemy aircraft for the fighters to get airborne and intercept them.

ABOVE LEFT: *A typical Luftwaffe bomber aircrewman. He is the equivalent of a top sergeant.*
BELOW LEFT: *Some of 'The Few' pose with a Spitfire. They are members of a Polish squadron. Three Polish squadrons fought during the Battle, with great gallantry.*
ABOVE: *Paul Nash's painting* Battle of Britain. *This is what the bombing looked like to the British people on the ground.*
RIGHT: *A Heinkel 111 bomber over the East End of London, late summer 1940. The bombers were aiming at the London docks, but the East End was also the poorest part of London and was to suffer grievously from the early German attacks on the capital.*

LEFT: *RAF Fighter Command headquarters at Stanmore, just north of London, was the British nerve center for the Battle of Britain. Here all the plots of German attacks were fed and decisions made as to how many squadrons of fighters should be put up against them.*
BELOW: *As an RAF fighter pilot climbs out of his Hurricane after a sortie, his ground crew are already at work, refueling and rearming his aircraft. Pilots were sometimes making seven or eight sorties a day during the height of the battle.*

During the last part of July Göring tried to lure the British fighters out over the Channel by attacking convoys. The British stopped sending convoys by this route and refused to be drawn. On 13 August the battle itself really started. Göring recognized the value of the radar stations and attacked these and airfields, the other obvious target. During the next three weeks the blue skies – for it was a glorious summer – above the south of England were seldom free of contrails. The Germans were losing more aircraft than the RAF, but it was the

LEFT: *Luftwaffe fighter pilots also had their successes. Here one describes how he shot down an RAF fighter. In terms of quality, there was probably little to choose between the pilots of either side.*
BELOW: *An RAF man inspects the nosecone of an He111, which has been shot down and refurbished. The only way really to establish the weak points of an enemy aircraft is to be able to fly it and put it through its paces.*

loss of pilots rather than machines which was worrying the British and more so as each day passed. It became a question of how many more days the RAF could hold out against the constant pressure. Then, on 7 September, the Germans made a fatal tactical mistake.

Two weeks earlier a German bomber had released its bombload on London through a navigational error. Believing that the enemy was now beginning to attack cities Churchill ordered retaliation in kind, and on the night of 25/26 August RAF Bomber Command attacked Berlin.

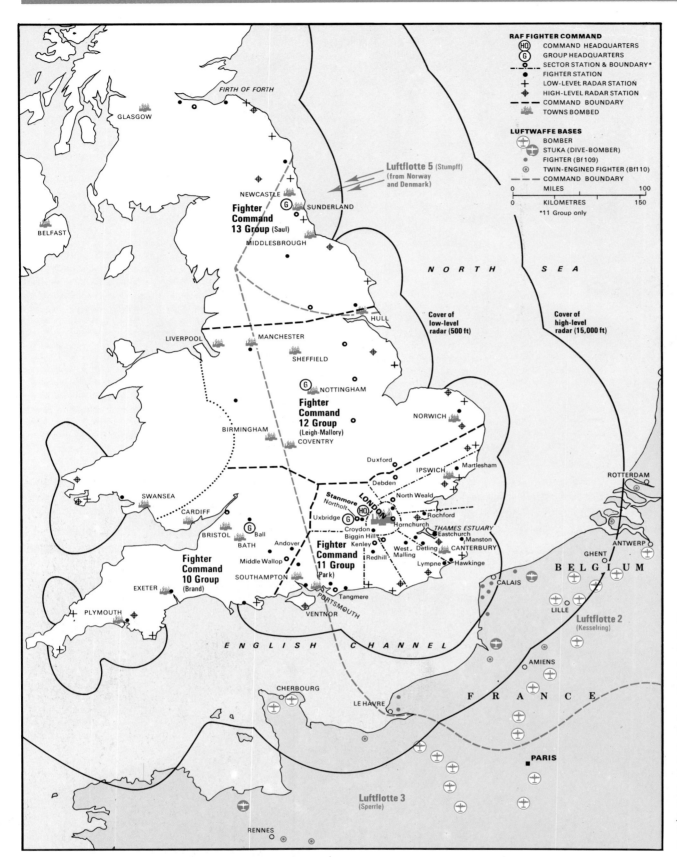

RAF FIGHTER COMMAND
(HQ) COMMAND HEADQUARTERS
(G) GROUP HEADQUARTERS
SECTOR STATION & BOUNDARY*
• FIGHTER STATION
+ LOW-LEVEL RADAR STATION
✚ HIGH-LEVEL RADAR STATION
COMMAND BOUNDARY
TOWNS BOMBED

LUFTWAFFE BASES
BOMBER
STUKA (DIVE-BOMBER)
• FIGHTER (Bf 109)
TWIN-ENGINED FIGHTER (Bf110)
COMMAND BOUNDARY

MILES 0 ——— 100
KILOMETRES 0 ——— 150
*11 Group only

LEFT: *This map shows how the Battle of Britain was fought. No 11 Group consistently took the brunt of the Luftwaffe's attacks, with No 12 especially and No 10 providing an immediate reserve. No 13, after Luftflotte 5 had suffered heavy casualties in the early phases, became relatively quiet, and was used to rest exhausted squadrons who had been in the front line.*
BELOW LEFT: *Heinkels in formation over British skies. If they were to have any chance of warding off RAF fighters, it was essential that they flew in tight formation in order to provide allround protection.*

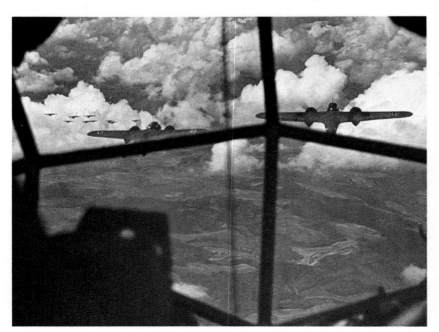

Furious because Göring had boasted that Germany's capital was impregnable, Hitler ordered the bombing of London. Consequently, on 7 September the Germans began daylight and night attacks on the city. This gave the RAF airfields and the radar stations a much needed breathing space.

The climax of the battle came on 15 September. Göring sent over two large waves of bombers, each with a big fighter escort. Both were broken up by the RAF before they reached their targets. This caused Göring to believe that this was one battle that he could not win. Hitler was forced to postpone his invasion indefinitely and now, still using the Luftwaffe, set about trying to break the will of the British people.

'Never has so much been owed by so many to so few,' declaimed Churchill, and forevermore the Battle of Britain pilots were to be known as 'The Few.' Yet they represented not just the RAF but the dominions of Canada, Australia and New Zealand, as well as other parts of the British Empire. Pilots from the occupied countries in Europe, especially Poland and France, took part, and last, but not least, there was a band of United States volunteer pilots, who fought in the RAF's two Eagle squadrons, a number of whom gave their lives.

LEFT: *For those Luftwaffe aircrew who were forced to bale out over England, their reception committee would inevitably consist of members of the Home Guard, a part-time force and Churchill's last ditch in the event of invasion, and, as seen here, the village 'bobby' who is taking down the bewildered German's particulars in this photograph.*
BELOW: *A graphic shot of a Heinkel nosegunner engaging a Spitfire which has just dived through his formation. With their better performance, Spitfires normally took on the German fighters, leaving the Hurricanes to tackle the bombers.*

The Blitz

Based on the very limited experience of World War I, it had been widely held between the wars that 'the bomber will always get through' and that it could, on its own, win wars by direct attacks on the civil population. While radar had shown that the bomber was not invincible, the second argument was not yet proved one way or the other, although the destruction of Warsaw and Rotterdam seemed to indicate that it could be so. Hitler and Göring now intended to put the theory to the test.

Since 1938 when war clouds had first begun to loom, the British had been making preparations to minimize casualties from air attack. Every member of the population, including children, had been issued with a gasmask – it was firmly believed that the Germans would use gas bombs. Air-raid shelters had been constructed, manuals on protection of houses issued on a wide scale, a civil defense organization set up and plans for evacuating children from the cities to safer rural areas set in motion. Thus, when the bombing of London and other cities began in September 1940, it did not take the British public by surprise, and civilian morale remained high.

BELOW: *Children being evacuated from London. A mass evacuation took place at the outbreak of war, but most children returned when no bombing took place. Thus another evacuation was organized in summer 1940.*

RIGHT: *One of the classic photographs of the London Blitz. St Paul's Cathedral stands defiant amid the destruction all around it.*

ABOVE: *Two Dornier 17 bombers over London during the Luftwaffe's daylight attacks of early September 1940. Heavy casualties forced Göring to switch to night operations.*

LEFT: *Londoners shelter from the bombs for the night in the Elephant & Castle underground station. Not only did they have the discomfort to contend with, but they also suffered the constant worry of returning home next morning perhaps to find their houses destroyed.*

BELOW: *This YMCA tea van was provided by the US Allied Relief Fund to Britain. Many Americans were deeply sympathetic to Britain's plight and charities were set up to provide food, clothing and other essentials.*

The Blitz, as the British called it, lasted without halt until May 1941 and even then bombing attacks continued intermittently. London was the main target throughout and suffered accordingly. Indeed, there were few nights when the air-raid warning sirens did not sound. For Londoners this meant sheltering in the basements of their houses or in garden or communal shelters. Indeed, many took to sleeping in the communal shelters every night, air raid or not, and the underground stations remained open for this purpose. The damage, however, was enormous and in the first six weeks of the Blitz alone some 225,000 people were made homeless, which put a grievous strain on the welfare services. Many businesses moved out of the capital. However, all the major towns and cities suffered and for the effects of one attack there is no better illustration than what happened to the Midland city of Coventry on the night of 14/15 November. Almost one third of the city's houses were destroyed and nearly 600 people killed. A new word, 'Coventrate,' meaning the physical and psychological destruction of a city, entered the English language.

Yet, prewar theories that such attacks could rip the heart out of a nation did not hold up in practice. The British people generally endured the terror, discomfort and disruption of the Blitz with stoicism, as they did food rationing and the other restrictions of life in wartime. Indeed, in many ways, the war brought out the best qualities of the human character, especially that of unselfishness, and the fact that rich and poor faced equal risks did help to bind the nation together. Some comfort was also to be gained from the fact that RAF Bomber Command was striking back in kind, as will be described in Part II. As for Hitler, the fact that he was unable to break the morale of the British people finally convinced him that invasion was not possible and, while continuing to keep a wary eye on Britain, he turned his attention to the European mainland.

ABOVE LEFT: *A tethered barrage balloon. These were used to prevent enemy aircraft from flying low and thus bombing more accurately. They were a familiar part of the British wartime landscape.*
ABOVE RIGHT: *In the belief that the Germans would strike at British cities from the onset of war, much effort had been made in the years leading up to 1939 to build up a sizeable anti-aircraft command. By the time the Blitz started every city and town was literally ringed with guns and searchlights.*
LEFT: *Bomb damage in the City of London. Many fine and historic buildings were destroyed in the Blitz.*
RIGHT: *'The morning after.' Fleet Street, home of British newspapers, with St Paul's Cathedral in the background. Fire hoses littering the ground and a still-burning fractured gas main indicate a hectic night, but for Londoners it is still 'business as usual.'*

North Africa

Italy's entry into the war in June 1940 created fresh problems for the British. The most serious was the threat to their lines of communication through the Mediterranean and Suez Canal to India and to their possessions in Southeast Asia and the Far East. This was both from Italian maritime forces and the large garrisons in Libya, Eritrea and Abyssinia. While the British had traditionally maintained a large fleet in the Mediterranean, their land and air forces were comparatively small. These were based in Egypt and Palestine, where, during 1936-39, they had had to deal with an Arab insurrection brought about by an increased influx of Jews from Europe.

The British commander in the Middle East, General Sir Archibald Wavell, recognized from the outset that his lack of strength meant that he would have to wait for the Italians to make the first move. In Egypt his small Western Desert Force closed up to the border with Libya and prepared for an Italian attack, but nothing happened. In the meantime British attention became focussed on French North Africa to which much of the French fleet had withdrawn after the fall of France. Fearful that the Germans might get their hands on North Africa and after the French refused to sail their fleet to British ports, the Royal Navy successfully bombarded it at Dakar, Mers-El-Kebir and Oran in early July. The resultant loss of life embittered relations between Britain and the Vichy government in France.

Not until the beginning of August did Mussolini finally make a move, but not against Egypt. Instead, he struck at weakly defended British Somaliland, quickly overrunning it, and also established lodgments in British-administered Sudan. Finally, on 13 September, the Italian Tenth Army began its long-awaited advance across the Egyptian-Libyan border. The British withdrew in front of it, not willing to give battle until they were forced back to terrain more suitable for defense. After an advance of 60 miles, the Italians halted and set up a number of fortified camps. There now followed another lull, during which Wavell set about planning the restoration of British fortunes in East Africa.

As fall turned to winter and the Italians in Egypt continued to make no move, Wavell began to think about taking offensive action against them. He was cheered, too, by the attack by Royal Navy aircraft on the Italian Fleet at Taranto on 11 November, which destroyed or damaged almost half of it. He noted that the Italian camps were too far from one another to be mutually supporting and decided on a five day 'raid' to capture them. In great secrecy, Operation Compass was launched on 9 December and was overwhelmingly successful, catching the Italians by surprise and sending them flying back into Libya. The opportunity to capitalize on this was too good to miss, but it could not be taken immediately, as one of the two divisions involved was urgently required in East Africa and had to be replaced by a newly arrived Australian division. Not until early January was the offensive

ABOVE LEFT: *Marshal Rodolfo Graziani, Governor of Libya and Commander-in-Chief of the Italian forces in North Africa. He was relieved of his command in February 1941, but remained faithful to Mussolini to the bitter end, even after Italy had gone over to the Allies.*
LEFT: *These 11th Hussar officers, with their Morris armored car, have brought a souvenir of a Cairo café out into the desert with them. As a reconnaissance regiment, the 11th Hussars were to fight throughout the campaign in North Africa and then in Italy and Northwest Europe.*

resumed. Bardia and then Tobruk fell and the campaign culminated in the Battle of Beda Fomm in early February, which resulted in the destruction of much of the Italian Tenth Army and the removal of the Italian presence in Cyrenaica. Largely external factors now intervened to prevent further exploitation.

For a start, Churchill decided to remove troops from the Middle East and send them to help Greece (see page 56). The counteroffensive in East Africa was now well underway, with twin thrusts being launched from Kenya and the Sudan to squeeze the Italians. The troops which had taken part in the Libyan offensive were also in urgent need of refurbishment and had to be replaced by formations fresh from England. Finally, a new actor had appeared on the North African stage.

In view of the Italian reverses in Egypt and Libya, Hitler had decided that stiffening by German troops was required. Accordingly, in February 1941, two German divisions, the Afrika Korps, were dispatched to Libya under Erwin Rommel. He was not a man to let the grass grow under his feet and toward the end of March attacked the now weakened Western Desert Force in the Cyrenaican 'bulge'. Within a month he had driven most of the British forces back into Egypt. The only remaining British toehold in Libya was the port of Tobruk, which now came under a siege which would last until November. Under pressure from Churchill, Wavell did mount two small offensives in May and June to drive Rommel back, but both failed.

ABOVE LEFT: *Destroyed British armor outside Tobruk, May 1941. The tank is an A13 Cruiser Mark IV. Behind this tank can be seen two Marmon-Herrington armored cars.*

ABOVE: *Stukas high over the Western Desert. During the first part of the war in the desert the Axis enjoyed air superiority, the British being forced to rely on obsolete types of aircraft.*

BELOW: *Indian infantry watch from the outskirts of Tobruk as port installations burn, 22 January 1941.*

RIGHT: *Artillery of the Deutsches Afrika Korps in action in Libya. The gun is a 150mm howitzer with a range of 14,600 yards.*
BELOW: *British airmen enjoy a wash. Water was always at a premium in the desert and when it was short washing became a low priority. Often, washed-in water would be used to top up vehicle radiators.*
FACING PAGE: *Luftwaffe aircrew on standby relax under the shade of the wing of their Me110. Many of the landing grounds in North Africa were simply strips of flat desert.*

In East Africa the British fared better. The twin offensives made good progress. The Italian lodgments in the Sudan were erased and Eritrea captured by the end of March 1941. Now began the clearance of Abyssinia where, assisted by the Abyssinian Patriots, the British restored the Emperor Haile Selassie to his throne in the capital, Addis Ababa, in May. But, mainly because of the barren and mountainous terrain, it would not be until toward the end of November that the last Italian resistance would be overcome.

During this time, though, Wavell also had problems to occupy him elsewhere. In April 1941 there was a pro-fascist revolt in the British mandate of Iraq which had to be put down. Then, at the end of May, it became apparent that Vichy French Syria was about to allow Axis forces into the country. This had to be forestalled, and in early June a force invaded the country and, after some surprisingly bitter fighting against an erstwhile ally, overran it. North, across the Mediterranean, there were further crises to be faced.

The Mediterranean and the Balkans

By the fall of 1940 the idea was already in Hitler's mind to invade Russia, but much preliminary preparation was needed. Vital to the German war machine was oil and in October 1940 he carried out a peaceful occupation of the Rumanian oilfields, Rumania herself joining the Axis. This, however, incensed Mussolini, who considered that the Balkans lay in his sphere of influence. Accordingly, he countered by launching an invasion of Greece from Albania. To his surprise this proved to be no walkover. Indeed, Greek resistance was such that by early 1941 not only had the Italians been repulsed, but were in danger of being driven out of Albania. The Greeks were realistic enough to appreciate that their success might well bring German revenge on their country and asked for British troops to be sent to help them against possible attack. This Churchill agreed to, even though it meant giving up the opportunity of clearing Libya of the Italian presence.

ABOVE: *Italian troops on the Albanian front, January 1941. The severe winter weather, inhospitable country and Greek successes had a grievous effect on Italian morale.*
RIGHT: *German infantry and horsedrawn artillery on their way through Bulgaria to attack Greece. This shows only too clearly that much of the German Army was not mechanized.*

LEFT: *British troops, with a 3.7 inch howitzer, pass through a Greek village on their way to the front. They did little to stop the German onrush and their absence was sorely felt in the Western Desert.*

BELOW LEFT: *German mountain troops in action on the Metaxas Line, a Greek defense position which ran southeast from the Yugoslav border facing into Macedonia. It was named for Marshal Ioannis Metaxas, the head of the Greek government.*

BELOW: *Exhausted British troops en route from Greece to Suda Bay, Crete. The lucky ones would find themselves carrying out a similar evacuation just over a month later.*

The Greeks were right. In the context of his projected attack on Russia, Hitler was concerned to secure his southern flank. True, Hungary, Bulgaria, and Rumania now had pro-Axis regimes and in early 1941 he was also able to conclude a pact with Yugoslavia. A hostile Greece, however, especially with a British military presence there, could well endanger his plans and accordingly Hitler ordered a plan for an attack on Greece to be drawn up. Then, on 27 March 1941, his plans were further upset by a coup in Yugoslavia and the installation of a pro-Allied government.

On 6 April the Germans struck both countries from Bulgaria, Hungary and Rumania. Yugoslavia succumbed in less than a week, and Greece lasted only two weeks longer. Once again the German blitzkrieg proved to be overwhelming. One Allied defensive line after

RIGHT: *German paratroopers dropping over Crete. Although the Germans enjoyed almost overwhelming air superiority, well over 50 percent of General Karl Student's men were killed before they reached the ground.*
BELOW: *Bemused and curious Cretans examine a German paratrooper. Fiercely independent by nature, the Cretans, encouraged by British agents, would make life very difficult for the German occupiers of their island.*

another was turned, and the Royal Navy had to be called upon to evacuate the 60,000 British, Australian and New Zealand troops who had been sent there. Thus the Balkans were now secure, but the need to mount Operation Marita meant that the German attack on Russia had to be delayed and this was to prove a significant factor in the outcome of the campaign.

The bulk of the Allied forces evacuated from Greece were sent to the island of Crete, which occupies a vital position in the eastern Mediterranean and which had had a British garrison since the previous

November. The Germans, too, recognized Crete's strategic significance and marked it as their next target. On 20 May 1941 the skies above the island were suddenly filled with German aircraft disgorging parachute troops. It was the first major airborne assault in history and after 24 hours' fierce fighting the Germans succeeded in capturing the vital airfield at Máleme. This enabled them to fly in reinforcements and from then on the outcome was a foregone conclusion. The British and Commonwealth forces were forced to retreat to the south coast of the island and the Royal Navy was once more called upon to evacuate

RIGHT: *Malta under one of its frequent Axis air attacks. The island was crucial to the British hold on the western Mediterranean and came under increasing Axis pressure. Such was the courage of her people that in 1942 King George VI awarded the island the George Cross, Britain's highest civilian decoration for bravery.*
BELOW: *The ruin of defeat. A German vehicle passes wrecked RAF Blenheim bombers on a Greek roadside.*

them, but this time with heavy losses from Axis air attacks which sank a large number of ships.

The German ability now to dominate the eastern Mediterranean from the air effectively closed this region to the Royal Navy, so that convoys entering the Mediterranean could proceed no farther east than Malta. Instead, they had to use the very much longer Cape route round the tip of South Africa. Indeed, the only maritime success which the British Mediterranean Fleet had enjoyed in the spring of 1941 had come at the end of March when, in a skillful night action off Cape

Matapan, the Fleet sank three Italian cruisers and two destroyers and seriously damaged the battleship *Vittorio Veneto*. Never again would the Italian Fleet venture out of its bases. Crete, too, although a spectacular victory, had not been without cost to the Germans. The casualties in men and transport aircraft meant that never again would they mount a major airborne operation and, indeed, the loss of aircraft was later to have a serious effect on their operations in Russia.

All this, however, lay in the future and in mid-1941 British prospects almost everywhere seemed bleak.

1941-1942

The War Becomes Global

Chronology 1941-1942

1941

June 22	Hitler invades Russia
August 9-12	Roosevelt and Churchill meet off Newfoundland
September 8	Leningrad surrounded
November 18	British launch Crusader offensive in Libya
December 4	German drive on Moscow halted
December 7	Japan attacks Pearl Harbor
December 11	Germany and Italy declare war on USA
December 22	Roosevelt and Churchill meet at the Arcadia Conference

1942

January 1	26 nations sign UN Declaration in Washington DC
January 21	Rommel attacks in Libya
January 31	Japanese clear British from Malaya
February 15	Singapore surrenders
March 7	Japanese enter Rangoon, Burma
April 18	Doolittle raid on Tokyo
May 4-8	Battle of the Coral Sea
May 6	US forces on Corregidor, Philippines, surrender
May 19-28	German victory at Kharkov, Eastern Front
May 26	Rommel attacks British Gazala Line, Libya
June 4-7	Battle of Midway
July 1-27	First Battle of El Alamein, Egypt
July 4	Germans secure Sevastopol, Crimea
August 7	Americans land at Guadacanal, Solomons
August 9	Germans capture Caucasus oilfields
August 30	Rommel repulsed at Alam Halfa, Egypt
September 1	Germans reach outskirts of Stalingrad
October 23	Montgomery begins his attack at El Alamein
November 8	Anglo-US landings in French North Africa (Torch)
November 11	Germans occupy Vichy France
November 19	Soviet counteroffensive at Stalingrad

The caption for this Soviet cartoon reads: '1942 must become the year of the enemy's final rout.' The Russians desperately wanted the Western Allies to open a second front in Europe in order to relieve them of the almost unbearable pressure they found themselves under. It was more easily said than done.

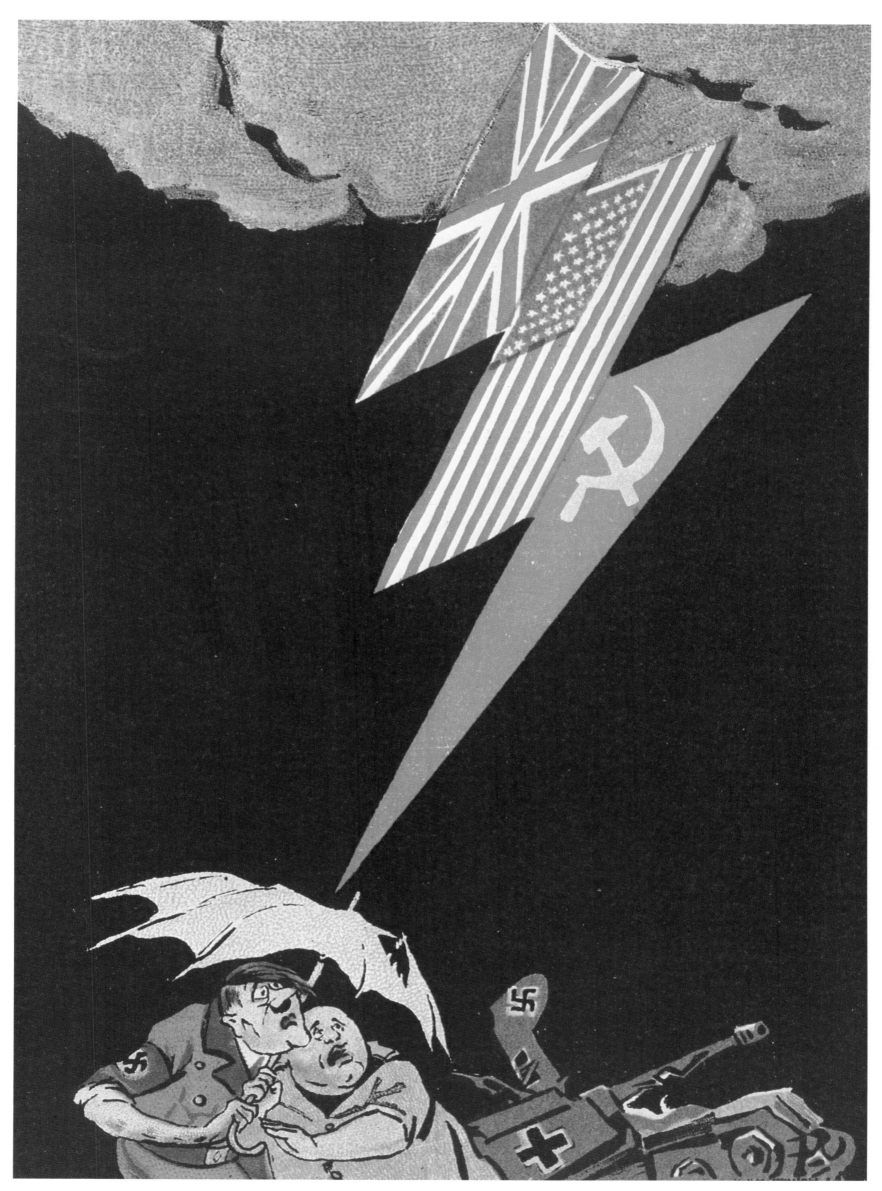

Outline of Events

On 22 June 1941, Hitler stunned the world by invading Russia, thus breaking the 1939 non-aggression pact. For Britain this meant that she at last had an ally again, albeit an unlikely one. Russia, herself, however, initially proved as incapable of handling blitzkrieg as the other victims of it. By the fall she had suffered enormous losses of men and material and the Germans were approaching Moscow. The weather now took a hand. Firstly the rains and then the snow slowed the Germans down and gave the Russians time to recover and by year's end the Germans had been forced to give ground in front of the capital.

There was little direct help which Britain could give her new ally, although Stalin demanded from very early on that Britain open the Second Front by invading France, something Britain was in no position to do. The British did, however, send supplies by sea – the Arctic convoys – to the northern Russian ports, but at a cost in loss of ships, and the RAF's bombing offensive against Germany was helping indirectly by tying down German aircraft. Otherwise, apart from the continuing struggle against the U-boats in the Atlantic, her attention was mainly fixed on North Africa. Here, after much pressurizing by Churchill, a major offensive was finally launched in November 1941, which once again drove the Axis out of Cyrenaica.

An encouraging trend, however, was the growing relationship between Churchill and Roosevelt. In August 1941 the two leaders met on a warship off Newfoundland and signed the Atlantic Charter, the foundation stone of today's United Nations. In essence it declared that once Nazi oppression had been eradicated, all nations, great and small, would have the right to choose their own form of government, which would be respected by the others. Eventually all the Allies and many neutral nations would sign it. There was also growing United States involvement in the Battle of the Atlantic and by November American warships were escorting convoys to the mid-Atlantic and thus being attacked by U-boats. The question of if and when the United States would enter the war was, however, rudely taken out of her hands.

Japan had been bent on forming an empire in the Far East for some years. Casting envious eyes over the wealth-producing colonies of the Western powers in the region, she planned to create a Great East Asia Co-prosperity Sphere, taking in the Dutch East Indies, Burma, Malaya and Singapore. In July 1941 she occupied French Indo-China and tried to persuade the United States to give her a free hand in the region. This resulted in a worsening of relations between her, Britain and the United States and she decided that peaceful means could no longer achieve her aim. On 7 December 1941, she launched an air strike against the United States Pacific Fleet base at Pearl Harbor in Hawaii and simultaneously attacked British and American possessions in the Pacific and Far East. Four days later, Hitler declared war on the United States. Thus America was now finally in the war, which had become truly global.

The first decision that the Western Allies had to make was over where the priority now lay, Germany or Japan. At a conference held in Washington DC two weeks after Pearl Harbor, between Roosevelt, Churchill and their military staffs, it was decided that Germany must be defeated first. To this end American troops and materiel would be sent across to Britain with a view to creating the Second Front.

ABOVE: *7 December 1941. A Japanese Nakajima B5N torpedo bomber takes off from a carrier, cheered on by the crew, its destination Pearl Harbor.*
RIGHT: *The Dieppe raid, 18 August 1942, with landing craft heading for the beaches. For the 2nd Canadian Division which carried out the operation the raid was a disaster, but valuable lessons were learned which were put to good use in June 1944.*
LEFT: *Roosevelt and Churchill on board HMS* Prince of Wales, *later sunk off Malaya, during their historic meeting in Argentia Bay, Newfoundland in August 1941. Behind them (left to right) are George C Marshall, Ernest J King and Harold R Stark.*

RIGHT: *Survivors of the Dieppe raid transshipping from their landing craft. The controversy over this raid rages even today.*
BELOW: *A British 6x4 three-ton truck on the quayside of the northern Russian port of Murmansk. Much British and American material aid to Russia came through this port, but the cost in merchant ships was high.*

The first few months of the alliance were, however, disastrous. Nothing seemed to stop the Japanese, who speedily overran United States Pacific islands, the British colony of Hong Kong, Malaya, Singapore, the Dutch East Indies and, finally, Burma and the Philippines. In North Africa, Rommel turned and struck the British once more in January 1942, driving them out of the Cyrenaican bulge. Then, after a pause, he attacked again in May and the British soon found themselves with their backs to Cairo and the Suez Canal. On the Eastern Front, too, after the Russians had successfully recaptured Kharkov in May, the Germans quickly recaptured it and launched a new offensive aimed at the Caucasus. At sea the situation was equally grim, with the U-boats taking maximum advantage of lax defenses on the United States eastern seaboard in what their crews called their 'second happy time.'

Matters did, however, slowly improve. In the Pacific the US Navy first halted the Japanese Fleet at the Battle of the Coral Sea and then defeated the Japanese at Midway, while the Australians managed to hold the Japanese on New Guinea. The Chinese, too, were not only holding the Japanese at home, but also beginning to cooperate with the British in the projected reconquest of Burma. The British successfully

ABOVE: *Preparing for the inevitable. Anti-aircraft gunners of the US Coast Artillery in training.*

RIGHT: *President Roosevelt broadcasts to the nation. His 'fireside chats' did much to help prepare the American people for war as well as to maintain his own popularity.*

invaded the French island of Madagascar in the Indian Ocean to prevent the Japanese using it as a submarine base. They also held Rommel in Egypt. Furthermore, there were improvements in the situation in the Atlantic and in midsummer some spectacular RAF Bomber Command raids against Germany.

Yet, there was discord among the Allies. Stalin was becoming increasingly insistent that the Second Front be created in 1942 and the American military planners tended to agree with him. The British did not consider that they and the Americans were ready for this, and the disastrous cross-Channel raid on Dieppe tended to support this. They felt it more important to clear North Africa of the enemy, and Roosevelt sided with them. The result was that in early November a joint Anglo-American task force was landed in French North Africa, while 2000 miles to the east, the British struck at Rommel and began to pursue him for the last time through Libya.

On the Eastern Front, as the fall wore on, Hitler became mesmerized by Stalingrad and his forces were embroiled in a costly battle here. By the end of the year a complete German army had been surrounded in the city. In the Pacific, too, the tide was on the turn. In August, United States Marines landed on Guadalcanal in the Solomons and American and Australian troops began to push the Japanese back slowly in New Guinea. Furthermore, the first hesitant steps were being taken to recapture Burma.

Hitler Invades Russia

From the time that Hitler had formulated his political creed, as set out in his book *Mein Kampf*, which he wrote while in prison after his abortive 1923 Munich coup, he believed that communism, as exemplified by Russia, was the world's greatest enemy and had to be crushed. Thus he saw an invasion of Russia as inevitable at some point in Germany's struggle. Stalin thought much the same about Nazism,

but in August 1939, since neither was militarily ready to take the other on, it suited each to have a pact with the other. This pact also had economic benefits in that there was an exchange of German industrial plant for grain from the Ukraine. It was only after Hitler's plans for the invasion of Britain had come to naught that he was in a position to begin to give serious consideration to invading Russia.

ABOVE: *Georgi Zhukov (center), who was to become perhaps the most distinguished Russian commander of the war, seen here during the Battle of Khalkin Gal, a border squabble with the Japanese in Outer Mongolia in August 1939.*
RIGHT: *22 June 1941. German infantry cross the River Prut on the Rumanian-Russian border.*

FAR RIGHT, ABOVE: *German Panzer Grenadiers in Russia ride forward on a* Sturmgeschutz *(Assault gun)* III. *Developed for infantry support, these vehicles were often used as tank destroyers.*
FAR RIGHT, BELOW: *German infantry dragging ammunition carts through the mud of the Donets Basin. When the fall rains came a severe brake was put on the German offensive.*

Nevertheless he had intimated to his generals what was on his mind as early as July 1940. They drew up a plan for two major thrusts, one directed on Moscow and the other on Kiev in the Ukraine. Once these two cities had been captured the two thrusts would join hands, thus sealing the Russian armies in one huge pocket. Bearing in mind the unimpressive performance of the Russians against the Finns, the German General Staff believed that the campaign could be completed in 19 weeks. But a prerequisite of success was the creation of more Panzer and motorized divisions.

Accordingly, during the winter of 1940-41, the number of Panzer divisions was doubled, but this could only be done by reducing the number of tanks in each division, although the models were heavier

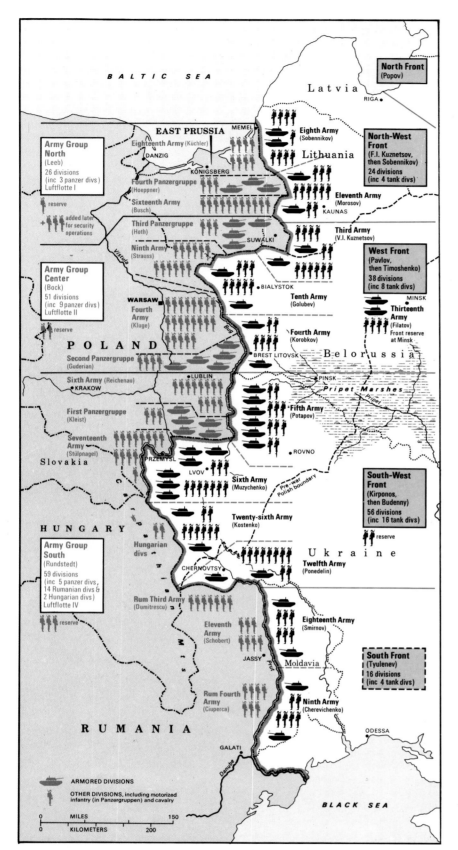

The map labels, reading top to bottom and left to right:

BALTIC SEA

Latvia

RIGA

North Front (Popov)

EAST PRUSSIA — MEMEL

Army Group North (Leeb)
26 divisions (inc 3 panzer divs)
Luftflotte I
reserve
+ added later for security operations

Eighteenth Army (Küchler)
DANZIG
KÖNIGSBERG

Eighth Army (Sobennikov)

Lithuania

North-West Front (F.I. Kuznetsov, then Sobennikov)
24 divisions (inc 4 tank divs)

Fourth Panzergruppe (Hoeppner)
Sixteenth Army (Busch)

Eleventh Army (Morosov)
KAUNAS

Third Panzergruppe (Hoth)
SUWALKI

Third Army (V.I. Kuznetsov)

Ninth Army (Strauss)

Army Group Center (Bock)
51 divisions (inc 9 panzer divs)
Luftflotte II
reserve

WARSAW
Fourth Army (Kluge)

West Front (Pavlov, then Timoshenko)
38 divisions (inc 8 tank divs)

BIALYSTOK

Tenth Army (Golubev)

MINSK
Thirteenth Army (Filatov)
Front reserve at Minsk

POLAND

Second Panzergruppe (Guderian)

BREST LITOVSK

Belorussia

Sixth Army (Reichenau)
LUBLIN
KRAKOW

PINSK
Pripet Marshes

First Panzergruppe (Kleist)

Fifth Army (Potapov)

Seventeenth Army (Stülpnagel)

Slovakia

ROVNO

PRZEMYSL
LVOV

Sixth Army (Muzychenko)

Pre-war Polish boundary

South-West Front (Kirponos, then Budenny)
56 divisions (inc 16 tank divs)

Twenty-sixth Army (Kostenko)

HUNGARY

Army Group South (Rundstedt)
59 divisions (inc 5 panzer divs, 14 Rumanian divs & 2 Hungarian divs)
Luftflotte IV
reserve

Hungarian divs

CHERNOVTSY

Ukraine

reserve

Twelfth Army (Ponedelin)

Rum Third Army (Dumitrescu)

Eleventh Army (Schobert)

JASSY
Moldavia

Eighteenth Army (Smirnov)

South Front (Tyulenev)
16 divisions (inc 4 tank divs)

Rum Fourth Army (Ciuperca)

Ninth Army (Cherevichenko)

RUMANIA
ODESSA
GALATI

BLACK SEA

ARMORED DIVISIONS
OTHER DIVISIONS, including motorized infantry (in Panzergruppen) and cavalry

0 MILES 150
0 KILOMETERS 200

than in the original Panzer division organization. This plan was then presented to Hitler in mid-December 1940, but he made a significant major amendment. Once the northern thrust had reached Smolensk, part of the forces were to drive north to seize Leningrad. Only when this city had been taken would Moscow be tackled. His directive, issued the following day, called for preparations for Operation Barbarossa to be completed by mid-May. The reason for this timing was that the attack could not be launched until after the ground had dried out after the spring thaw and the Germans had to be firm on their final line on the River Volga before the fall rains began in October. Given the 19 week estimate for the duration of the complete campaign, this meant that time was very tight.

As we have seen, Hitler's attention was diverted to the Balkans in the early months of 1941 and to deal with them he had to use forces earmarked for Russia. This meant that the timetable had to be put back and it was not until the second half of June that the Germans were finally ready. In the meantime the plan was changed so that Leningrad became the objective of an entirely independent thrust to that directed on Smolensk and Moscow.

Including two Rumanian armies, the Germans had gathered together 105 infantry, 17 Panzer and 12 motorized divisions. They were organized into three army groups – North (von Leeb), Center (von Bock) and South (von Rundstedt). Facing them were 150 Russian divisions split into four fronts (the Russian equivalent of an army group). Unfortunately, the Russians were still in the midst of a major reorganization brought about by the lessons learned against Finland. Their defensive layout also played into the German hands since the bulk of their forces were on the border, with little attempt at defense in depth. Yet, both the British Government and Soviet spy rings had been warning Stalin for some months that the Germans were about to mount an offensive.

As it was, it was not until the evening of 21 June that the Russian armies were put on alert. At 0200 hours next morning a grain train steamed cross the River Bug into German-occupied Poland. One and a quarter hours later the German preliminary bombardment started and 15 minutes later German troops crossed into Russian territory.

LEFT: *The lineup for Barbarossa. While both sides appeared evenly matched, the Russians were in the throes of a major reorganization and were ill-prepared to resist the German attack.*
BELOW LEFT: *'Target!' – a German 37mm antitank gun in action during the early days of Barbarossa.*

BELOW: *Cossack horsemen in German service. As the Poles had discovered, horse cavalry was no match against tanks, although cavalry could still play a useful role in broken terrain.*
RIGHT: *Stiffening the resolve of the defenders of Moscow. The capital would certainly have become another Stalingrad if the Germans had succeeded in reaching it.*

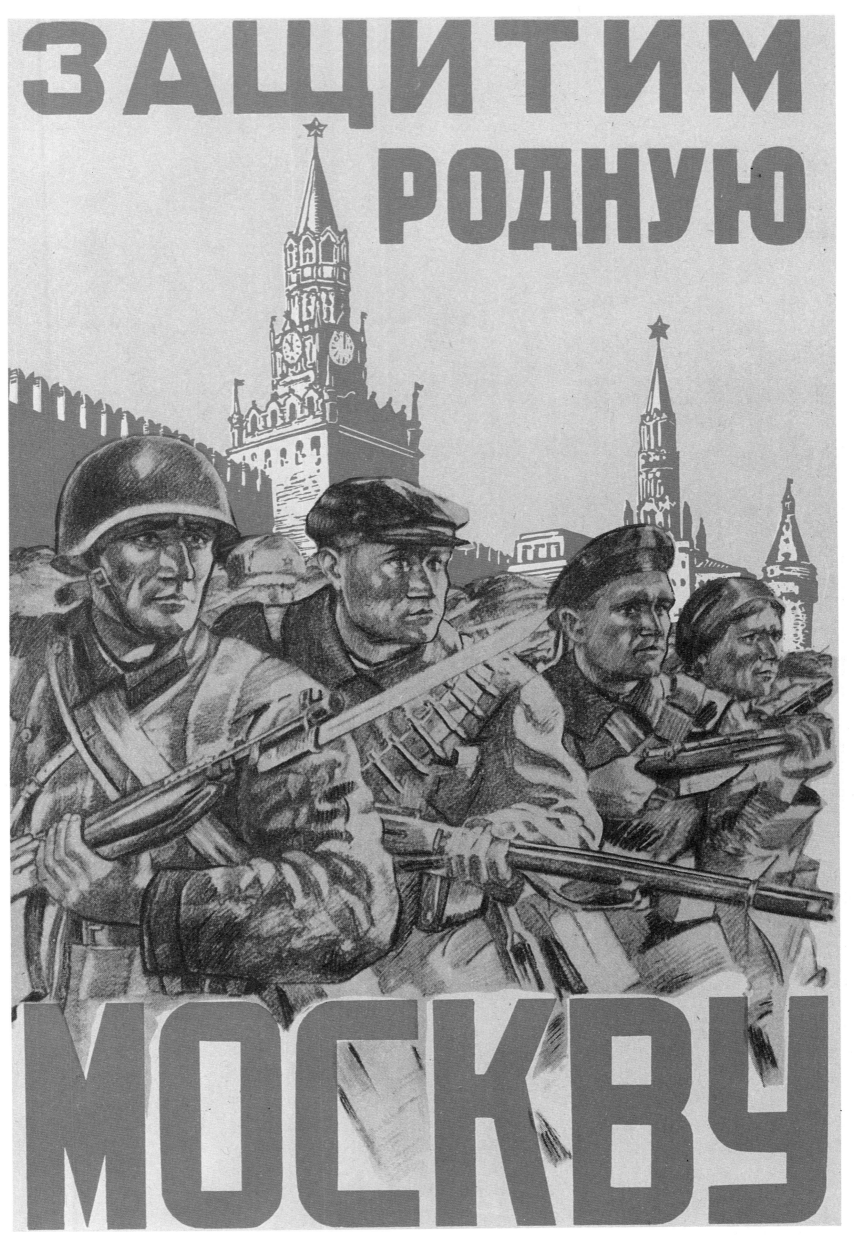

LEFT: *'How many more kilometers to Moscow?' By allowing his attention to be diverted to the Ukraine, Hitler ensured that Army Group Center would never reach Moscow.*
RIGHT: *Some of the many thousands of Russian troops captured in the Kharkov pocket in October 1941, just before the fall rains came.*
BELOW: *Initially many of the Russian peasants, fed up with the suffocating restrictions of life in Stalin's Russia, welcomed the German invader with open arms. It was only when Hitler's racial policy started to bite that they changed their attitude.*

The Russians were taken almost entirely by surprise. Worse, many of their aircraft were caught on the ground and by the end of the first day they had lost 1200. Army Group North swept through the former Baltic republics, but was slowed by the forests and bogs on the approaches to Leningrad. In the center significant pockets were created around Minsk and Bialystock, but the Russians at Brest-Litovsk resisted stoutly and did not surrender until mid-July. Yet the problems of the widely different pace between the Panzer and infantry divisions meant that the former were continually having to be halted to allow the latter to catch up. The Russians, too, were belatedly recognizing the need to have forces in the depth. Nevertheless another huge pocket had been created around Smolensk by mid-July. In the south, on the other hand, the Russian defense was conducted with much more skill and, try as he might, von Rundstedt was unable to create any form of pocket until he reached Kiev in mid-July.

At this stage Hitler stepped in personally and ordered Army Group Center to give up some divisions to von Leeb and others to von Rundstedt, leaving von Bock with merely infantry divisions with which to continue the advance to Moscow. Von Rundstedt succeeded in trapping two Russian armies southeast of Kiev and advanced toward the Crimea and Donets basin. In the north, the additional armor made little difference because of the terrain difficulties. Hitler, however, did order the Luftwaffe to bomb both Leningrad and Moscow, but this showed up a major weakness. The ground forces believed that the Luftwaffe's prime role was to support them, and hence it proved difficult to find sufficient aircraft to make these strategic bombing attacks effective, there being few occasions when 100 aircraft took part, most raids consisting of no more than 10. During this time, Army Group Center had been able to make little progress and indeed had to face fierce attacks from Timoshenko's West Front. Consequently, when it got its armor back in September Army Group Center was still 200 miles from Moscow and time was running out.

The Gates of Moscow

Between Smolensk and Moscow lay an estimated 100 Russian divisions, and Hitler decreed that these must be destroyed before Moscow was tackled. By the end of the first week in October, Army Group Center had succeeded in creating two pockets, at Bryansk and Vyazma, the latter yielding a record bag of 650,000 prisoners. On 14 October Hitler ordered that Moscow be encircled rather than attacked frontally, in spite of protests by von Bock that this would disperse his forces too much.

In the meantime the Russians had not been idle. Marshal Georgi Zhukov had taken over the defense of the capital and had constructed a defense line 80 miles west of it. Fresh troops were brought in and citizens' militias called up. While much of the machinery of government had been moved behind the Urals, as had also the bulk of Russian industry, Moscow would not be given up easily. Nevertheless the Mozhaysk Line had been penetrated in three places by 18 October and there seemed little that could save the city.

It was now that the fall rains came and the German advance literally became bogged down in the glutinous mud, with Moscow still 30 miles away. German hopes were restored with the coming of the frosts at the beginning of November, and on the 16th the advance was renewed. Snow and falling temperatures followed. The German supply system, which had become more and more overstretched as the advance had continued, foundered. Worse, there was no winter clothing available as Hitler had refused to countenance the possibility of the campaign lasting into the winter. Thus, on 1 December, von Bock, his troops now 18 miles from Moscow, was forced to concede that no further advance would be possible. Immediately the Russians

BELOW: *When the snows came in November 1941, the Germans found themselves singularly ill equipped to combat the Russian winter, especially in terms of winter clothing. The Winter Relief Fund was used to make good this deficiency.*

RIGHT: *A poster aimed at Russian workers. The Luftwaffe's lack of long-range strategic bombers came home to roost in Russia since the war industries that the Russians set up in new factories beyond the Urals could not be touched by the Germans.*

began a series of fierce counterattacks, with the object of paying the Germans back in kind with an encircling operation of their own. Hitler ordered that there should be no withdrawals but the encirclement was not achieved, despite extremely heavy German casualties.

Elsewhere, Leningrad was under siege and would remain so until early in 1944, but in the south the Germans were forced to withdraw from Rostov to behind the River Mius. So furious was Hitler that it cost von Rundstedt his command.

ABOVE: *Under heavy artillery fire a Russian soldier attends to his wounded comrade. The Russian soldier was inured to hardship and displayed large reserves of courage. At the same time he could be intensely pessimistic.*
RIGHT: *The defenses of Moscow. Men and women dig an antitank ditch. Russian women proved themselves as tough as their menfolk and many, unlike their Western counterparts, were in combat branches of the armed forces.*

Blitzkrieg had met its match for the first time, not because of superior tactics, but the very vastness of Russia and the severity of her climate. For the Germans it was now a question of waiting for the spring and, in the meantime, enduring the harsh winter as best they could. This gave the Russians the vital breathing-space that they needed and the chance to digest the lessons which they had learned.

TOP: *Reinforcements for the battle in front of Moscow. Siberian ski troops march through the city. Many of the reinforcements were purposely marched through the center in order to stiffen both their resolve and that of Muscovites.*

LEFT: *The factories behind the Urals operated round the clock in order to produce the weapons needed to turn back the invader. Here women assemble PPSh-1941G machine pistols.*

ABOVE: *Ilyushin Il-2 Stormoviks (armored attackers) patrol the skies above Moscow. Very similar in appearance to the British Fairey Battle, these aircraft were used for close support of the ground forces.*

RIGHT: *A German soldier endures a temperature of −35°C. The incidence of frostbite during the winter of 1941-42 on the Eastern Front was very high among the German armies.*

The U-boat Menace

During the summer of 1941 it seemed as though the Royal Navy was beginning to get to grips with the U-boats. Indeed, Admiral Karl Dönitz, who commanded the U-boat arm, was becoming concerned that the increase in the number of boats in commission was not being matched by the rate of sinkings of merchant vessels. There were a number of reasons for this. For a start, the British were now beginning to be able to read the German top secret Ultra ciphers, which were used to transmit orders to the U-boats. This meant that to an extent they were able to guide convoys away from areas known to contain U-boats. Escort vessels were becoming more effective, both in anti-submarine drills and in equipment, and more and more were being built. The expansion of the U-boat arm also meant that there were more inexperienced skippers and crews.

There was, too, the increasing role being played by the United States. In July 1941, American troops relieved the British garrison on Iceland, which increased the United States presence in the western Atlantic, and, indeed, American warships began to carry out convoy escort duties in this area on the pretext that some of the ships in the convoys were bound for Iceland. Inevitably, this meant brushes with the U-boats. The first of these involved the USS *Greer* on 4 September 1941, as a result of which Roosevelt warned the Axis that any of their warships entering the waters south of the Canadian port of Halifax would do so at their own peril. Hitler, anxious not to provoke the United States too much, imposed a ban on U-boats operating there, but this did not stop incidents with US warships. On 17 October USS *Kearny* was torpedoed and badly damaged and two weeks later the USS *Reuben James* was sunk by a U-boat while on escort duties.

U-boat deployments also reduced the sinkings. Fearful that the British were contemplating an invasion of Norway, Hitler insisted on a strong force of U-boats being retained there, which meant that they were largely unavailable for deployment in the mid-Atlantic. Together with Norwegian-based aircraft, they did, however, cause much damage to the convoys bound for Russia. In September 1941 Hitler also insisted, in the face of Dönitz's protests, on moving a large number of

ABOVE: *Posters like this were common. This one refers particularly to the Battle of the Atlantic and convoy sailings. In fact, the Germans had precise knowledge by other means since up until 1943 they were able to read the British merchant ship codes.*
LEFT: *Grand Admiral Karl Dönitz, a World War I U-boat ace, who as Flag Officer, U-boats until 1943 and then Commander-in-Chief of the German Navy conducted the U-boat campaign. Here he inspects submariners.*

boats to the Mediterranean. Furthermore there was the question of endurance. In order to operate for any length of time in the Atlantic, the U-boats had to be resupplied at sea. This had been done by specially adapted merchant vessels, but, thanks to Ultra intercepts, during the course of 1941, the British were able to locate and sink them. The German answer was to build supply U-boats, called 'milk cows,' but these were not available until 1942.

With the declaration of war on the United States, Hitler lifted his ban on U-boats operating in US territorial waters and they soon discovered rich pickings along the eastern seaboard. In spite of the experience of the past two years, vessels were allowed to sail independently and convoying was not instituted, the reason being lack of escort vessels. The submarine chasers used were hopelessly inadequate and could only operate in calm waters, and the absence of a blackout on land made navigation and identification of targets very easy for the U-boats. Consequently, sinkings rose from 40 in this area in January 1942 to 121 in June, and it was only then that convoying was introduced and the losses became smaller. The U-boats then moved to the Caribbean and the Gulf of Mexico.

The threat of German surface ships still remained, especially from the *Scharnhorst* and *Gneisenau* in Brest. RAF attempts to bomb them had failed, but in February 1942, as a precaution against an attack on Norway, Hitler ordered them back to Germany. Accordingly, together with the *Prinz Eugen*, they boldly sailed up the English Channel. Because of a series of mishaps, British efforts to stop them failed, and they arrived safely in the Baltic, apart from the *Gneisenau*, which was damaged by a mine off the Dutch coast and never went to sea again.

The introduction of the 'milk cows,' beginning in March 1942, significantly increased the time which the U-boats could spend on patrol and meant that more could be kept on station. They also hunted more in groups, the so-called 'wolf packs,' and the German ability to read the Allied merchant shipping code, meant that these could be guided on to convoys. Nevertheless it was usually only where the escort was weak and inexperienced that they achieved notable successes. Dönitz now recognized, once the Americans had tightened up their procedures, that the mid-Atlantic, the Black Gap which aircraft could not reach, was potentially the most fruitful area and began to concentrate on this. A further advantage which Dönitz enjoyed for most of 1942 was that the British were unable to read his Ultra signals. The reason for this was a modification to the Enigma cipher machines. Nevertheless, he was badly caught out at the beginning of November

ABOVE LEFT: *A U-boat crewman. A cruise could last as long as six weeks and the very cramped confines proved a test of both courage and endurance.*
LEFT: *Until the development of the schnorkel and Walther turbine power plant, U-boats were forced to spend much time on the surface. They were very vulnerable to attack, especially from the air, and it was vital to have alert lookouts.*

1942, when his boats failed to intercept any of the convoys sailing from the United States and Scotland for the Allied landings in French North Africa and when he did deploy some to the western Mediterranean in the aftermath of the landings, seven were sunk in one week.

Yet, while 1941 and 1942 saw a number of crisis points for both sides in the Atlantic, it was to be in the first part of 1943 that the battle would really be decided. In the first months of 1943 the U-boats would concentrate their attacks at the decisive point – the North Atlantic convoys.

ABOVE: *A U-boat in typical mid-Atlantic seas. This is a Type VIIC, the most common boat during the first half of the war. It had a surface range of 6500 nautical miles at 12 knots and a submerged range of 80 nautical miles at 4 knots. The complement of a Type VIIC was 44 men, they had four torpedo tubes and carried 14 torpedoes.*

LEFT: *A typical convoy. The box formation was the best for escort control and protection. Much of the escort vessels' time was taken up in shepherding stragglers, which were very vulnerable to U-boats.*

ABOVE RIGHT: *British submarines were also active, especially in the Mediterranean and Baltic approaches. The executive officer of* HMS Tribune *stands at the periscope while other crew members wait anxiously.*

RIGHT: *In order not to reveal a convoy's location to the U-boats, messages between ships were usually passed by Aldis lamp. Sometimes, though, especially in fog, loud hailers had to be used.*

Strategic Bombing

At the outbreak of war in 1939 none of the combatant countries was prepared to countenance the bombing of civilian targets, in spite of what the prewar air theorists had advocated, and their air forces had been given strict instructions to concentrate on military targets. The Germans bombed Warsaw and Rotterdam on the grounds that, having refused to surrender, they had become military targets. While the accidental bombing of London by a German aircraft in August 1940 was the spark that initiated the intentional bombing of British and German cities, there were other, technical factors which brought this about.

In 1939 both sides believed that most bombing would take place by day when navigation was easier, when bombers, provided they flew in formation, could defend themselves against fighter attack, and when the bombing would be more accurate. By the end of the year, RAF Bomber Command was forced to accept, after very costly attacks on German naval targets in the Baltic, that attacks by day could be prohibitive and the emphasis was switched to night. The Germans learned the same lesson during the Battle of Britain.

Once the Germans had attacked in the west in May 1940, the RAF was allowed to attack targets within Germany, but concentrated on precision ones, mainly marshalling yards and oil installations. These were joined by a whole variety of other targets affecting Germany's ability to wage war. The creep into what the RAF called 'area bombing' was gradual. Even the RAF's first raid on Berlin at the end of August was directed at industrial targets which were on the outskirts and not at the city itself.

LEFT: *Sir Arthur Harris, leader of RAF Bomber Command 1942-45. He remorselessly pursued his aim of bringing Germany to her knees through bombing.*

BELOW: *Bombing up Lancaster S for Sugar for a raid. This particular aircraft flew on no less than 137 operations and now resides in the RAF Museum at Hendon, London.*

Indeed, it was Churchill himself who first seriously considered the intentional bombing of cities as the only way of bringing the meaning of war home to the German people. Yet it was not until December 1940, in retaliation for the Luftwaffe's devastating attack on Coventry the month before, that RAF bomber crews were specifically ordered to aim for the center of a city, in this case Mannheim. The object, however, was not to kill civilians, but to destroy their homes and disrupt their lives. Nevertheless the RAF firmly believed that they could bomb accurately by night, and the main priority rested with precision oil targets, urban areas only being attacked on nights when there was no moon.

By early 1941 the British had two concerns over bombing. The first was that there were not enough bombers to make a significant impact and the second concern was the mounting loss of aircraft. By now the Germans were constructing a defense line, called the Kammhuber Line' after the Luftwaffe general responsible for setting it up. This consisted of a network of radars, searchlights and anti-aircraft guns, as well as ground stations to control their night fighters. These last, as the British had done to counter the Blitz, were equipped with airborne radar. As the year wore on, however, a further worry surfaced as to whether RAF Bomber Command was actually hitting its targets. By now bombers had been equipped with cameras and an analysis of raid photographs showed that a frighteningly small proportion of them were doing so. By now, while the RAF was arguing that it should concentrate on destroying cities and that this could be decisive, Churchill was less enthusiastic and believed that the Command should husband its strength until it was better equipped.

In February 1942 RAF Bomber Command received a new leader, Arthur 'Bomber' Harris. It also began to receive new technical aids to improve navigational and bombing accuracy and a new family of four-engined bombers with increased range and payload. Harris was dedicated to the belief that area bombing of German cities could win the war, but only when he had enough bombers. To demonstrate this he launched a raid at the end of May with over 1000 bombers taking part, flying in a concentrated stream, against the city of Cologne. The results were impressive, but two subsequent raids of the same size did not fare so well because of the weather, and since to mass such a force meant stripping the training organization and borrowing from other

ABOVE: *German girls manning a sound location device. The German anti-aircraft defenses were formidable and by the end of the war no less than 8000 RAF bombers had been lost on operations.*

RIGHT: *'Your target for tonight.' RAF bomber crews being briefed prior to a raid. Bomber aircrews, if they survived that long, completed a tour of 30 operations and were then 'rested' for six months in the training organization before returning to combat flying.*

commands it had to be disbanded and Harris reverted to smaller-sized raids. Nevertheless he had restored Churchill's faith in bombing.

In summer 1942 the US Army Air Force's (USAAF) bombers under General Carl Spaatz began to arrive in Britain. The Americans were still firmly wedded to the idea of daylight bombing and believed that their heavily armed bombers, especially the B-17 Flying Fortress, could ward off the German fighters. The British had their doubts, but it would not be until well into the following year that this belief would be fully tested, mainly because the build-up of United States forces was slow and, in order to break in their crews they concentrated initially on short-range targets and did not penetrate German air space.

ABOVE: *An 8th USAAF crew. General Ira C Eaker led the first raid by the 8th AF, on 17 August 1942 on a French target.*

LEFT: *The crew of a Stirling bomber returns from a flying test.*

TOP: *The rear and mid-upper turrets of a heavy bomber. The rear gunner was the loneliest member of the crew, but his job in spotting and warding off enemy fighters was vital.*

Ebb and Flow in North Africa

After the second British attempt, in June 1941, to drive Rommel out of Egypt and relieve Tobruk, there was a lull in the fighting in the North African desert. Both sides badly needed to draw breath: General Sir Claude Auchinleck, who had replaced Wavell, needed to gather his strength in order to ensure that the next blow against Rommel was successful; the Axis forces wanted to rest so that they could concentrate their efforts on Tobruk. At the same time the Axis began to apply pressure through constant air attack on Malta, for if the British lost this essential island stronghold they would not be able to maintain a naval presence in the Mediterranean. Not until November would the desert armies clash again.

Auchinleck drew up a plan, Crusader, which had two objectives – to relieve Tobruk and destroy the Axis armor. During the late summer and early autumn he received considerable reinforcements, including supplies of the US M3 light tank, the General Stuart, which the British renamed the Honey, and the Western Desert Force was retitled the Eighth Army. He set the date for the launching of his attack as 18 November.

When it came, it took Rommel temporarily by surprise since he thought that the British were too concerned by the German threat to the Caucasus to contemplate an attack. The Eighth Army commander, General Sir Alan Cunningham, had, however, made a fatal mistake. His basic concept of an infantry-heavy assault toward Tobruk while his armor drew the Axis tanks into battle farther south was sound, but the flaw was that he did not keep his armor concentrated, which enabled the Axis to defeat it in detail. The most intense fighting took place around the airfield at Sidi Rizegh, where the British lost a complete armored brigade. Cunningham now wanted to call off the battle, and Rommel, seeing the British now off balance, gathered up his Panzers and personally led them on a charge toward the Egyptian frontier. Auchinleck, keeping his nerve, replaced Cunningham with his own deputy chief of staff, General Ritchie, and ordered the thrust toward Tobruk to continue. In the meantime, Rommel, out of contact

with his own headquarters and faced with increasing casualties, shortage of fuel and determined resistance, fought on. When he did regain contact with his staff on the 27th, he realized that the situation around Tobruk was serious and that he would have to retrace his steps. The British advance was gaining momentum and, to avoid being outflanked from the south, Rommel began to pull his forces back to prepared

ABOVE: *Sir Claude Auchinleck, known as 'The Auk' by his men, who commanded in the Middle East 1941-42. Relieved by Alexander in August 1942, he went on to spend the rest of the war as Commander-in-Chief in India.*

LEFT: *British tank crews put their newly issued M3 General Grant medium tanks through their paces. These tanks began arriving in the Middle East in spring 1942 and were much welcomed by the Eighth Army, although the position of the 75mm gun in the sponson meant that almost the whole tank was exposed to the enemy when it was used.*

positions around Gazala. Tobruk was finally relieved on 10 December, and Rommel retired to Tripolitania in order to draw breath and force the British to operate on extended lines of communication. The British now reoccupied the Cyrenaican bulge and, as they had done the previous year, sent many units back to the Delta to refit.

Rommel waited little time and struck once more on 21 January.

Within two weeks he had once more driven the Eighth Army out of the bulge and it had taken up a defensive position along the line Gazala-Bir Hacheim. There was now a pause for almost four months while both sides made plans. These revolved around Malta, against which the Axis air forces had stepped up their attacks since the beginning of the year. For the Axis, the capture of Malta meant that their convoys

ABOVE: *The greatest fear of British tank crews in the desert was the German 88mm flak gun used in the antitank role. It was a German tactic to use their tanks to draw the British onto these guns which had a killing range of 2000 yards.*
RIGHT: *Erwin Rommel (second from right), the Desert Fox. He was so revered by both his own men and his foes, that Auchinleck had to issue an order to the Eighth Army stating that Rommel was not superhuman!*

LEFT: *German PzKw Mk IIIs await the order to move forward. This version mounts a 50mm gun. One major advantage which German tanks enjoyed over their enemy was that they had both solid shot and high explosive ammunition, unlike the British tank guns which only fired solid shot. This was acceptable for engaging tanks, but not against antitank guns.*

across the Mediterranean would suffer fewer losses, but Rommel successfully argued that if he was to make use of this for seizing the Suez Canal, he needed to recapture Tobruk first in order to keep his lines of communication as short as possible. Conversely, Churchill saw the recapture of the airfields in western Cyrenaica as vital if Malta was to hold out. Auchinleck, however, was not prepared to attack again until he had restored his losses in tanks during the recent fighting.

As it happened, it was Rommel who struck first, early on 27 May. On the surface the Eighth Army appeared to have a strong defense, but it was fatally flawed in that it consisted of a series of fortified positions which were too far apart to support one another. Also, once again the British had failed to concentrate their armor. Thus, Rommel was able to penetrate and, in spite of desperate efforts by the Eighth Army, especially at Bir Hacheim, which was gallantly defended by the Free French, it was gradually forced back. As the confusion generated by a series a fluid tank battles increased, so the British lost their grip on the situation and by the middle of June they were beginning to

withdraw. This quickly gave way to a wholesale retreat. Tobruk was once more invested, but this time it held out only for a few days, its defenses having been allowed to deteriorate since the first siege. Ritchie decided to stake all on standing on a defense at Mersa Matruh, but Auchinleck countermanded this, sacked Ritchie and took personal control of the Eighth Army. Instead, he decided to stand fast at El Alamein, the last defendable position before Cairo and, if need be, continue the fight across the Suez Canal into Palestine. By the end of June the Eighth Army was back at Alamein.

Although Rommel had had an advantage in recent months of being able to gauge British intentions through intercepts of the coded traffic with Washington of the United States military attaché in Cairo, the British had Ultra, which was invaluable, especially for a setpiece battle such as was just about to be fought.

Rommel attacked Auchinleck on 1 July 1942, but did not make the progress for which he had hoped, being held up until evening by an Indian brigade of whose presence he had been unaware. Next day he

LEFT: *Unlike the previous year, in June 1942, Tobruk fell quickly to Rommel. Here the defenders are marched away into captivity. This event marked the lowest ebb of British fortunes in North Africa.*
BELOW: *New brooms in the desert, August 1942. Left to right: Alexander (Commander-in-Chief Middle East), Churchill, Montgomery (commanding Eighth Army), Brooke (Chief of the Imperial General Staff).*

tried again, but was bothered both by British counterattacks and the Desert Air Force, which was making its presence felt. Throughout the next two weeks counterattack followed attack, but neither side was able to make an impression. Thereafter it was just the British who were attacking, but with the same result. Eventually, on 27 July, both sides fell back exhausted. Auchinleck had stopped Rommel, but had not been able to wrest the initiative from him.

A week later Churchill arrived in Cairo to see for himself and he decided that fresh blood was needed. Less than two weeks later General Sir Harold Alexander arrived to take over as Commander-in-Chief Middle East and, with him, came General Bernard Montgomery, who had seen no action since distinguishing himself as the best of the divisional commanders in France in 1940. Between them, they set to to overhaul the Eighth Army. They did not have much time, for Ultra told them that Rommel intended to launch a further offensive sooner rather than later.

Pearl Harbor

The Japanese strike on Pearl Harbor on 7 December 1941 was no sudden rush of blood to the head, but the result of months, even years, of careful planning. While they had hoped to fulfill their ambitions of a Far Eastern empire as much as possible through peaceful means, and certainly did not want to confront the United States militarily unless they had to, the Japanese had to be prepared for the worst case.

The driving force behind the plan was Admiral Isoroku Yamamoto, who had been Commander-in-Chief of the Japanese Combined Fleet since August 1939. Unlike most naval men of the time, he was a great believer in the aircraft carrier, seeing it, rather than the battleship, as the decisive weapon in the war at sea. The aircraft carrier gave a fleet the ability to strike at an enemy at a great distance, far outranging the 16-inch gun. In the event of war with the United States the main threat to Japan was the US Pacific Fleet and if this could be destroyed before it had a chance to come into action Japan would create herself a major advantage which would be difficult to offset.

Until early 1941, however, the accepted plan was to seize the Philippines first and then wait for the Americans to react. This, too, was what the American planners expected to happen, and the Japanese seizure of Indo-China in July 1941 seemed to confirm this. The British success at Taranto against the Italian Fleet in November 1940 had shown that an attack by carrier-borne aircraft against a fleet in its base was certainly feasible, and Yamamoto took careful note of it, using it successfully to persuade the Japanese government to change to the Pearl Harbor option.

When the United States, Britain, and also the Dutch Government-in-Exile froze Japanese assets at the end of July 1941, it meant an automatic embargo on trade with Japan. For Japan, what was crucial about this was oil, for she was almost totally reliant on imports of this commodity. Admittedly she had three years' worth of stocks at peacetime usage rates at the time of the embargo, but these would be swallowed up in half the time if she was at war. Therefore she pleaded with the United States to lift the ban, but in vain. There was hope that perhaps the United States, given her isolationist attitude, might give in or perhaps stand aside while Japan seized oil-rich colonies from the British or Dutch, but an American decision to defend the Philippines in time of war and her sending of reinforcements there indicated otherwise. In the meantime Japanese agents throughout the world were gathering information, much of it very accurate, on the precise dispositions and plans of the Western colonial powers in the East.

For some time the Americans had been able to read the Japanese top secret codes, the equivalent of the German Ultra and called Magic. This was especially so with the diplomatic communications between Tokyo and the Japanese ambassador to Washington DC. Thus, every time the ambassador made a demand, the US State Department knew about it beforehand.

BELOW: *Pearl Harbor, Hawaii, base of the US Pacific Fleet, as seen in a photograph taken in October 1941. A similar tranquil scene would have greeted the attacking Japanese a few weeks later.*

In mid-October 1941, a new Japanese prime minister was appointed, General Hideki Tojo. He had a reputation as a hardliner and he quickly decided that the United States must be given an ultimatum to accede to Japanese demands by the end of November or face the consequences. Ambassador Nomura in Washington was warned on 20 November that war was likely and through this the Americans were also alerted, but they had no inkling that the first Japanese blow would be against Pearl Harbor. The Japanese fleet itself set sail on the 26th, but while United States Signals intelligence was able to detect movement of ships toward Hong Kong, Indo-China and Malaya, there was no sound from the six aircraft carriers with the fleet. On the night of 6/7 December it became clear to the Americans that war was about to break out when they intercepted another signal from Tokyo to Ambassador Nomura telling him to tell the American authorities that negotiations were at an end. But there was still no indication of where the Japanese would strike first.

Meanwhile the Japanese carriers had now arrived, as yet undetected, within range of Pearl Harbor. They had purposely chosen a Sunday to attack because they knew that the Pacific Fleet would be in port. To their disappointment, however, the three carriers which they viewed as the primary target were not there. Nevertheless the attack was to go ahead.

LEFT: *The aftermath of the attack. The destroyers* Cassin *and* Downes *lie wrecked in the foreground. The battleship* Pennsylvania, *although seriously damaged in the stern, flies Old Glory in defiance.*
BELOW: *The* West Virginia *and* Tennessee *would have sunk completely, had it not been for the fact that they were moored in shallow water.*

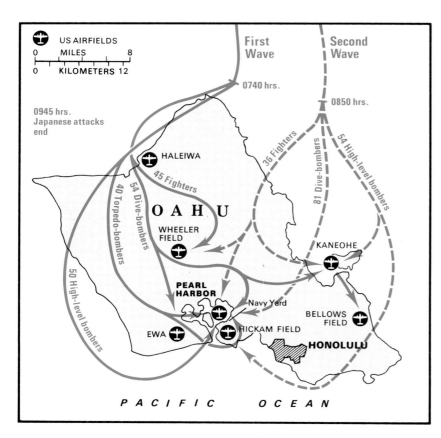

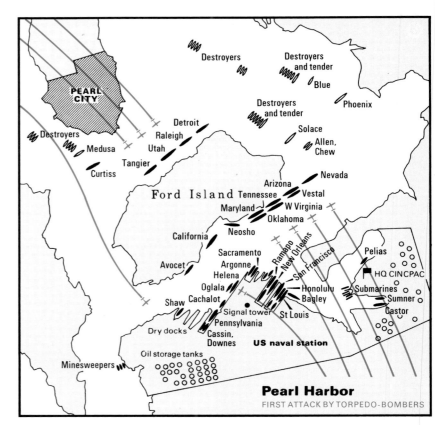

Pearl Harbor
FIRST ATTACK BY TORPEDO-BOMBERS

ABOVE LEFT AND RIGHT: *How the Japanese made their attack. They attacked not just the ships but the air bases as well.*

At 0700 hours local time a radar station on Oahu Island spotted a swarm of unidentified aircraft approaching the base. This was reported, but no action was taken on the assumption that they were friendly. Half an hour later, coming in from the north, they were over Pearl Harbor and attacking. Then came another attack from the east. In two hours, of the eight United States battleships present, four were sunk and four badly damaged. Three destroyers were also sunk, as were four smaller vessels, and four other ships badly damaged. The Americans also lost 188 aircraft, mostly on the ground, a further 63 were damaged, and almost 3500 people were killed or wounded. The Japanese, on the other hand, lost a mere 29 out of 340 aircraft engaged, plus five midget submarines, but they had failed to locate the three American carriers, which for the future was to be significant. They were also at war with a nation whose material and human resources they could never hope to match.

BELOW: *The first news of the attack carried in an Hawaiian newspaper. No information on American ship or aircraft losses is given for obvious reasons. The death toll was much higher than indicated here.*

BELOW: *An American battleship engulfed in flames. The crew of a boat looks vainly for survivors. Luckily, with the fleet being in port and it being a Sunday, many of the sailors were ashore.*

ABOVE LEFT: *Yet another view of the carnage from the attack. While surprise was complete, the Japanese failed to catch their prime target, the carriers, and also did not attack the oil storage tanks.*

ABOVE: *A grim-faced Roosevelt signs the United States declaration of war on Japan. Hitler saved him a dilemma over going to war with Germany as well.*

LEFT: *The US Navy buries its dead. They would in time be revenged.*

The Japanese Onrush

The attack on Pearl Harbor was not an isolated strike by the Japanese. Their object was to launch a number of simultaneous attacks in order to achieve their aim of the Greater East Asia Co-prosperity Sphere before the Allies had time to react and then hold it against whatever the Allies might throw at them.

On 7 December 1941, as Pearl Harbor was being attacked, two United States outposts, the islands of Wake and Guam, far to the west of Pearl Harbor, were attacked from the air, and Midway, some 1000 miles northwest of Hawaii, was subjected to naval bombardment. But this was not all. Japanese troops crossed the border from China to invade the British colony of Hong Kong. British airfields in Malaya and on the island of Singapore came under air attack, as did Clark Field in the Philippines. Amphibious landings were also made in southern Thailand and northern Malaya.

First to fall into Japanese hands was Guam, on 10 December. Two weeks later, in spite of a gallant defense by the US garrison, which had no hope of reinforcement, Wake, too, was overrun. Hong Kong was in much the same situation and the British General Staff had been well aware that no reinforcement would be possible for at least 90 days. The British, Indian and Canadian garrison was quickly forced to withdraw to Hong Kong island and surrendered on Christmas Day.

In Malaya, the British, Australian, Indian and Malay troops outnumbered their attackers, but were not as well equipped. Since, too, the RAF had overall responsibility for defense, the force was primarily and wrongly deployed to guard airfields. Furthermore, little jungle training had been carried out. The Japanese quickly seized the airfields in the north, but worse followed on 10 December. Japanese aircraft based in Indo-China attacked and sank the Royal Navy's two largest warships in the theater, the *Prince of Wales* and *Repulse*, which were steaming to intercept further Japanese landings, once again demonstrating the potency of aircraft against surface warships. Using the jungle to outflank the Allied positions, the Japanese cleared Malaya by the end of January, driving the defenders across the causeway to Singapore island. During the 1930s large coastal guns had been emplaced on the island which was generally held to be impenetrable. What the planners

ABOVE: *Admiral Isoroku Yamamoto who masterminded the attack on Pearl Harbor and the Japanese Pacific onrush.*

BELOW: *Japanese troops, after overrunning the new Territories and crossing over to the island of Hong Kong.*

had not catered for, though, was an attack across the causeway, and when this happened, Singapore surrendered shortly afterward on 15 February.

Toward the end of December, the Allies formed a joint command, ABDA (American, British, Dutch, Australian) under British general, Archibald Wavell, in order to develop a coherent defense, but it was too late. It was, however, only in Java in the Dutch East Indies which the Japanese now invaded, that the opportunity came to put this into effect with troops of all four countries involved. Not that it had much effect, since the Japanese soon captured these territories.

ABOVE LEFT: *Mitsubishi Ki-21 heavy bombers attack Rangoon, capital of Burma. The British had few aircraft to defend Burma, as elsewhere in the Far East.*
ABOVE RIGHT: *The humiliation of defeat. Canadian defenders of Hong Kong after its surrender on Christmas Day, 1941. At this stage they probably had little idea of what lay in store for them as prisoners of the Japanese.*
LEFT: *Japanese soldiers enter Rangoon's railway station, 8 March 1942. The British defenders, in danger of being cut off, had withdrawn the previous day.*

LEFT: *The surrender of Singapore, 15 February 1942. 70,000 Australian, British and Indian troops were taken prisoner. The surrender came as a severe shock to the British people.*
BELOW: *General Douglas MacArthur with his celebrated corncob pipe. He conducted a grim defense on the Bataan peninsula. Evacuated to Australia on Roosevelt's orders to become commander SW Pacific Area, he declared: 'I came through and I shall return.' Two-and-one-half years later he fulfilled this vow.*
RIGHT: *The Japanese celebrate yet another victory. In spring 1942 they seemed to the Allies to be unstoppable, but soon the tide would start to turn.*

The Japanese also had their eye on Burma and had been subjecting it to air attack since mid-December. The invasion proper began on 20 January. The story here was much the same as in Malaya, with the defenders outnumbering the attackers, but the latter proving overwhelmingly superior in tactics and equipment suitable for jungle warfare. Rangoon, the capital, was evacuated on 7 March and in April the Burma Road, the one land line of communication between China and India, was cut. From then on it was virtually a rout, with the last of the Allied troops crossing the border in nothing more than they stood up in in mid-May. Simultaneously the Japanese began to make their presence felt in the Indian Ocean, raiding the British naval base in Ceylon from the air and sinking merchant shipping in the Bay of Bengal. They also landed troops in Papua New Guinea and launched air attacks on Darwin in northern Australia.

This left the Philippines, whose defense was entrusted to General Douglas MacArthur, World War I hero and former US Army Chief of Staff, who had then retired to become military adviser to the Filipino government, but had been recalled to United States Army active duty in July 1941. Much of his 140,000 man garrison consisted of poorly trained and equipped Filipinos and he relied on the 30,000 United States troops and Filipino Scouts, whom he positioned around Manila, the capital. The initial Japanese landings were made on the northern and outlying Batan group of islands in order to give them airfields from which to operate shorter range aircraft. This was followed by landings on the north and southeast coasts of the main island of Luzon and, on 22 December, a major landing was made 120 miles north of Manila. Four days later the capital was declared an open city and the defenders withdrew to the fortified Bataan peninsula to the west. Here the initial Japanese attacks were easily repulsed and, although MacArthur was not aware of it, by early February the defenders significantly outnumbered the attackers thanks to malaria and the transfer of one of the two Japanese divisions to the Dutch East Indies. The defenders, however, had their problems. Supplies were limited and it also became clear that no effort was being made by Washington to send a relief force. Furthermore, in early March, MacArthur was ordered to Australia to take over the newly formed Southwest Pacific command. All this caused a lowering of morale and, at the beginning of April, when the Japanese, now heavily reinforced with fresh troops, renewed their attacks, the defense quickly caved in. General Jonathan Wainright, now in command, withdrew the survivors to the fortified island of

Corregidor, two miles offshore. After three weeks heavy artillery and air pounding, the Japanese landed on the night of 5/6 May. In spite of mounting a fierce resistance in the initial stages of the attack, Wainright was forced to surrender within hours.

Within six months the Japanese had achieved almost all their territorial ambitions. That they had done so with such apparent ease was in no small measure due to the way in which the Western powers had underestimated their military capabilities. Those who had to pay the greatest penalty for this were the captured Allied soldiers. The Japanese regarded surrender as dishonorable and reflected this in the inhuman treatment meted out to their prisoners. Yet in spring 1942 there were two glimmers of light for the Allies. The first was an audacious raid by carrier-launched B-25 bombers led by Lieutenant Colonel James H Doolittle on three Japanese cities, including Tokyo, on 18 April, and the second the first proper clash between the opposing battle fleets in the Pacific.

The Arsenal of Democracy

What President Roosevelt called 'a day that will live in infamy,' 7 December 1941, did not catch the United States totally unprepared for war. While as late as May 1941 a Gallup poll showed that 79 percent of Americans were against voluntary entry into the war, the majority expected that the United States would be dragged in sooner or later. More important, American industry had, since the passing of the Lend Lease bill, been gearing itself up for wartime production.

The first two beneficiaries of Lend Lease were Britain and China, but increasingly they had to compete with the requirements of the United States' own armed forces which began to expand in preparation for the war that became increasingly inevitable. In particular China suffered, although in part this was because Roosevelt hoped that some sort of peace could be maintained in the Far East so that he could concentrate on Europe.

Where the United States had a major advantage over the rest of the world was in her natural resources. At the time she produced two thirds of the world's petroleum supplies and half of the world's cotton and copper, and had to import only a few essential minerals. Combined with this was a flair for efficient management. Thus the transformation from a peace to war footing was carried out relatively painlessly. Soon factories were turning out the tanks, guns, ships, planes and all the other paraphernalia of war in ever increasing quantities.

What was especially significant was the ability to streamline manufacturing processes, reflecting ingenuity and the efficient use of resources. No better example of this exists than in the Liberty ships. During the crisis years of the Battle of the Atlantic the U-boats were sinking merchant ships at a faster rate than they could be built. American shipbuilders therefore evolved the idea of manufacturing prefabricated sections which could be done by plants well inland. These were then transported to the yards on the coast, where they were put together to create a ship. This radically reduced building time and was one factor which led the Allies finally to gain ascendancy in the Atlantic in spring 1943.

ABOVE LEFT: *Hollywood stars do their bit for the war effort – Lt Clark Gable USAAF. Many joined the US armed forces, while others gave their services as entertainers.*
LEFT: *Assembling B-29 Superfortresses, which were to help to bring Japan finally to her knees, at the Boeing plant at Wichita, Kansas. Development began in March 1938, and the first combat mission was flown on 5 June 1944. By the end of the war no less than 3000 B-29 Superfortresses had been delivered.*

With Russia's forced entry into the war on the side of Britain in June 1941, there came further demands for American aid. To begin with, this was limited and had to make use of the Arctic convoy route. In September 1941, however, the British and Russians occupied Persia (Iran) and the British were able to give the Russians on the Caucasian front some aid using the railroad running from Basra to the Caspian. During 1942 they expanded this and also built a highway, which crossed the border with Russia east of the Caspian. The Americans began to use this route more and more, although it was not until 1943 that their contribution began to be significant, especially in terms of trucks. Indeed, although the Russians themselves would never admit it, they became almost totally reliant on American mechanical transport vehicles. Likewise, the United States also opened up another route from Alaska to Siberia which was used to supply bombers.

Yet while America's allies became increasingly dependent on her material support, her own armed forces did not go short, and her ability to maintain production and supply was one of the truly great achievements of the war. Before the war ended America had built well over 600,000 Willys Jeeps and almost 50,000 M4 General Sherman tanks. For General Eisenhower final victory could be attributed to the production and supply of Willy's Jeeps, C-47 Skytrain (Dakota) transport aircraft and landing craft.

This massive industrial effort helped to ensure eventual victory, but it also greatly benefitted the United States domestically. The large expansion required brought about a boom which overshadowed that of the 1920s, providing full employment for the first time for years and a significant increase in the living standards of the average American. It also meant that at the end of the war America came out economically stronger than before, while her allies were financially crippled and exhausted.

ABOVE: *An unusual US recruiting poster, reflecting one of the cornerstones of democracy. The American-Jewish element had been significantly enlarged by the arrival of refugees from Nazi dominated countries in the late 1930s.*
LEFT: *US Army recruits at drill. As part of his preparations for war, President Roosevelt introduced his Selective Service Act in 1940. This meant that the US Army already had over 1.6 million men under arms at the time of Pearl Harbor, compared with 210,000 in September 1939.*

Life in Occupied Europe

The darkness which engulfed the continent of Europe during 1940 and 1941 affected different people in different ways. Much of it depended on the German attitude to the country concerned. Thus the nations of the east, especially Poland and occupied Russia, suffered much more harsh treatment than, say, Denmark, whose king and government were left, at least until 1943, to run the country with little German interference. It also depended on the individual's political persuasion. Those who espoused fascism – there were a significant number in all the occupied countries – and were prepared to collaborate with the Germans, enjoyed perks and privileges which others did not. On the other hand, members of the various resistance movements, those with leftwing leanings and, above all, Jews, were virtually under constant threat.

In most cases, the German system of government was based on the appointment of a Reich commissioner for each occupied state. He in turn gave orders through the existing government machinery, both at national and local levels. While the Germans made some use of indigenous fascist elements, they often distrusted them, and their main activity became recruitment for the foreign legions of the Waffen-SS, the military arm of Himmler's political 'shock troops.' There were, however, exceptions to this. Denmark, as we have already seen, was one and Vichy France, until November 1942, was another.

In each occupied territory, whether or not there was a Reich commissioner, German armed forces were stationed and, in collaboration with the local police force, were generally responsible for maintaining law and order. Two other organizations also had a hand in this, the Abwehr and the Allgemeine-SS. The former was the main intelligence-gathering agency and spent its time trying to penetrate resistance groups. The Allgemeine, or 'General' SS, on the other hand, was much more concerned with rooting out Jews and other political undesirables, but the latter included the Resistance. Often, though, it would operate independently of the Reich commissioner and the Abwehr, a symptom of the constant rivalry to be found among the tools of government within the Third Reich.

The general effect of the occupation on the local population was marked by restrictions of movement, with sensitive military areas, such as coastlines, being placed out of bounds, and the disappearance of many items from store shelves. This was partly because overseas trade had come to a halt, but also because many foodstuffs and other vital commodities, such as fuel, were commandeered by the Germans for their own use. Civilians could be and often were called upon to carry out laboring tasks for the occupation forces and most factories were adapted to the manufacture of war material. As the war went on, the Germans turned increasingly to the occupied countries to provide labor within Germany itself. Men were conscripted for this, but they were treated comparatively well unless they were from the territories of the east.

Hitler regarded the Slavs as subhumans and, unlike the populations of Western Europe, totally expendable. They were therefore to be used as slave labor and treated as such; their conditions were appalling and millions died. Indeed, it was one of the fatal errors that the Germans made when they invaded Russia. Many of the peasants, for whom communism was abhorrent because it did not allow them to work their own land, had welcomed the German troops with open arms and were happy to work for them. The appearance of the SS, though, who treated the local population ruthlessly, quickly drove the majority of the peasantry back into Stalin's arms, and many of them joined the partisans.

LEFT: *Youthful members of the Danish Resistance. Two of them are armed with British Sten guns, probably dropped in by parachute. Some, however, were produced in underground arms' factories.*
FACING PAGE, ABOVE LEFT: *German soldiers sightseeing in Paris. Up until 1944 many of the divisions making up the German garrison of the occupied countries came for short spells to recover from combat on the Eastern front.*
FACING PAGE, ABOVE RIGHT: *In spite of the shortages, Parisiennes still managed to maintain their traditional chic.*
FACING PAGE, BELOW: *Those with fascist leanings often volunteered for service with the foreign legions of the Waffen-SS, believing Russia to be the main enemy. Here French volunteers of the SS Charlemagne Division depart for the Eastern Front.*

Most of those under German occupation were prepared to endure it until such time as liberation came. Others, brave men and women, resented the German presence from the start and were determined to take positive action, both to make life uncomfortable for their uninvited guests and to accelerate liberation. To assist them the British created the Special Operations Executive (SOE) in the summer of 1940, and when the Americans entered the war in 1941 they formed a similar organization, the Office of Strategic Services (OSS). Their task was to foster and encourage these resistance movements through the supply of equipment and the training of agents. The main activities of the Resistance were sabotage and the gathering of intelligence, but it was a dangerous game to play. Members knew that if they were caught they would have to pay with their lives and endure torture, especially if they fell into the hands of Himmler's dreaded secret police, the

RIGHT: *Two youthful Russian partisans are summarily executed. The partisan movement in German-occupied Russia began with soldiers who had been cut off during Barbarossa. It grew rapidly once the true face of the Third Reich was revealed to the Russian people.*
BELOW: *French workers employed as forced labor by the Germans to build fortifications. The penalty for trying to evade this labor was the concentration camp.*

Gestapo. Many suffered this fate through betrayal or penetration by the Abwehr.

Initially the communists in the occupied countries stayed out of the Resistance, but after the invasion of Russia, they became wholehearted supporters. Often, though, there was little love lost between the communists and other resistance groups. This was especially so in the Balkans. In Yugoslavia, for instance, Josef Broz Tito's communist partisans clashed violently with the royalist Ustachi to such an extent that the latter often sided with the Germans. It was the same, although not to such an extreme, in Greece. The communists

LEFT: *One means of passive resistance was the painting of 'V for Victory' signs on walls. This one also has a 'Death to Hitler' symbol.*
BELOW: *On 29 May 1942, Reinhard Heydrich, Protector of Bohemia and Moravia, was mortally wounded by two Czech agents in Prague. Twelve days later, as one of many reprisals, the Germans shot the entire male population of the village of Lidice and shipped the women to Ravensbruck concentration camp. The children, half of whom are shown here in a school photograph, were sent to Germany and brought up under different names. Many were never traced. The village was razed to the ground.*

were also suspicious of both SOE and OSS and it was often very difficult for Allied agents to strike up any rapport with them. Nevertheless the part played by the resistance movements, both non-communist and communist, was vital in tying down German forces and in providing valuable intelligence.

It was, however, the Jewish communities which suffered most in occupied Europe, especially once the Nazis became bent on their total extermination and began building death camps. Their horrific sufferings are covered in the third section of this book (see *The Final Solution* p 158).

103

Coral Sea and Midway

Flushed with their recent successes, in May 1942 the Japanese decided to enlarge their perimeter in the Pacific by capturing further groups of islands, including Midway, the Gilbert and Ellice islands, New Hebrides, Fiji, New Caledonia, the Solomons, Papua and Port Moresby on New Guinea. The Japanese plan envisaged firstly a landing on the small island of Tulagi, one of the more southerly of the Solomons, in order to establish a seaplane base there, and then a landing at Port Moresby. Tulagi, which the Australians had evacuated, was occupied on 3 May, and the Japanese then turned their attention to Port Moresby.

The American codebreakers had, however, managed to ascertain the gist of the Japanese intentions. Accordingly Admiral Chester Nimitz, now commanding the Pacific Ocean area as opposed to MacArthur's Southwest Pacific command, dispatched a naval task force under Rear Admiral Frank Fletcher to intercept the Japanese landings. This was built around the two available aircraft carriers, *Lexington* and *Yorktown* (the other two carriers in commission, *Enterprise* and *Hornet*, were still involved with the Doolittle raid on Japan), and two cruiser escort groups. The Japanese naval force had one small and two large carriers. What was about to happen was the first naval battle in which the opposing ships never set eyes on one another.

BELOW: *A B-25 Mitchell takes off from the carrier USS* Hornet *for Colonel James H Doolittle's raid on Japanese cities on 18 April 1942. Although the raid proved successful, bad weather caused most aircraft to crash in China.*

RIGHT: *Frank J Fletcher who commanded the US carrier task force at Coral Sea.*

LEFT: *The Battle of Midway. Japanese aircraft strike the carrier* Yorktown. *She had been damaged during the Battle of the Coral Sea, but was now sunk. Revenge was gained next day when the* Hiryu, *whose aircraft had attacked her, was herself sunk.*
BELOW: *USS* Lexington *during the Battle of the Coral Sea. Most of her crew managed to get off and she remained afloat for some hours before a US torpedo finally sank her.*

Fletcher missed striking the Japanese carriers during the Tulagi landing, although the day after his aircraft did sink a Japanese destroyer. This, however, made the Japanese aware of his presence, and they reacted by sending their carriers southward, to the east of the Solomons, hoping to catch Fletcher in the rear. He, meanwhile, moved to intercept the force bound for Port Moresby. Early on 7 May Japanese aircraft thought they had spotted a carrier and cruiser, but these were actually a destroyer and tanker, and both were sunk. Late that day Fletcher retaliated by sinking the light carrier *Shoho* en route to Port Moresby. The significance of this was that it caused the Japanese to postpone their landing, the first time that they had been thwarted. The battle, however, was not yet over. Next day the two forces finally came to grips properly. The subsequent air strikes resulted in the Japanese carrier *Shokaku* being badly damaged; and on the American side the carrier *Lexington* was so badly hit that she sank and the *Yorktown* suffered some damage. Fletcher then withdrew his force, and thus ended the Battle of the Coral Sea. At the time matters appeared inconclusive, although the Japanese were forced to turn away from Port Moresby. But the sequel to this drawn battle was not long in coming.

ABOVE: *Admiral Chuichi Nagumo, the driving force behind Japanese naval aviation. He refused to leave his flagship, the carrier* Akagi, *after she was struck at Midway, and went down with her.*

BELOW: *'Pilots, man your planes!' US Navy pilots dash to their Grumman Wildcats in order to strike again at the Japanese fleet.*

The Japanese now turned to Midway. The aim here was twofold, to capture the island and to destroy the United States Pacific Fleet. In order to achieve the latter they decided to make a subsidiary landing on the Aleutians, far to the north and off the coast of Alaska. This was to be a preliminary designed to fix the attention of the United States fleet. The bulk of their navy was concentrated on Midway itself, hoping to be able to catch Nimitz's ships as they sailed north to the Aleutians, and then trap them between the two task forces. Nimitz's main concern was his inferiority in numbers of ships. Because of Pearl Harbor, he had no battleships, while the Japanese were fielding eleven for the combined operation, and he only had three carriers compared with eight Japanese. The one major advantage which he did have was, with the breaking of the Japanese code, better intelligence.

On 3 June the Aleutians task force arrived off the islands and launched air attacks which were repeated the next day, but caused little significant damage. In the meantime Nimitz had positioned his carriers well to the north of Midway so that they could take the task force headed for the island in the flank. On 4 June Admiral Nagumo, who had commanded the Pearl Harbor task force, launched air attacks against Midway, causing considerable damage. Midway-based American aircraft struck back at him, and he ordered a second wave to attack the airfields so as to neutralize this threat. By now Nimitz was aware of his presence and launched waves of aircraft to attack Nagumo's carriers. Three out of four were sunk, but the one survivor, the *Hiryu*, struck the *Yorktown* with her aircraft and destroyed her. *Hiryu* did not, however, survive for long, being hit by American aircraft and eventually sinking in the early hours of the 5th.

If the Coral Sea was possibly indecisive, there was no doubt of the outcome of the Battle of Midway. It was a clearcut American victory. Although the Japanese did land on three islands in the Aleutian chain, it was of little advantage to them, since the inhospitable climate and unfriendly terrain meant the islands had little strategic value. Japanese losses off Midway, on the other hand, meant that the capture of the island was no longer possible, but, more importantly in the final analysis, these sunken carriers caused the Japanese to be much more circumspect in the employment of their fleet, and gave the Americans time to enlarge the Pacific Fleet.

LEFT: *Damaged or out of fuel, a Douglas Dauntless divebomber ditches alongside a US cruiser after a sortie during the Battle of Midway. Note the cruiser's floatplane, used for reconnaissance.*
BELOW: *The USS* Yorktown, *with a destroyer standing by to take off any crew still on board, slowly settles and sinks.*

This did not mean to say that Midway halted the Japanese advance. The landings in the northeast of New Guinea in March 1942 at Lae were reinforced in July by landings at Buna in an attempt to seize Port Moresby from the landward side by advancing over the Owen Stanley Mountains. The Australian defenders were driven back to only 30 miles from Port Moresby before, in the most inhospitable conditions, they began to drive the Japanese back over what had now become known as the Kokoda trail. Meanwhile, in August, the Japanese made

another landing at Milne Bay in the extreme southeast of Papua, but this was contained and the Japanese were eventually driven back into the sea.

In the Solomons, the Japanese gradually worked their way down the chain, using aircraft from one island to support the landing on the next one. But this was to be brought to a halt in August 1942 when the Americans began to counterattack. The tide in the Pacific was now beginning to turn in favor of the Allies.

Stilwell and China

On 23 January 1942 General Joseph Stilwell was appointed Commanding General United States Army Forces in the China-Burma-India Theater, Chief of Staff to the Supreme Commander China Theater, supervisor of Lend-Lease, and United States representative on any Allied war council in the region. His tasks were to keep open the Burma Road, command such Chinese forces as might be assigned to him, improve the combat efficiency of the Chinese Army and increase the effectiveness of American aid to China.

The news of Pearl Harbor had been greeted with unconcealed delight by the Chinese, who, of course, had been at war with Japan for some ten years. On the very day of the attack Chiang Kai-shek summoned British and American representatives to a meeting at Chungking, his seat of government, and proposed that all the Allies, including Russia, should make the defeat of Japan their priority, concentrating all available airpower to do this. This ran counter to what the United States and Britain were about to agree in Washington, namely that Germany must come first, but, as a sop to the Chinese, Chiang Kai-shek was appointed Supreme Commander China Theater, and General Wavell, as the newly appointed head of ABDA, met him in Chungking on 23 December.

The meeting was not a success. The Chinese were very concerned over the stockpile of Lend-Lease supplies accumulating in Rangoon harbor, especially since Wavell wanted to use them for the defense of Burma. Likewise, there was an argument over who should have the right to the one United States combat formation already in China. This was a band of volunteer pilots under Colonel Claire Chennault, and known as Chennault's Flying Tigers. Concerned about Burma, Chiang Kai-shek offered Chinese troops to help in its defense, but this offer was turned down on the grounds that Burma could not feed the troops and the British did not want foreign troops fighting on their territory. It was thus understandable that the Chinese leader should turn to the Americans. They, in their turn, considered it important to prop the Chinese up for fear that they might make a separate peace with Japan.

BELOW: *Lt Gen Joseph W Stilwell confers with one of his Chinese divisional commanders. Dealing with the enigmatic Chinese was often frustrating, but Stilwell was well versed in their ways.*

ABOVE: *Chiang Kai-shek, Madame Chiang Kai-shek (whom many Americans believed was the 'power behind the throne') and General Claire L Chennault of Flying Tigers fame.*

Stilwell himself was an old China hand, who had first visited the country during the 1911 revolution, had been an intelligence officer there just after World War I, had later in the 1920s served with the 15th Infantry in Tientsin, and finally had been United States military attaché there in the late 1930s. There was therefore little that he did not know about the country or its people. His nickname of Vinegar Joe aptly summed up his character, and he had an almost pathological hatred of all things British.

Stilwell arrived in India at the end of February, in time to witness the disasters that were befalling the British in Burma. After discussions with Wavell, he flew on to Chungking and reported to Chiang Kai-shek. He was forcibly struck by the Chinese dislike of the British and that the Allied policy seemed to be to let the Japanese keep the initiative. Nevertheless, Chiang Kai-shek did agree to place two armies under his command, although there were strings attached, and he was allowed to employ some of these troops in northern Burma, north of Mandalay, to help the British, who were desperately trying to hold on to the western half of the country. This was in vain and, like the British, Stilwell found himself walking out of Burma and back into China on foot. The Japanese now tried to invade China along the Burma road, but the Chinese armies in the Yunnan, strongly supported by Chennault's aircraft, managed to stop them.

Although Stilwell wanted Chiang Kai-shek to set about planning a re-entry into Burma, the latter was now content to let his allies do his fighting for him. At the same time he demanded a stepping up of Lend-Lease. With Burma no longer available, the only way that this could be achieved was by air from India. To begin with, the United States Air Transport Command had only 25 aircraft for this purpose.

RIGHT: *Flying Tiger pilots scramble. They painted sharks' noses on their aircraft to taunt the Japanese, who had a traditional fear of them. Such was their success that they destroyed nearly 300 Japanese aircraft in six months fighting.*
BELOW: *Casualties of the war against the Japanese. Chinese Red Cross nurses with wounded soldiers in Chungking. After training, and given sufficient equipment, the Chinese soldier proved himself a match for the Japanese.*

The route over what the pilots called the 'Hump' was one of the most uncomfortable in the world because of the constant air turbulence, and many aircraft were to be lost.

The British, as well as Stilwell, were determined to re-enter Burma, but they needed Chinese military cooperation in the north. Stilwell recognized that for this to be effective the Chinese Army must be overhauled in order to make it a more modern and effective fighting force. For the rest of 1942 he was almost entirely involved in trying to persuade Chiang Kai-shek to let this happen. The Chinese leader's view, however, was that if the Americans boosted their as yet slender airpower in the country, this alone would be sufficient to defeat the Japanese. He also continuously complained about the small amount of supplies coming to him over the 'Hump,' but it was apparent that he wanted these more to secure and strengthen his own regime than to help in the Allied war effort.

During the fall of 1942, it seemed as though the Chinese were at last coming round to an offensive into Burma, but then, at the beginning of January 1943 they did an about-turn, complaining that the British and Americans did not have their hearts in what they were doing and that the Chinese could not afford another reverse in Burma. True, the British had launched a limited offensive in the Arakan in November 1942, which had quickly become bogged down, and Japanese airpower still dominated the Bay of Bengal. The Americans, too, because of commitments elsewhere, were unable to give Chiang Kai-shek the support that he wanted. For Stilwell, who was caught in the middle, it was a gloomy and frustrating time.

Special Forces

One of the most marked contrasts between World Wars I and II was the plethora of unorthodox forces raised by both sides in World War II. The reasons for this are many and varied.

Improved technology was one reason, and this is well reflected in the development of airborne troops. The concept had first been put forward by the American airman Billy Mitchell in France in 1918 as a means of disrupting the German rear areas. It was, however, not until the 1930s that serious attention was paid to the idea, and then by the Germans and the Russians. The early successes by the Germans during 1939-41 inspired all the combatant nations to raise airborne forces. It was the advent of suitable parachutes and aircraft which had made all this possible.

The fact too that World War II involved dictatorships which would stop at nothing to achieve their ends brought in a new ruthlessness. Less serious attention being paid to the traditional laws of war added to this ruthless tendency. Thus, at the outset of their invasion of Poland in 1939 the Germans used sabotage squads dressed in civilian clothes. Likewise, their Brandenburgers operated at times in Allied uniforms, as for example during the Ardennes counteroffensive in December 1944. The Allies, too, were also guilty of this. In 1942 in North Africa, the British employed a group of German-speaking Palestinian Jews, the Special Interrogation Group, who, dressed in Afrika Korps uniforms and using captured trucks, infiltrated the Axis lines.

There was also the need to give active support to the Resistance and this meant OSS and SOE teams operating with the Resistance groups and partisans, both to encourage and train them, as well as to ensure that they received the necessary supplies. These were usually delivered by air or sea. In the latter case, especially in the Aegean and Adriatic Seas, there were a number of clandestine naval forces. The OSS ran a fleet of schooners in the Adriatic and the Royal Navy had a similar fleet of local caiques operating in the eastern Mediterranean.

BELOW: *British Commandos with German prisoners after a successful raiding operation on the River Garigliano in Italy at the end of 1943.*

ABOVE: *A paratrooper of the US 17th Airborne Division ready to board his aircraft prior to the airborne drop in support of the 21st Army group crossing of the Rhine in March 1945.*

The constant need for accurate intelligence was another driving force behind Special Forces. Apart from the activities of the OSS and SOE in this field, there were many other organizations involved. In the Pacific the Australians organized their Coastwatchers, brave men who positioned themselves on the coasts of Japanese-held islands and monitored enemy shipping. The Germans were the first to recognize the need for trained intelligence personnel to operate with forward combat units in order to secure documents and equipment before they were destroyed, and they raised the Abwehrkommando, which was first used in the Balkans in 1941, for this purpose. The British followed suit with their 30 Assault Unit (alias No 30 Commando). Another British unit, Phantom, provided higher commanders with direct information on the progress of their forward troops.

Another sector of Special Forces had its origins in Churchill's urge to hit back at the Germans with any means available after the fall of France in 1940. This resulted in the raising of the Commandos, whose original role was raiding on the coasts of occupied Europe. Commandos were intially raised from volunteers from the armies in Britain and the Middle East, and they were later mirrored by the United States Rangers, who indeed initially did their training at the Commando depot in Scotland. Gradually, though, their role changed. Their expertise in amphibious operations meant that they came to be used more and more as the spearhead for the major Allied landings on the coasts of Europe. Nevertheless they continued to carry out raids.

In their turn the Commandos spawned many other Special Forces units and the North African desert was a popular birthplace. It was a young Commando officer, David Stirling, who conceived the idea of a specialist force for infiltrating the Axis lines and destroying aircraft on the ground. This was the original role of the Special Air Service (SAS) which he formed in the late summer of 1941. A sister organization was

RIGHT: *David Stirling (standing) with a patrol of his Special Air Service in North Africa, 1942. He was captured in Tunisia in January 1943, but the SAS rose to brigade strength by the end of the war.*
BELOW: *Men of Merrill's Marauders in northern Burma. Like the Chindits, they operated behind the Japanese lines. Their crowning feat was the capture of Myitkyina airfield in May 1944.*

the Special Boat Squadron (SBS), which specialized in using canoes launched from submarines to attack targets on enemy shores. Earlier than both the SAS and SBS in North Africa was the Long Range Desert Group (LRDG), which was formed in summer 1940 to operate as an intelligence-gathering unit behind the enemy lines, and the Italians had a similar unit in their AutoSaharan Group.

The concept of long-range penetration of the enemy lines was also used in Burma, both by Wingate's Chindits and Merrill's Marauders (see pp 162-5). Other Special Force units were formed specifically to support the maintenance of main force operations once ashore. Two examples of these were the United States Navy's construction battalions, or Seabees, who cleared obstructions in harbors and on beaches and airfields, often under enemy fire, on Pacific islands, and the RAF Servicing Commandos who performed a similar task on newly captured airfields. Beach reconnaissance prior to a landing was another highly specialized task, and for the British this highly dangerous and secret work was carried out by the Combined Operations Pilotage Parties (COPPs).

There were many other Special Forces units used by both sides, but space does not permit mention of them. That Special Forces played an important role in the war, there is no doubt, and no better proof of this is seen than in the importance attached to them to this day. At times, it is true, there seemed to be too many 'private armies' in existence and the result was confusion and muddle, the lesson being that to be effective they had to be carefully controlled and coordinated. Conventional forces, too, often resented them, especially since it was invariably their best men who volunteered for Special Forces duty. A popular image of Special Forces is that they contained the misfits who could not be employed anywhere else. True, they attracted many who found conventional soldiering constricting, but the high standards of self- and corporate discipline required were such that there was no place in them for the man who merely wanted to do his own thing.

The Tide Turns in North Africa

During August 1942 Rommel and the British Eighth Army stood glowering at one another at El Alamein in Egypt. Rommel was preparing for a last desperate bid to break through to the Suez Canal, while Montgomery was racing against time to reorganize his army so that Rommel would be stopped in his tracks. Montgomery's forceful personality quickly made itself felt by the men of the Eighth Army and his positiveness was a tonic after the seeming confusion and indecision of the previous months.

Ultra intercepts told Montgomery of the progress of his adversary's preparations and also when he was about to launch his attack. Ultra also helped the Royal Navy to intercept Rommel's supply ships as they crossed the Mediterranean, and the result was that Rommel was very short of fuel and realized that the only way he could reach Cairo was by capturing British stocks. Therefore on the night of 30/31 August his troops moved through their own minefields and began their attack. By the end of 1 September Rommel had had enough and pulled back to behind his own minefields. The British tried to follow up before he closed the gaps in the minefields, but without success. The Battle of Alam Halfa Ridge marked the final turn in Rommel's wheel of fortune in Egypt and Libya and the future held out nothing but retreat. Yet there would now be a pause before this happened, for Montgomery did not consider his army ready for offensive operations.

A new element was about to enter the war in North Africa, however. One of the courses of action considered at the Anglo-American Washington conference of December 1941 was an invasion of French North Africa. The British were attracted to it because it would remove the Axis presence from North Africa, establish an outer cordon around Germany and help secure British maritime communications through the Mediterranean. The American view was that it merely detracted from the primary objective of establishing the Second Front as soon as possible. Indeed they wanted it to take place in 1942, although the British thought this over optimistic. The British, however, had an ally in Roosevelt and, at the end of July he overrode his planners and

directed that Torch, as the operation was codenamed, was to take place by, if possible, 30 October. Appointed to command Torch was General Dwight D Eisenhower.

Eisenhower was ordered to secure the whole of French Morocco, Algeria and Tunisia and then bring about the annihilation of the Axis forces facing the British in the Western Desert. Three landings were to be made, at Casablanca in Morocco and at Oran and Algiers in Algeria. That at Casablanca was to be made by troops coming directly from the United States, while the other two task forces would sail from Scotland. The Algiers landing would be made by British and US troops, while the other two would be by American troops only.

ABOVE: *A near miss for the crew of this British 6-pounder antitank gun. The British used three types of antitank gun during the war, the 2-pounder, the 6-pounder and later the 17-pounder, which first made its appearance in Tunisia. Unlike the Germans, they never used anti-aircraft guns in the antitank role.*
LEFT: *Australian infantry in action during the last stages of the Battle of El Alamein. It was the last victory of the war to be won by the British alone. From now on they would fight closely with the Americans.*

RIGHT: *French Algerian native troops, Goums. They were excellent soldiers and, in spite of being short of equipment, if the French had decided to offer more than token resistance the Torch story might have been very different. Later the Goums would distinguish themselves in Tunisia and Italy.*
BELOW: *The Torch landings. Few of the Allied amphibious landings were to be as peaceful as these were.*

Much of the success of the landings depended on how the Vichy French defenders would react. Ever since Dakar there had been no love lost between the British and Vichy France, but the United States had maintained diplomatic relations with Pétain's government. For some months the United States consul general in French North Africa, Robert C Murphy, had been involved in delicate negotiations with the French commanders in an attempt to woo them over to the Allies, but no real progress was made until mid-October. By this time the date of Torch had been fixed as 8 November. General Mast, commanding the Algerian division of the Vichy forces, was very friendly with General Giraud, who had made a spectacular escape from a German prison camp in 1940 and was now living in Vichy France. It was thus arranged to bring Giraud across to Algeria in order to rally the French behind him once Torch had taken place. To reinforce these intentions, Eisenhower's deputy, General Mark Clark, was taken across by submarine to meet Mast in secret, and the latter agreed that his troops would offer only token resistance.

Thus all was now set and the optimism was increased by the news that on the night of 23/24 October Montgomery had launched his long-awaited attack on the Axis positions at El Alamein. It was, however, no walkover. Rommel's troops resisted fiercely, and it was

only after 12 days' bitter fighting that Montgomery was able to pass his armored divisions through the minefields and Rommel began to withdraw. Poor handling of the armor, and heavy rains which literally bogged down the pursuit, meant that Rommel was able to make good his escape, and there now began a long drive through Libya.

The Torch landings themselves went in almost exactly on schedule in the early hours of 8 November. The Germans were taken totally by surprise, Hitler being too preoccupied by the recent events in Egypt and on the Eastern Front. His first step, however, was to order the German occupation of Vichy France. French resistance to the landings was fiercer than expected. At Casablanca, shore batteries engaged the United States naval covering force and French ships counterattacked, which for a time seriously threatened the troop transports. The Center Task Force had problems in securing the port of Oran and also met opposition as they advanced inland, while at Algiers, the port also proved difficult to capture. Sporadic fighting went on for the next three days, and it was only on the 11th that an armistice arranged between Mark Clark and the French high commissioner in North Africa, Admiral Jean Darlan, finally came into effect. The next task was to secure Tunisia, but valuable time had already been lost and the Axis powers were beginning to fly in troops from Italy and Sicily.

New Guinea and Guadalcanal

When the Australians turned the Japanese back from in front of Port Moresby, New Guinea during the latter half of September 1942, they little imagined how long it was going to take to clear the Japanese from the island. True, by the beginning of November they had driven the Japanese back along the Kokoda trail to their startpoint, Buna, but here and around Gona they dug in and refused to budge. MacArthur sent in American reinforcements under a new commander, General Robert Eichelberger, whom he drove remorselessly, with apparently little understanding of the conditions which his troops were experiencing. Exhausted, short of rations and artillery, and riddled with disease, they were finding it an uphill struggle. Eventually, on 9 December, the Australians stormed and took Gona, but it was not until toward the end of January 1943 that Buna fell, and MacArthur could set about removing the enemy from the Lae region in the northeast of New Guinea.

Throughout all this time the Americans were also concerned with operations in the Solomon Islands. They were naturally very keen to exploit their victory at Midway and on 2 July the Joint Chiefs of Staff issued a directive. This called for a three stage offensive. First, Nimitz was to capture the Santa Cruz Islands and eastern Solomons, especially Tulagi and Guadalcanal, and then MacArthur was to clear the Japanese from Lae and regain the remainder of the Solomons, prior to capturing the main Japanese base in the southwest Pacific, Rabaul. There was some opposition from MacArthur to this as he wanted to go directly to Rabaul, but it was pointed out to him that he did not have the forces available to do this with any reasonable chance of success. Three days after the directive had been issued, however, news came that the Japanese were constructing an airfield on Guadalcanal, which would later become well known as Henderson Field. The implications for the American plans of bombers operating from here were serious, and it was decided that Guadalcanal must be taken before the airfield became operational.

On 7 August 1942 General Alexander Vandegrift's 1st United States Marine Division carried out an unopposed landing close to the airfield on Guadalcanal. Simultaneous landings were also made on Tulagi and two other islands, but only on Tulagi did the Japanese try to resist the landings. Henderson Field was quickly abandoned by the Japanese, who withdrew into the jungle. Their first positive reaction came on the night of 8/9 August, when, in an attempt to destroy the transports standing off the beaches, they sent a naval task force in from the northwest, which managed to slip through the American destroyer screen and sink four cruisers, damaging a fifth. The Battle of Savo Island was the first of many naval clashes which accompanied the fighting on Guadalcanal, and the American reaction was to withdraw

ABOVE: *Australia became the base for MacArthur's Southwest Pacific command and US formations were initially sent here from stateside before being committed to operations. GIs like these, however, would find it difficult at first to adapt to the steamy jungle heat.*
LEFT: *The campaign in New Guinea. Casualties from sickness were as high as from combat. Many lives were saved thanks to the dedication of the native stretcher-bearers struggling down the Kokoda Trail.*

RIGHT: *An Australian 3-inch mortar crew in action in New Guinea. The campaign here, in terms of both the terrain and logistics, was one of the toughest of the war.*
BELOW: *Men of 1st US Marine Division coming ashore at Guadalcanal in August 1942. Their attitudes and the tracks already on the beach indicate that they are reinforcements rather than leading waves.*

their naval forces to the south, leaving the marines on short rations and starved of air cover until Henderson Field was reactivated on the 20th.

Having initially underestimated the size of the landing, the Japanese now tried to run in reinforcements from Rabaul. One regiment was landed at Taivu, east of Henderson Field, on the 18th and immediately attacked the marines but was destroyed. Five days later came the next naval clash, when Fletcher's carriers intercepted a Japanese attempt to draw them into a trap. The result was that the Japanese lost a carrier and destroyer, while the carrier *Enterprise* was damaged. From now on the Japanese were reduced to running in reinforcements and sup-

plies by night. On 7 September the United States Marines carried out a successful raid on Taivu and gained warning of an impending Japanese attack. This came five days later when the Japanese were beaten back with heavy losses. There was now a lull while both sides brought in reinforcements. Then, on the night of 11/12 October came a further naval action, the United States Navy losing a destroyer to a cruiser and destroyer. This delayed the next land attack, which came in from the west on 23 October and was again beaten back. Three days later came the Battle of Santa Cruz, another clash between carriers, in which the *Hornet* was lost and the *Shokaku* and *Zuiho* severely damaged.

RIGHT: *A B-17 Flying Fortress over Sizo Island in early October 1942. US airpower played a crucial part in the campaign in the Solomons, especially in neutralizing Rabaul.*
BELOW: *The effects of US airpower. A Japanese base on Tanambogo, one of the smaller islands off Guadalcanal, after a strike by US Navy aircraft in early August 1942.*

Determined to hang on to Guadalcanal, the Japanese continued to ship in reinforcements during November, while the United States Navy tried to intercept them. One such interception, called the First Battle of Guadalcanal, occurred on the night of 12/13 November and resulted in two United States cruisers and four destroyers being sunk, while the Japanese lost a battleship and a destroyer, but were unable to land their troops. Nevertheless these actions showed that the

Japanese were superior at night. The sequel came on the 14th, when aircraft from Henderson Field sank a cruiser and seven transports, but that night two American destroyers were sunk and a battleship and two destroyers were damaged in exchange for sinking a Japanese battleship and a destroyer.

The final naval action, the Battle of Tassafaronga, took place on the night of 30 November/1 December, when eight Japanese destroyers

RIGHT: *Some of the defenders of Guadalcanal. A Taisho 6.5mm machine-gun crew of the Japanese Naval Landing Force (equivalent to the US Marines). The Taisho was based very much on the French 1897 Hotchkiss.*
BELOW: *Japanese casualties from one of their counterattacks on Guadalcanal. It was here that the US Marines became aware of the fanatical and suicidal bravery of their opponents.*

were surprised by a United States task force. The latter lost a cruiser and three others damaged, while the only Japanese casualty was a destroyer which sank. In early December, the exhausted marines were finally relieved and by the end of the month the Japanese realized that their casualties were too great for Guadalcanal to be held for much longer, and began a slow evacuation of troops which was eventually completed by early February.

Guadalcanal demonstrated the fanatical bravery and obstinacy of the Japanese in both attack and defense. The battle was a clear indication that the reconquest of the Pacific would be no easy matter and a long road lay ahead. On the other hand, American troops had shown that physically and mentally they were a match for their adversary. The American naval losses showed that the US Navy, on the other hand, needed an urgent overhaul of its night fighting techniques.

The Eastern Front 1942

The Germans began planning for their 1942 offensive as early as November 1941 when it became clear that they were not going to capture Moscow. It was not, however, until the beginning of April 1942 that Hitler issued his directive. Accepting that there had been failure in the center in 1941, he turned to the south. The main objective was to be the Caucasian oilfields and the passes through the Caucasian mountains. Simultaneously, Leningrad was to be seized and a link-up achieved with the Finns. The key to overrunning the Caucasus was seen in the destruction of the Russian armies in the Veronezh area, but this was not to be done by creating vast pockets as previously, but through close pincer movements.

Because of the casualties which they had suffered the year before, the Germans were becoming much more dependent on their allies. There were now Hungarian, Italian, Rumanian, and even a Spanish volunteer formation, the Blue Division, and the idea was that these should guard the flanks of the German thrusts. The Panzer divisions were almost all below their 1941 strengths, and the Luftwaffe, too, because of demands elsewhere, did not have the same number of aircraft available.

Stalin, encouraged by the fact that he had forced the Germans on to the defensive during the winter, decided, in spite of opposition from his generals, who did not believe that their forces were yet strong enough, to launch a counteroffensive directed on Kharkov. This task was given to Marshal Semyon Timoshenko's Southwest Front.

Timoshenko struck on 12 May 1942, catching the Germans poised to launch their own attack, and penetrated to a depth of 30 miles, creating a large salient south of Kharkov. The Germans then counter-attacked the southern flank of the salient, catching Timoshenko totally off balance, with his armor off well to the west and without an adequate reserve. Stalin refused to allow Timoshenko to halt his attack and the result was that the bulk of his forces were surrounded. It was now the turn of the Germans.

Von Bock, now commanding Army Group South, which was to carry out the drive into the Caucasus, split his command into two – Army Groups A and B. The main effort was to be made by Army Group A. Its initial task was to clear the Donets Basin and recapture Rostov. Army Group B, setting off from Kharkov, would seize Voronezh and then

ABOVE LEFT: *Marshal Semyon Timoshenko. During 1941, it was he who forced the Germans to a halt in front of Moscow. He was, however, unable to stop the German advance on Stalingrad.*
LEFT: *A German 75mm Pak 40 Panzerjäger (tank hunter) Marder in a typical Russian village during the fall rainy season. The Marder used the Pak 40 antitank gun on a PzKw Mk II chassis.*
ABOVE RIGHT: *A Soviet antitank rifle team. The weapon is the PTRD 1941 which fired a 14.5mm round. The submachine-gunner was there to provide close protection.*
RIGHT: *PzKw Mk IIIs outside Sevastapol after its fall on 4 July 1942. The Russian defenders had held the city, their key port on the Black Sea, against the Germans for eight months.*

wheel southeast, coming up on Army Group A's left flank to squeeze the remains of Timoshenko's Southwest Front between them.

The operation began on 28 June. Unfortunately the Russians had captured an operation order as a result of a staff officer being shot down, and were able to withdraw most of their forces before they became trapped. Thus, while Voronezh and Rostov were captured, most of the German blows appeared to strike thin air, and von Bock became increasingly cautious and Hitler frustrated. Failing to catch the Russians in the Donets corridor, Hitler sacked von Bock for his dilatoriness, and replaced him with Maximilian von Weichs. Hitler also began to switch armor from Army Group B to A, but at the same time

he wanted to create a pocket west of Stalingrad. Friedrich Paulus' Sixth Army was now expected to advance toward this city without any armor, and not surprisingly his progress was slow. Hence Hitler stepped in once more.

Because of Stalingrad's name, Hitler was increasingly convinced that Stalin would not give it up without a struggle and that it was here that he could destroy the Russian forces. Toward the end of July he therefore switched armor back from Army Group A to B, but at the same time, in view of the lack of progress around Leningrad, made Army Group A send much of its artillery north. Furthermore, priority of air support was now given to Army Group B. The denuded Army

LEFT: *Russian assault infantry, well equipped for combat in the extreme cold, on the Eastern Front, winter 1942-43. By this time the Germans, too, had proper winter clothing.*
RIGHT: *The fighting in the Leningrad area in 1942. The caption of this Russian photograph states that these are destroyed German tanks. The foreground chassis looks like that of a T-34, possibly with a BT turret on it. The dead trees give an indication of the severity of the combat.*

Group A thus found the overrunning of the Caucasus an impossible task, and its drive gradually petered out, although reconnaissance elements did actually reach the highest peak in the Caucasus Mountains, Mount Elbrus.

As far as the now totally divergent drive on Stalingrad was concerned, Hitler was right in his belief that the Russians would stand fast and fight for the city. On 23 August Paulus reached the River Volga north of the city and drove the Russians into it. Instead of getting round behind Stalingrad, he now chose to assault it frontally, but the Russians stood their ground. Throughout the fall and into November, Paulus battered his head against the city, much of which was soon reduced to rubble. By this time, the Germans held the western part of the city, but could get no farther. Stalin had sent down one of his best generals, Marshal Georgi Zhukov, to oversee the defense and he

noted that the German Sixth Army was now in a salient, with Rumanian armies holding each shoulder. Consequently, on 19 November, he struck the northern shoulder, following this the next day with a similar blow in the south. The Rumanians were thrown back in confusion. On 23 November the Russian forces joined hands and Paulus was now cut off.

Paulus' natural inclination was to mount a breakout operation but Hitler instead ordered him to stand fast. He was encouraged in this decision by Göring's assurance that he keep could Paulus supplied by air. In the meantime, Erich von Manstein's newly created Army Group Don organized a relief operation, which was launched on 12 December. It managed to struggle to within 30 miles of the city in the face of mounting resistance, but was then flung back by a Russian counterblow. Paulus was now well and truly on his own and his situation looked bleak. The Germans were about to suffer their greatest reverse since the outbreak of war.

LEFT: *Another Russian attack, this time using T-34 tanks to cover the infantry. The T-34, which they first encountered in July 1941, gave the Germans a nasty surprise. Robust, simple to manufacture, with good armament and armor, it was one of the outstanding tanks of the war.*
RIGHT: *German dead outside Leningrad. In spite of besieging the city for over three years, the Germans never captured Leningrad.*

1943-1944

The Path to Victory

Chronology 1943-1944

1943

January 14-23	Anglo-US conference at Casablanca
January 31	German Sixth Army surrenders at Stalingrad
February 14-22	Battle of Kasserine, Tunisia
April 23	Anglo-US HQ set up in London to plan invasion of Europe
May 13	Axis forces surrender in Tunisia
May 24	Dönitz orders his U-boats to leave the Atlantic
June 21	US Marines land at New Georgia, Solomons
July 5-12	Battle of Kursk, Eastern Front
July 10	Allied landings in Sicily
July 25	Mussolini overthrown
August 14-24	Allied conference, Quebec (Quadrant)
August 23	Russians recapture Kharkov
September 3	Allied landings in toe of Italy
September 8	Italy makes peace with the Allies
September 9	Allied landings Salerno, Italy
October 13	Italy declares war on Germany
November 6	Russians retake Kiev
November 20	US landings on Tarawa and Makin, Gilberts
November 28 – December 1	Roosevelt, Stalin and Churchill meet at Teheran, Persia

1944

January 22	Allied landings Anzio, Italy
January 27	Russians raise siege of Leningrad
January 31	US landings on the Marshalls
February 29	US landings on the Admiralty Islands
March 8	Japanese mount offensive in Burma
March 29	Russian troops enter Rumania
May 18	Allies capture Monte Cassino, Italy
June 4	Rome liberated
June 6	Allied landings in Normandy
June 15	US landings on Saipan, Marianas
June 19-20	Battle of the Philippine Sea
July 9	German Army Group North cut off in the Baltic
July 20	Attempt on Hitler's life fails
July 25	US troops break out of Normandy beachhead
August 1	Polish uprising in Warsaw
August 15	Allied landings in South of France
August 23	Rumania surrenders to USSR
August 25	Paris liberated
September 8	Bulgaria declares war on Germany
September 15	US troops enter Germany
September 17-24	Allied airborne operation to seize river crossings in Holland (Operation Market-Garden)
September 19	Finland signs armistice with Allies
October 20	US landings on Leyte, Philippines
October 23-26	Battle of Leyte Gulf
December 15	US forces land on Mindoro, Philippines
December 16	German counteroffensive in the Ardennes begins

The invasion armada moves toward Normandy, 6 June 1944.

Outline of Events 1943-1944

On 14 January 1943 Churchill and Roosevelt, together with their advisers, began their third meeting of the war, this time at Casablanca in Morocco. With the Axis forces now sandwiched between Allied armies on either side, the end in North Africa could not be far off, and the object of the meeting was to decide what to do next and formulate the overall strategy for winning the war.

The policy of 'Germany first' was reaffirmed, but Roosevelt also wanted, and this was agreed, the unconditional surrender of both Germany and Japan. Unlike in 1918, both enemies would have to be totally overrun and occupied and their military power crushed forever. Once again there was an argument over the opening of the Second Front for which Stalin had continued his agitation. The American planners were insistent that this must take place in 1943, but the British argued that it would be better to knock out Italy, the weakest of the Axis powers, first. Roosevelt, however, again sided with Churchill, and it was agreed that, once North Africa had been cleared of the enemy, Sicily would be invaded in order to provide a springboard for tackling the Italian mainland. Preparations for the invasions of France, including the buildup of American forces in Britain would, however, continue. For the necessary buildup to be achieved as quickly as possible, it was essential that the U-boat threat in the Atlantic be eliminated, and this was given high priority. It was also agreed that, in order to weaken Germany and pave the way for the invasion, a joint strategic bombing offensive would be mounted against her. Thus the way ahead was now clear.

FAR LEFT: *A German comment on the Teheran Conference of the Big Three in November 1943. It is captioned 'The more we are together . . . ,' implying that the Western Allies were foolish to put their trust in Stalin.*

BELOW LEFT: *Total war comes to the United States. Members of the Women's Army Corps at drill.*

RIGHT: *Casablanca, January 1943. Surrounding Churchill are (right to left) Montgomery, Eisenhower, Marshall, Alexander, Cunningham (British naval commander in the Mediterranean), Tedder (British air commander, Mediterranean), Brooke and Eden (British Foreign Secretary).*

BELOW: *Civil war in Athens, fall 1944. Members of ELAS, the communist Resistance Group, using captured German equipment.*

In January 1943 there was stalemate in Tunisia, but Montgomery had pursued Rommel across Libya and into Tunisia. February and early March were marked by Axis attacks, but then the Allies began to squeeze the Axis forces tighter and tighter and the end came in early May. British and American eyes now turned on Sicily, which was invaded in July. This also took longer than expected to overrun and the Italian mainland was not invaded until September. Italy now sued for an armistice and changed sides.

The Battle of the Atlantic reached a new crisis point in March 1943 with a dramatic rise in sinkings of Allied ships. In May, however, came the turning point and by the end of the month Dönitz was forced to withdraw his boats temporarily. From now on, although the battle was to continue until the end of the war, the Allies were to remain on top. At the same time the Combined Bomber Offensive against Germany began to get underway and would continue until April 1944, when the strategic air forces would switch to bombing targets directly affecting the invasion of Normandy. Planning for the invasion got properly under way in April 1943.

On the Eastern Front, Paulus's army surrendered at Stalingrad at the end of January 1943 and by the end of March the Germans had been driven back to the River Donets, thus giving up all their gains of the previous summer. Hitler now planned twin attacks to pinch out the large Russian salient centered on Kursk. Delays and Russian awareness of the plan meant that when it was finally launched in early July it gained the Germans little and they could ill afford the losses incurred in this, the largest tank battle of the war. This was the last major German attack in the East and from now on the Russians were to be permanently on the offensive.

As for the war against Japan in 1943, the fighting to clear northeast New Guinea of the Japanese continued into the fall, but this still left them secure in Dutch New Guinea. After the final securing of Guadalcanal in early February, MacArthur embarked on an 'island hopping' campaign to clear the remainder of the Solomons and this culminated in the landings on Bougainville in November. Meanwhile Admiral Nimitz collected together ships and men for a similar drive in the Central Pacific. This got underway in November with landings in the Gilberts. In Burma the British offensive in the Arakan, which had become bogged down at the end of 1942, made no further progress and in March, after the launching of a Japanese counterattack, the British were forced to withdraw. In the early months of 1943, however, the first of the Chindit operations, which caused the Japanese some discomfort, occurred. The big fighting in Burma would not come, though, until 1944.

In November 1943, the Allied leaders, this time with Stalin as well, met in Teheran, Persia. Stalin continued to press for the Second Front, being unimpressed by Allied progress in Italy which had ground to a halt with the coming of winter. He extracted a promise that France would be invaded by the end of May 1944. In return he undertook to enter the war against Japan two months after the defeat of Germany. The postwar map of Europe was also discussed and it was agreed that

Germany should be partitioned among the Allies. Stalin also stated that Poland lay within his sphere of influence. Although this was the last thing that the Polish Government-in-Exile in London wanted, Churchill and Roosevelt could not object if Allied unity was to be maintained.

The attention of the Western Allies was now firmly fixed on France and after months of preparation the invasion was mounted on 6 June 1944. After two months of bitter fighting in Normandy, the Allies

LEFT: *Sicily, like many other parts of liberated Europe, suffered extensive combat damage. Usually it was the Allied forces who had to organize the repair of public facilities and get life going once more.*

ABOVE RIGHT: *Industry at war – a British factory. Women took over many jobs normally performed by men so as to release men for service in the armed forces.*

RIGHT: *These women are preparing artillery shells which will next be filled with high explosive.*

LEFT: *During the second half of the war, Anglo-US operations were dominated by amphibious landings. Here US Marines undertake a practice landing. Note how the wartime censor has scratched out the men's shoulder badges.*

ABOVE: *Omaha Beach, Normandy, shortly after D-Day. The Mulberry harbor is not yet in position and hence landing ships are beached to unload their supplies. They will float off with the tide.*

broke out and, in conjunction with a further landing in the South of France in August, quickly liberated the country and much of Belgium as well. An ambitious airborne operation in southern Holland in September mounted in order to maintain momentum, just failed, and stretched supply lines slowed down the advance, allowing the Germans to recover. Nevertheless by the beginning of December the borders of Germany were close. Hitler, in a last desperate bid, now mounted a surprise counteroffensive in the Ardennes. Italy, meanwhile, had become a backwater, a situation not helped by the switch of troops to France and the defensive nature of the terrain.

On the Eastern Front, by fall 1943, the Germans were back on the line of the River Dnieper. Leningrad was finally relieved in January 1944 and the Polish border crossed. The Russians were now launching attacks all along the wide front, and as one died down they attacked elsewhere. During the early summer of 1944 they cleared eastern Poland and by August had closed up to Warsaw. The Polish Home Army now rose up against the Germans in the capital, but not until long after it had been crushed did the Russians attack and take Warsaw. Farther south, also in August, the Russians entered Rumania, bringing about its surrender and that of Bulgaria as well. Assisted by Tito's Partisans, the Russians also took Belgrade and entered the plains of Hungary, but were held up from capturing the capital, Budapest, by unexpected German resistance.

The twin thrusts in the Pacific made good progress during 1944. The island hopping continued, with both Nimitz and MacArthur edging ever closer to the Philippines. Landings here were finally made in October 1944, and this triggered the final major naval battle in the Pacific at Leyte Gulf, which broke the back of Japan's maritime power. By late summer, China-based United States bombers had started attacking Japan itself, but had to be switched to the Marianas, when the bases came under threat from a Japanese offensive. The only question that now remained was how finally to defeat Japan. In Burma, too, there were dramatic happenings during 1944. A Japanese counteroffensive to a further British attack in the Arakan was held. On the central front, the Japanese launched a determined attack in March 1944. Two months' desperate fighting saw it finally repulsed and the Japanese in retreat. Now the Allies, the Chinese in the north, and the British in the center and south, began to drive the Japanese back. Victory was in the air.

The Fall of Stalingrad

Stalingrad in early January 1943 was a grim place in which to be. The intense cold of the Russian winter was but one problem for the soldiers of Paulus's Sixth German Army. Göring's boast that he could keep Paulus's men supplied by air proved as empty as his belief that the Luftwaffe could destroy the BEF at Dunkirk. There were only two airfields in the pocket that could be used and these were within range of the Russian guns, and the Luftwaffe simply did not have the aircraft to keep the 200,000 men in the pocket adequately supplied. Consequently the garrison was now desperately short of food and ammunition, and was reduced to living mainly off its transport animals. With the failure of von Manstein's relief operation in December, prospects looked increasingly dark, and Hitler's declaration that they were the heroes of the hour was of little comfort.

The Russians, now under Marshal Konstantin Rokossovsky, were preparing for their final assault. On 8 January, Rokossovsky sent a message urging Paulus to surrender or otherwise suffer total destruction. Paulus referred this to Hitler, requesting freedom of action, but, not surprisingly, this was denied him. He was assured that plans for another relief operation were being drawn up, with Panzer divisions being switched from France for this purpose. It was a slender straw, but Paulus clutched at it.

On 10 January, preceded by a massive bombardment to which the Germans had no answer, the final attack began. It came in from the west and south, driving the Germans back toward the ruins of Stalingrad. On the 16th the airfield at Pitomnik fell, which meant that the defenders merely had the airfield at Gumrak left in operation. A trickle of supplies was still arriving here, and wounded, the lucky ones, were flown out. By the 24th even these lifelines had gone and the German survivors were now totally cut off from the outside world, save by radio. The Russians had driven the remnants of the Sixth Army back into Stalingrad itself and they were confined in two small pockets. The end was now nigh.

Yet on 30 January 1943, the tenth anniversary of Hitler's accession to power, Paulus could still send him a congratulatory message. In return Hitler promoted him to Field Marshal, but it was an empty honor. Next day, Paulus, realizing that any further resistance was hopeless, surrendered. The other pocket, in the northern part of the

ABOVE: *Russian soldiers in combat in the streets of Stalingrad, fall 1942, before the German Sixth Army was cut off. The fighting within the city was intense, with many casualties on both sides.*
LEFT: *German troops await the order for their next attack. Little did they know of the fate that would befall them a few months later.*

city, fought on for another two days before finally giving in. Some 107,000 Germans went into captivity at Stalingrad, and about the same number had been killed. Of those who surrendered, only some 5000 ever saw their homes again. It was the greatest disaster suffered by the Germans to date, and the blame for it lay at the door of one man, Adolf Hitler, for his sheer obstinacy. Together with the British victory at El Alamein and the Torch landings in North Africa, it marked the turning point of the war against Germany.

ABOVE LEFT: *As the battle for Stalingrad drags on so the state of exhaustion of the German troops of Sixth Army increases.*
ABOVE RIGHT: *The face of defeat. The newly promoted Field Marshal Friedrich Paulus (left) goes into captivity. His blind obedience to Hitler and worries over lack of fuel to enable a break-out to be made condemned many of his men to death.*
LEFT: *Paulus's surrender was taken by General Shumilov, commander of the 64th Army. Soon Shumilov would take over 7th Guards Army, which he would lead for the rest of the war.*

LEFT: *The last days in Stalingrad. Russian soldiers winkling Germans out of a wrecked factory.*

ABOVE: *The moment of victory. Stalingrad was reduced to a mere shell, but was quickly rebuilt.*

BELOW: *The prisoners from Stalingrad were paraded through Moscow prior to being moved to Siberian labor camps from which few returned.*

Pacific Island Hopping

At the beginning of February 1943, with Guadalcanal finally secured, MacArthur could set in motion the next stage of his plan to recapture the Solomons. His concept of operations was based on the need to have land-based air cover for his landings, and hence was necessarily a step-by-step process. Combined with the operations around Lae in New Guinea, the idea was to isolate the main Japanese base at Rabaul.

The next main target in the Solomons was New Georgia, but prior to this, unopposed landings were carried out on the islands of Pavuvu and Banika, between Guadalcanal and New Georgia, and airfields were constructed. There was now a pause while the Americans gathered their strength. In April, however, thanks to a Magic intercept, they had a significant coup. On the 18th American aircraft intercepted a plane carrying Admiral Yamamoto over Bougainville and shot it down.

LEFT: *US infantry wade ashore at Makin Atoll. The shallow shelving of the beach meant that their landing craft could not get in close.*
BELOW: *A B-25 strafes a merchant vessel in the harbor at Rabaul.*

RIGHT: *The campaign in the Solomons and New Guinea.*
FACING PAGE, BELOW: *A US 37mm gun in action in the Solomons.*

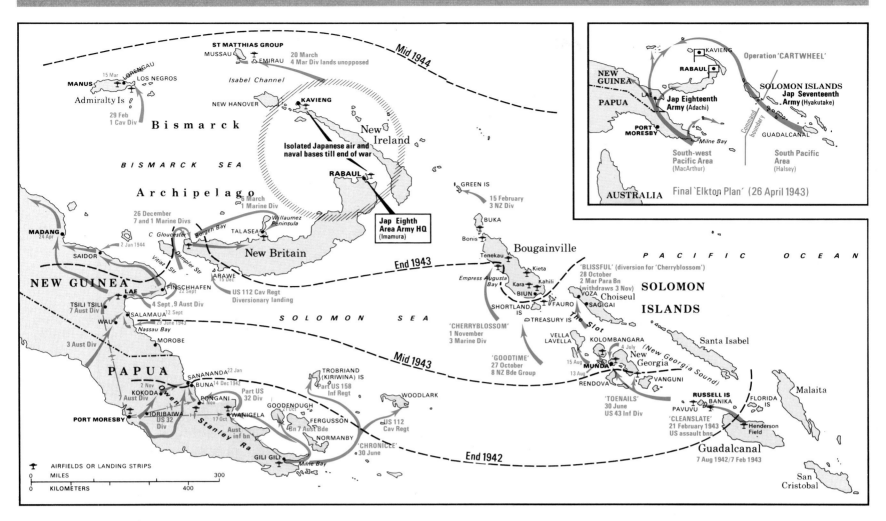

As Japan's foremost strategist, he was a grievous loss. In the meantime operations against Japanese-held northeast New Guinea had begun in January, but it was to be the end of the year before the region was totally secured and the Americans and Australians could land on New Britain at the other end of the island from Rabaul.

Operations against New Georgia began on 21 June 1943 with landings by US Marines at Segi in the southeast. Their target was the main airfield on the island, Munda, in the southwest corner. Further landings, by United States Army elements, took place during the first week of July, but the Japanese fought fiercely and it was not until 5 August that Munda was taken. During this time the Japanese, as they had done at Guadalcanal, tried to run in reinforcements by sea and there were two naval clashes. In the first, on the night of 5/6 July, the Americans lost a light cruiser and a destroyer, while two Japanese destroyers were sunk. In the second, on the night of 6/7 August, the United States Navy bested what was called the Tokyo Night Express, sinking three out of four destroyers without loss to themselves. This and the loss of Munda airfield finally convinced the Japanese that New Georgia was lost and they now evacuated their remaining troops.

The next and last major objective in the Solomons was Bougainville, but it was not until the end of October that this was tackled. To ensure success, MacArthur wanted to seize the Treasury Islands lying to the southeast as a staging post. This was achieved by the New Zealanders, while United States Marines made a feint landing on Choiseul to the north. Then, on 1 November 3rd United States Marine Division landed on the south coast of Bougainville in Empress Augusta Bay. The Japanese immediately struck back with air attacks, and while they lost almost all their aircraft engaged, they did damage a destroyer and several transports. On land, resistance was light and the beachhead was soon secured. On 7 November the Tokyo Night Express brought in a small contingent which was landed north of the beachhead and repulsed with most of the Japanese being killed. Rather than setting about clearing the remainder of the island, the priority lay with developing Empress Augusta Bay so that by the end of the year it had good port facilities and three operational airstrips. With the landings on New Britain, as well as others on the Admiralty islands and the St Matthias group early in 1944, Rabaul was now totally isolated.

The Allied planners had believed from the outset that final victory in the Pacific could only be achieved by an invasion of mainland Japan. The operations in the southwest Pacific were progressing well and had removed the threat to Australia, but the drive here was a very indirect one toward Japan, and a more direct route needed to be opened up.

FACING PAGE, ABOVE: *Always a tense moment: US infantry transship to their landing craft in Empress Augusta Bay, Bougainville, the last major objective in the Solomons.*
RIGHT: *US aircraft attacking Japanese shipping off Bougainville. Below a Nakajima Ki-84 Hayate fighter-bomber which has just dived through the attacking bombers one of which is taking the photograph. The large ship under attack is the seaplane tender* Akitsushima.

Until the naval losses at Pearl Harbor had been made good, it had not been possible to support a second axis of attack, but by the fall of 1943 Nimitz had built up his forces and could begin offensive operations in the Central Pacific.

His first objective was the Gilbert Islands and, after a week's intensive naval and air bombardment, the 2nd United States Marine Division landed at Betio on the Tarawa Atoll on 20 November. Tarawa was defended by 4700 Japanese troops, who, knowing that no support or relief was possible, fought with fanatical bravery. There were three days of intense combat before the atoll was finally cleared. It cost the United States Marines 1000 casualties, but there were only 100

Japanese alive at the end of the fight. In contrast, a parallel landing on Makin Atoll was carried out with little difficulty.

Nimitz's next target was the Marshalls. Landings were made on Majuro on 30 January 1944, and on the two main atolls of Kwajalein, on 1 February, and Eniwetok on 17 February. Here again, Japanese resistance was fierce and on Eniwetok not one of the 2000 Japanese defenders was left alive at the end.

In the northern Pacific, during the spring and summer of 1943, the Japanese had been successfully removed from Attu and Kiska in the Aleutians, and, thus, by early 1944, the noose around Japan was beginning to be pulled tighter and tighter.

LEFT: *Mopping up on Bougainville: M4 General Sherman medium tanks with infantry following up behind. Mopping up could be a nervewracking business as Japanese snipers would often lie doggo for days.*
RIGHT: *Japanese prisoners captured on the Solomons. They were a rare breed since the Japanese considered surrender dishonorable, which was why they treated Allied POWs so badly.*

139

Tunisia

With the Torch landings successfully achieved and Morocco and Algeria secured, the immediate task was now to move into Tunisia. This was to be the responsibility of the British and US troops who had landed at Algiers. They were organized as the British First Army under General Kenneth Anderson, but, to start with, it was an army in name only, having the strength of no more than a strong division. The hope was that, in conjunction with the French forces based there, Tunisia could be secured before the Axis reacted.

As it was, the Germans reacted very quickly and began to fly in reinforcements from Sicily to the airfields around Tunis and Bizerta the day after the Torch landings had taken place. The distance from Algiers to Tunis was some 500 miles, and there were few good east-west roads, which created some enormous logistic difficulties, especially since all supplies had to come from Britain. The odds were therefore stacked against Anderson.

As soon as the armistice with the French in Algeria had been arranged, Anderson set to. British Commandos seized the port at Bougie, although the Luftwaffe then bombed it, destroying much shipping. Next day, the 12th, British airborne forces landed on Bône airfield and secured it, and on the 15th carried out a similar operation at Youks les Bains further inland, and another the next day at Souk el Arba. Two parallel brigade-sized columns then set off by road toward Bizerta and Tunis. The Germans had not been idle and sent columns west to meet them. They clashed in a series of engagements east of Sedjenane in the north, at Medjez el Bab, at Tebourba, just 20 miles from Tunis, and, farther south, just north of Pont du Fahs. In each case the Allies were rebuffed. Matters were not helped by the fact that the Germans were enjoying air superiority, their airfields being nearer the front, with metalled runways, as opposed to the muddy strips available to the Allies.

By the end of December the Allies had been pushed back to a line running north-south and some 30 miles from Tunis. Both sides initially

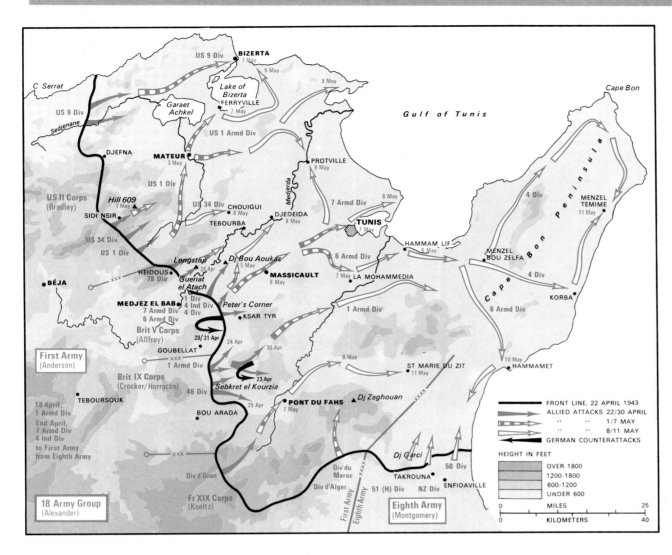

The map labels include:

C Serrat, US 9 Div, BIZERTA 7 May, 9 May, 9 May, Cape Bon, Lake of Bizerta, FERRYVILLE 7 May, US 9 Div, Sedjenane, Garaet Achkel, US 1 Armd Div, Gulf of Tunis, DJEFNA, MATEUR 3 May, PROTVILLE 8 May, US 1 Div, 4 Div, MENZEL TEMIME 11 May, US II Corps (Bradley), Hill 609 1 May, US 34 Div CHOUIGUI 8 May, 7 Armd Div 8 May, Medjerda, SIDI NSIR, TEBOURBA, DJEDEIDA 8 May, TUNIS 7 May, US 34 Div, US 1 Div, HAMMAM LIF 8 May, MENZEL BOU ZELFA, Longston 26 Apr, Dj Bou Aoukaz 5 May, 6 Armd Div, 4 Div, BÉJA, HEIDOUS 78 Div, Gueriat el Atach, MASSICAULT 6 May, 7 May LA MOHAMMEDIA, 6 Armd Div, KORBA, MEDJEZ EL BAB 7 Armd Div 6 Armd Div, 1 Div 4 Ind Div 4 Div, Peter's Corner, 1 Armd Div, Cape Bon Peninsula, Brit V Corps (Allfrey), 20/21 Apr, KSAR TYR, First Army (Anderson), GOUBELLAT, 24 Apr, 30 Apr, 9 May, ST MARIE DU ZIT 11 May, 10 May HAMMAMET, 1 Armd Div, Brit IX Corps (Crocker/Horrocks), 46 Div, Sebkret el Kourzia 23 Apr, 18 April, 1 Armd Div End April, 7 Armd Div 4 Ind Div to First Army from Eighth Army, TEBOURSOUK, 25 Apr, BOU ARADA, PONT DU FAHS 7 May, Dj Zaghouan, Dj Garci, Div d'Oran, 50 Div, 18 Army Group (Alexander), Div du Maroc, TAKROUNA, Div d'Alger, Fr XIX Corps (Koeltz), 51 (H) Div, NZ Div, ENFIDAVILLE, First Army Eighth Army, Eighth Army (Montgomery)

Legend:
FRONT LINE, 22 APRIL 1943
ALLIED ATTACKS 22/30 APRIL
" " 1/7 MAY
" " 8/11 MAY
GERMAN COUNTERATTACKS

HEIGHT IN FEET
OVER 1800
1200-1800
600-1200
UNDER 600

MILES 0 — 25
KILOMETERS 0 — 40

LEFT: *The final stages of the Tunisian campaign. The British Eighth Army had difficulties in breaking through the successive defense lines at Mareth, Wadi Akarit and Enfidaville and hence Alexander's decision to entrust a reinforced First Army with the final attack.*

BELOW: *A British Bofors crew on the Goubellat Plain, south of Medjez el Bab, during the final stages of the campaign. This Swedish designed light anti-aircraft gun was in British service throughout the war.*

ABOVE LEFT: *General Sixt von Arnim, Commander-in-Chief Army Group Africa, goes into captivity at the end of the Tunisian campaign. With him went 250,000 German and Italian soldiers.*

LEFT: *The winter rains caused mobility problems for both sides. Here, Italian soldiers struggle to free a commandeered French truck from the mud.*

RIGHT: *The German paratroopers of the Hermann Göring Division were perhaps the toughest of the Axis troops. Both sides resorted to horse transport in the rugged terrain of Tunisia.*
BELOW: *The combatants in Tunisia. American, British and French soldiers with their Italian and German prisoners. Tunisia was the first campaign in which the British and Americans fought together and they had much to learn about each other.*

had too few troops to hold the 200 mile front, but only for the first half of January was there any significant lull in the fighting. Way to the east, however, Montgomery had been pursuing Rommel across Libya and on 23 January entered Tripoli, pausing to open the port to shipping so that he could improve his very stretched supply line and allowing Rommel to cross into Tunisia.

By this time both sides in Tunisia had received considerable reinforcements. First Army now had a British corps, an American corps and a French corps, still under Anderson's command, with Eisenhower, who was mainly tied up with political matters, providing higher direction. The Axis forces had, as their nominal supreme commander, Marshal Ambrosio, who was based in Rome. On the ground their forces were built round Sixt von Arnim's Fifth Panzer Army, but at the beginning of February 1943, with Rommel's arrival, there was a change. He was appointed to command Army Group Africa, with von Arnim's army and his own desert veterans, now renamed First Italian Army.

During the second half of January there were various probing attacks all along the front. These were in preparation for a major attack aimed at driving the Allies back into Algeria. The area chosen was the southern part of the front, which was held by the Americans. It must be pointed out that, apart from some Rangers who had taken part in the Dieppe raid of August 1942 and a few tank crews who had fought at Alma Halfa, for the American troops, Tunisia was their blooding in the European Theater. The Germans thus considered the Americans

the weak link among the Allies. The attack began on 14 February with a thrust by von Arnim against Sidi Bou Zid, which drove the Americans back toward Kasserine. Rommel now came up from the south, creating further confusion. The pass at Kasserine fell and it looked as though the Allied line was about to be peeled back. Anderson now stepped in and counterattacked. This, together with heavy rains, finally halted the enemy. The news of Kasserine came as a shock to the American people and did little for Anglo-American relations in Tunisia. Eisenhower sacked the United States corps commander and brought in instead George S Patton, who could be guaranteed to stiffen the resolve of the troops. At the same time First and Eighth Armies were combined into a new command, 18th Army Group, under Alexander.

Three days after the end of the Kasserine battle, on 26 February, von Arnim launched another series of attacks, this time against the British in the north. He made some gains, but nothing significant. Rommel, however, now turned east in order to deal with Montgomery. Forewarned by Ultra, Montgomery was ready for him, and when he struck at Medenine on 6 March he was bloodily repulsed. Worn out and disappointed, Rommel left North Africa for good.

It was now Montgomery's turn to attack. On 20 March he began to force the formidable Mareth Line. His frontal assault failed and so he switched to the left flank and was successful. But he was unable to trap the Axis forces, who now withdrew to their next defensive line, at Wadi Akarit. Montgomery attacked this on 5 April, but again the Axis forces were able to make good their escape.

By now First Army was also on the offensive. The Fondouk Pass was forced in early April and the approaches to Medjez el Bab were cleared. Then, on 11 April, came the first linkup between the two armies. On 19 April Eighth Army came up against the First Italian Army at Enfidaville, but made little initial progress. Next day, on the First Army front, von Arnim launched a spoiling attack at Medjez, which was repulsed. The stage was now set for the final offensive.

Alexander decided that First Army should take the lead part and formations were transferred from Montgomery. At the same time, he launched an air offensive against the Axis supply lines across the Mediterranean. During the last week of April, First Army attacked all along its front. In the north, the Americans seized Mateur and then, on 7 May, entered Bizerta. That same day, the British similarly captured Tunis, while the French drove up through Pont du Fahs. The final act of the drama was played out in the Cap Bon peninsula, with the last Axis forces, some 250,000 men, surrendering on 13 May. The North Africa shore was now completely in Allied hands and they could turn their attention north toward Europe.

ABOVE: *1st US Ranger Battalion, known as Darby's Rangers after their commander, in hilly Tunisian terrain. William O Darby himself was to be killed during the last weeks of fighting in Italy. In all, six Ranger battalions saw action during the war.*
RIGHT: *The liberation of Tunis, 7 May 1943. The British troops were given a rapturous welcome by the French inhabitants. Bizerta was liberated by the 9th US Infantry Division on the same day.*

Sicily

Planning for the invasion of Sicily, Operation Husky, had begun in early April 1943, some time before the Tunisian campaign had finished. The idea was to employ two armies, the newly created United States Seventh Army under Patton and Montgomery's Eighth Army. Patton was to land on the south coast and clear the western half of the island, while Montgomery assaulted the southeast corner and cleared the eastern half. The final objective for both armies was Messina, which would provide an ideal launching pad for the invasion of the Italian mainland a mere five miles away.

Before the invasion took place, the island of Pantelleria, an important Italian naval and air base which lay midway between Sicily and Tunisia, was subjected to ten days' air bombardment at the beginning of June. Such was its intensity that when British troops landed on 12 June the garrison surrendered without firing a shot. Another preparatory move involved a deception plan. A body dressed in a British officer's uniform was washed ashore on the Spanish coast. Papers planted on it suggested to the Germans that the Allies were about to invade Greece, and so seriously did they view this that they reinforced the garrison with a Panzer division sent from France.

The invasion itself took place on 10 July. Both armies got ashore with little difficulty and quickly secured their beachheads, taking the largely demoralized Italians holding the coast by surprise. The only aspect which did not go right was the airborne landings, in this the first major use of airborne forces by the Allies. High winds scattered the paratroopers over a wide area and many were lost. Nevertheless they helped to compound the Italian confusion. Further inland, though, lay two German divisions, and when the British and Americans came up against these progress became significantly slower. Matters were not

ABOVE: *Montgomery and Eisenhower discuss the invasion of Italy at Messina after the Allies had secured Sicily.*

BELOW: *British troops coming ashore on Sicily.*

ABOVE RIGHT: *George S Patton led the US Seventh Army with much dash in Sicily, but fell from favor for slapping a battle-fatigued soldier's face in hospital.*

RIGHT: *US troops enter Palermo to a warm welcome, 21 July 1943.*

helped by the mountainous terrain and few good roads, which favored the defenders.

Both Patton and Montgomery were forceful personalities, suspicious of each other, and each determined to beat the other to Messina. Patton had the initial disadvantage of the longer route, but Montgomery, after a few days, faced an additional airborne division, which the Germans dropped in south of Catania, and which quickly became engaged in a fierce tussle with British airborne and Commando troops sent in to seize a bridge over the River Simeto. Resistance grew and Montgomery was forced to shift his thrust more to the center of the island. In the meantime Patton managed to capture Palermo, the capital, on 22 July.

By 1 August, the Germans realized that they could not hold onto the island for much longer, and needed their forces there for the defense of Italy. Therefore, temporarily bringing in an additional division, they began a withdrawal operation through the northeast part of Sicily. Patton tried a number of short hooks from the sea, but in each case they hit thin air. Montgomery tried the same and with a similar result.

On the morning of 17 August, American patrols entered Messina, but the enemy had gone – some 100,000 men had been ferried back across the Straits of Messina, with virtually no losses. Yet the Allies could, apart from the capture of the island, take comfort in an event which had taken place in Italy on 25 July. In view of the worsening military situation, the Fascist Grand Council in Rome passed a vote of no confidence in Mussolini. King Victor Emmanuel appointed a new government under Marshal Pietro Badoglio and Mussolini was arrested. The King then instructed Badoglio to approach the Allies with a view to negotiating an armistice.

Atlantic Turning Point

One of the principal decisions which had been taken at the Allied conference at Casablanca in January 1943 was that the Battle of the Atlantic must be won, and won quickly. Bad weather that month resulted in only 14 ships being sunk. In February, the total rose to 34, but Dönitz was concerned that too many convoys were crossing the Atlantic without being spotted by his wolf packs. He was aware that the Allies had a good knowledge of U-boat movements, but refused to believe that it was because of their ability to read the Ultra traffic.

In March 1943, however, the picture changed dramatically. During the first three weeks of the month, no less than 97 ships were sunk, two-thirds of them in convoy, with most of the others being stragglers. For a short time, too, thanks to the Germans introducing an additional rotor into their naval Enigma machines, the British could not read Ultra. A gloom descended on the Allied navies, and the British even questioned the efficacy of convoying, but accepted that there was no alternative action they could take.

Stormy weather during the last third of the month brought about a lull, and 11 ships only were sunk. In the early part of April, the Germans had only one wolf pack operating in the Atlantic, and the lull continued, but during the month no less than 98 U-boats set sail, and it became clear that the battle was about to reach a crescendo.

On 22 April convoy ONS 5 set sail from Liverpool, England for Halifax, Canada. It consisted of 40 merchantmen and six escort vessels. In order to avoid the wolf packs, a northerly route had been selected, but this meant severe gales and for the first few days the ships were well and truly buffeted. Early on the 28th the U-boats first made contact, and that night they attacked the convoy, but were seen off. Also during that day, Catalina flying boats from Iceland spotted three U-boats south of the convoy and succeeded in damaging one. At dawn next day, Dönitz called the wolf pack off and ordered it to join with another farther west. During the next five days there was another bout of bad weather and the convoy became badly scattered. It meant that the escorts found it difficult to refuel from their accompanying tankers, and the escort commander himself was forced to leave the convoy and make for St John's, Newfoundland, because of a shortage of fuel.

ABOVE LEFT: *Admiral Ernest J King, Commander-in-Chief US Fleet and Chief of Naval Operations. While he believed that the Pacific Theater should take priority, he recognized that the Battle of the Atlantic had to be won.*
LEFT: *A British corvette struggles in heavy Atlantic seas. Bad weather made the escorts' task of keeping the convoy together very difficult. On the other hand, it kept the U-boats at bay.*

Realizing that a large concentration of U-boats lay ahead of the convoy and that no diversion was possible, a support group of four destroyers was sent to reinforce the escort, but, after 48 hours, three of them were also forced to seek harbor owing to a lack of fuel. During the period 4-5 May, the U-boats began to harry the convoy and, within 24 hours, 11 ships had been sunk at a cost of one U-boat destroyed by an RCAF Catalina, and one depth charged by an escort. The convoy seemed certain to be annihilated.

ABOVE: *A U-boat pen at the French Atlantic port of St Nazaire. Protected as they were by very thick concrete, Allied attempts to destroy them from the air proved fruitless. The only answer was to attack the sources of their manufacture.*

LEFT: *A U-boat, having been caught on the surface, is strafed by an Allied aircraft. It took a U-boat some 90 seconds to crash dive and so it needed very alert lookouts. More U-boats were sunk by aircraft than by any other single means.*

On the night of 5/6 May, there were as many as 24 separate U-boat attacks on the convoy. One more ship was sunk, but the escorts sank no less than four U-boats, badly damaging several others. In addition, two others collided and were also lost. At daylight the U-boats retired, having suffered a devastating defeat, and the convoy finished its voyage with no further losses.

ABOVE: *A possible U-boat has been identified on sonar. Captain Frederick Walker RN, called by Churchill 'our most outstanding U-boat killer,' hatless on the bridge of the destroyer HMS* Starling.
LEFT: *The Hedgehog, a British anti-U-boat weapon, which came into service in 1942. The projectiles each had 32 pounds of Torpex explosive and were fired over the bows. They fell in a pattern and had a contact fuze.*

ABOVE RIGHT: *Escort carriers like this one were first introduced into the battle in spring 1943 and made a significant contribution to winning the war.*
RIGHT: *Two Type XXIII U-boats. This was one of the smaller and later models, specifically for use in coastal waters. It had a schnorkel and a submerged range of 175 nautical miles at 4 knots. Only seven were operational at the end of the war.*

In all, during the first three weeks of May, 31 U-boats were lost, and among the crew casualties was Dönitz's own son. Indeed, such was the reverse of fortune that on 24 May Dönitz ordered the temporary withdrawal of his wolf packs from the Atlantic, but, even so, a further 10 U-boats were lost during the last part of the month.

May 1943 was the major turning point in the Battle of the Atlantic. In fact, to be more precise, it was the 24 hours covering the nights of 4/5 and 5/6 May, when ONS 5 turned from facing certain disaster to inflicting a crushing defeat on the U-boats. No one single factor was decisive. Ultra played its part in helping to steer the convoys around the wolf packs, but could not help once they were met. In these circumstances, it was well-drilled escort groups, with improved submarine locating devices and effective weapon systems which played a major part. But the role of aircraft cannot be underestimated. By this stage, the Black Gap had been plugged by longrange American, Canadian and British patrol planes, which were now inflicting as much damage from the air as the escorts were on the surface.

This victory did not, however, mark the end of the Battle of the Atlantic, which was to drag on until the war's end. First the Germans came back with the acoustic torpedo, which caused temporary problems, especially for escort vessels, until the technical means were developed to counter it. Then, the U-boat became more formidable with the introduction of schnorkel equipment, which meant that the U-boats no longer had to surface to recharge their batteries and take in fresh air; also, the Walther turbine enabled boats equipped with it to travel more quietly and at higher speeds underwater. These came too late in the war, however, to affect the outcome. By this time, too, the preponderance of escort groups in the Atlantic meant that the U-boats were hopelessly outnumbered. Nevertheless sinkings of merchant vessels continued until as late as 7 May 1945, when two were lost off the Firth of Forth in Scotland. Shipping losses, though, were a mere fraction of what they had been before spring 1943.

149

The Combined Bomber Offensive Against Germany

As a result of Casablanca, instructions were issued to Harris and Spaatz, commanding respectively RAF Bomber Command and the United States Eighth Air Force, for a combined bomber offensive. Its object was 'the progressive destruction and dislocation of the German military, industrial and economic system, and the undermining of morale of the German people to a point where their capacity for armed

ABOVE: '*Bomber' Harris and his staff examine photographs showing air raid damage. By 1943 all RAF bombers were equipped with cameras to photograph where their bombs fell. In this way bombing accuracy could be better established.*
LEFT: *B-17s of the US Eighth Army Air Force line up for takeoff at their base in East Anglia, England.*

ABOVE RIGHT: *467 (Australian) Squadron RAF Bomber Command celebrate Lancaster S for Sugar's 100th operation. Painted on her are the Distinguished Service Order, and three Distinguished Flying Crosses won by her crew.*
RIGHT: *General Carl Spaatz, one of the leading American 'bomber barons.' He originally commanded the Eighth and then went to North Africa prior to taking command of all US strategic air forces in Europe in January 1944. In July 1945 he took over the same post in the Pacific.*

resistance is fatally weakened.' A number of specific targets were listed, of which the most important were the U-boat construction yards, the aircraft industry, transportation and oil.

Although attacks on morale came low down on the target list, Bomber Harris continued to consider this as the RAF's prime role and the British Air Ministry did little to dissuade him. Consequently, on the night of 5/6 March, he launched the first of three major bombing offensives that he would carry out during the next 12 months. The target was the Ruhr. Attacks were to be mainly directed against this region until the end of May. Although considerable damage was done, many bombers were lost on the mission, since the area was strongly covered by air defenses.

As far as the Americans were concerned, before the summer of 1943 they lacked sufficient longrange bombers in Britain to do more than nibble around the edges. On 12 April, however, General Ira C Eaker, who had brought the first elements of the United States Eighth Air Force across to Britain the previous year, produced his own plan as to how the Americans should conduct the Combined Bomber Offensive. After careful analysis, he selected six critical German industries, which included those already listed, together with the ballbearing and synthetic rubber industries. Further analysis produced 76 individual targets. At the same time, he recognized the value of the RAF's night attacks on morale. If the Americans concentrated on precision attacks on his listed targets by day, the RAF could complement these with morale attacks by night. Hence the origins of 'round the clock' bombing. Yet unlike Harris who was still convinced that bombing could win the war, Eaker believed that a cross-Channel invasion would not work without an effective preliminary bombing campaign. He also argued that the American bombers could not effectively operate deep into

151

LEFT: *A squadron of B-17s high over Germany. Much more heavily armed than their RAF counterparts, their maximum bombload was significantly less. The B-17 had a crew of up to ten and no less than thirteen 0.50in Browning machine-guns.*
BELOW: *The Mohne Dam after the epic RAF Dambusters' raid of the night 16/17 May 1943. It was a triumph of scientific ingenuity and cold courage, and did much to raise the stock of RAF Bomber Command, although its impact on German war industry was much less damaging than expected.*

Germany without reducing the German fighter force, especially since at this time the Allies did not possess a longrange escort fighter. Thus the initial American phase (July-October 1943) saw bombers penetrating to a limit of 400 miles into Germany, and it was only after this that longer raids were undertaken.

At the end of July, Harris mounted the second of his attacks, this time on a single city, Hamburg. On four nights in a 10-day period a concentrated British bomber force unleashed its bombs on the city with the Americans following up by day. Much of Hamburg was destroyed, with fires raging uncontrollably. Two weeks later, on 17

LEFT: *Hamburg burns, late July 1943, during one of the two daylight raids on the north German city by US bombers. B-17s can be seen at the top and right of the picture while a German fighter appears lower left. These were to support the four RAF raids by night – a classic example of bombing round the clock. These attacks virtually destroyed Hamburg and killed almost 60,000 people.*
BELOW: *An RAF Halifax attacking the Wanne-Eickel oil refinery in the Ruhr on 12 October 1944, during the oil campaign by the strategic air forces. Even six months earlier the RAF would have mounted this by night, but by this stage the Luftwaffe was almost in ruins.*

August, came two significant operations. By day, 376 American bombers set off to bomb an aircraft factory at Regensburg and the ballbearing factory at Schweinfurt, both in southern Germany, in their first deep penetration raid. No less than 60 bombers were lost, mainly to German fighters. American confidence in daylight bombing was severely shaken. That night the RAF bombed Peenemunde on the Baltic coast, where Hitler was developing in great secrecy his surface-to-surface rockets, the V-bombs, and set the program back by some months.

The importance of Pointblank, as the Combined Bomber Offensive was called, in paving the way for invasion was reaffirmed by the Allied leaders when they met at Quebec in Canada in August. This encouraged Harris to begin preparations for his third major offensive. The target was Berlin. Preliminary attacks during the fall provided warning that it would be expensive in aircraft, but new technical aids were being introduced. Indeed, the bombing war had become very much a technological battle. The battle proper began in November 1943 and continued until the end of the following March, often in appalling weather and with heavy crew casualties. Much of Berlin was destroyed, but the morale of the Berliners was not broken.

The Americans gradually regained their confidence in day bombing after Schweinfurt-Regensburg and by the beginning of October 1943 were once more over German skies. On the 14th they mounted another attack against Schweinfurt, but again with heavy losses. Sixty out of 291 bombers were posted missing. It was this that finally confirmed the urgent need for a longrange escort fighter, and when the P51-B Mustang began to appear in early 1944 casualties dropped significantly. A reorganization during the fall of 1943 also introduced the United States Fifteenth Air Force into Italy, and this joined in Pointblank.

On the night of 30/31 March 1944, RAF Bomber Command suffered losses similar to the American casualties at Schweinfurt when 96 out of 795 bombers were lost in a raid on Nuremberg. Pointblank now ended and a new phase began.

Kursk

During the first months of 1943 on the Eastern Front, Stalingrad was not the only success which the Russians enjoyed. Simultaneously with their final attack on the German Sixth Army, they launched a massive counteroffensive aimed at recapturing all the territory which they had lost the previous summer. From mid-December they had been applying pressure in the Caucasus, and steadily driving von Kleist's Army Group A back toward Rostov. Here von Manstein managed to hold open a corridor through which the bulk of von Kleist's forces managed to escape, but the city finally fell on 14 February. To the north, and a week earlier, the Russians had liberated Kursk, and by 16 February they had recaptured Kharkov and Voroshilovgrad.

On 20 February, however, von Manstein mounted a counterblow. Noting that the Russian Sixth Army was in a dangerously exposed salient south of Kharkov, he struck from the south and overran it, driving the remnants back to the Donets. This was followed in early March by another attack, this time toward Kharkov, which von Manstein retook on the 15th, again restoring the line of the Donets in this area. The spring thaw prevented any further exploitation, and the Russians were left holding a huge salient centered on Kursk.

While Hitler acknowledged by this time that he could no longer win the war in the East, he was still determined to hold on to what he had left. It was inevitable that the Russians would continue their attacks once the ground dried out, and hence he was determined to forestall them by mounting an attack of his own. The object was the elimination of the Kursk salient.

Operation Citadel was originally due to be launched in mid-April, but various factors brought about fatal delays. The idea was that simultaneous attacks should be launched against the salient by Walther Model's Ninth Army from the north and Hermann Hoth's Fourth Panzer Army in the south. Model, however, was against the plan and complained that he had too few troops to overcome the Russian

defenses. Consequently, there were delays while his army was strengthened. Then, Hitler took a hand, insisting that the attack be delayed until new tanks, the Panther and Ferdinand, which he believed would tilt the scales further in his favor, were sent from Germany.

It was perhaps inevitable that the delay in mounting Citadel should result in the Russians learning about it. Indeed, they did so very quickly, largely thanks to one of the most effective espionage groups of the war, the so-called Lucy Ring based in Switzerland. Their reaction was not to try and pre-empt it, but merely to strengthen their defenses and wait for it to materialize. They calculated that the losses that they would inflict on the Germans would increase the chances of success of their own counteroffensive. They therefore massed some 12 armies in the salient, and, behind them in a newly constructed fortified line at the base of the salient, five further armies, which were to be used in a counterattack role. In all, the Russians had some 3000 tanks, and the Germans 1900.

On the afternoon of 4 July 1943, the Germans finally struck. Hoth gained tactical surprise in the south, but was quickly slowed down by increasing resistance and several torrential thunderstorms. Model, who attacked 12 hours later, managed to penetrate some six miles on the first day, but after that experienced the same problems as Hoth. By 12 July, Hoth was still 55 miles from Kursk and 90 miles separated him from Model. It was now that the Russians chose to counterattack.

ABOVE: *Kursk resulted in huge losses of materiel on both sides. Here a German PzKw Mk III passes an abandoned Russian 45mm antitank gun.*

LEFT: *The commander and gunner of a PzKw Mk IV search for a target.*
RIGHT: *A confident and proud looking T-34 crewman. It was at Kursk that the Russian tank arm really came of age.*

In what was the largest tank battle of the war, three Russian tank armies engaged two Panzer corps, while overhead flocks of fighter-bombers and ground attack aircraft joined in the fray. Many tank engagements were at pointblank range and the whole battlefield became covered in clouds of dense black smoke as more and more tanks were hit and caught fire. The next day Hitler called a halt to Operation Citadel.

The Allied invasion of Sicily on 10 July meant that a second front had been opened in Europe. Italy and France, where a further invasion must come soon, had to be reinforced and this could only be done at the expense of the Eastern Front. The Battle of Kursk had cost the Russians some 2000 tanks and the Germans 1000. The difference was that the Russians, with war production mounting steadily from factories beyond the Urals, could afford losses. The Germans could not.

Kursk was the last major German offensive flourish in the East. From now on it was the Russians who would be continuously on the attack and the pressure would never let up. Once an attack began to

lose momentum in one area, they would attack in another. On 15 July, two days after Hitler had called off his offensive, the Russians launched their first counterattack, driving Hoth and Model back to their original start lines and beyond. Kharkov was retaken in the south and in the north the Germans were forced back to Bryansk.

Now came the turn of von Kluge's Army Group Center, which during August and September was forced out of Smolensk. Bryansk fell, and by the beginning of October, von Kluge was only 50 miles east of the Dniepr. It was the same in the south, with Kiev being evacuated by the Germans on 6 November, and a large body of troops totally cut off in the Crimea. The tide had well and truly turned.

ABOVE LEFT: *German Panzer Grenadiers at Kursk. Columns of smoke in the background mark burning vehicles. In the center of the battlefield the obscuration was such that many engagements took place at almost pointblank range.*

BELOW: *Russian soldiers inspect captured German tanks. These are PzKw Mk IV s in the foreground and, without muzzle brakes, PzKw Mk IIIs.*

ABOVE: *Wrecked German armored fighting vehicles. Kursk marked the last major German attack on the Eastern Front. Compromised from the outset, the offensive had little chance of success.*

The Final Solution

ABOVE LEFT: *Heinrich Himmler, the second most powerful man in the Third Reich. A Hitler decree of October 1939 charged him with putting the racial policy into effect. He summed up his own attitude when he said: 'Whether nations live in prosperity or starve to death interests me only in so far as we need them for slaves to our* Kultur.'

ABOVE: *'Behind the enemy powers, the Jew.' It was a constant theme of Nazi propaganda that the Allies were being manipulated by the Jews. This tended to be more for domestic consumption than directed at the Allies themselves. Hitler on occasion referred to Churchill and Roosevelt as 'Jew lovers.'*

From the outset the Nazis had a pathological hatred of the Jewish race. According to Nazi mythology it was the Jews who had largely created the 'stab in the back' in 1918, and they had no loyalty to Germany, only to themselves. When Hitler came to power in 1933, he quickly began wholesale persecution of the German Jews. They were ostracized in public, their businesses were confiscated and their rights curtailed. Half the Jewish population of 600,000 in the country fled abroad during the 1930s, many to the United States. The prewar climax came late in 1938 when, after the murder of a German diplomat in Paris by a young Polish Jew, the Nazis instituted the Crystal Night pogroms of 9-10 November, when there was wholesale looting of Jewish-owned shops, schools and synagogues were burned down, and a number of Jews were murdered. From then, all Jews remaining in Germany were forced to wear the yellow Star of David, a practice that was to be applied in all occupied countries. This, however, was mild compared with what the war would bring.

When the Germans invaded Poland they found themselves with some three million Polish Jews on their hands. At the same time, they wanted to bring 500,000 ethnic Germans across from the Russian-occupied Baltic states. They therefore began to move the Jews as far east as possible, concentrating them into ghettoes within the towns and cities in preparation for deportation to a large reservation near Lublin. At this stage, even though as early as January 1939 Hitler had remarked in a speech that European Jewry must be eradicated, there was no policy of extermination in force.

The overrunning of Western Europe in 1940 added to the numbers of Jews under German control, and serious thought was given to establishing a large Jewish colony in Madagascar, to which the majority

of European Jews could be deported. It came to nothing. With the invasion of Russia, the policy of mass genocide became fact. The responsibility for carrying it out rested with Heinrich Himmler and his feared SS troops.

Himmler used two main tools, the concentration camps and the Einsatzgruppen or 'action groups.' The first concentration camp was established at Dachau in March 1933 and was built to house opponents of Hitler's regime, including Jews. By the fall of 1937, Dachau had been joined by three other camps – Lichtenburg, which was for women, Sachsenhausen and Buchenwald. After *Anschluss* a further camp was built at Mauthausen to cater for Austrians and later Czechs. The guards for these camps were provided by Theodor Eicke and his notorious SS Totenkopf (Death's Head). During the Polish campaign, the SS Totenkopf had employed three regiments in the rear areas and these had soon gained an infamous reputation for their excesses, and were the forerunners of the Einsatzgruppen. The Totenkopf were then organized into a division of what became the Waffen-SS, and concentration camp duties were handed over to the Allgemeine-SS.

ABOVE: *From the very start of the movement in the 1920s, the Nazis had played on the traditional gentile suspicion of the Jews, especially with regard to money matters. Here, in the 1930s SA stormtroopers plaster the windows of a Jewish-owned shop in Bayreuth with handbills to persuade the local population not to buy from it.*
LEFT: *A typical scene in the Warsaw Ghetto. By strictly limiting the food allowed into it the Germans sentenced many of its inhabitants to death by slow starvation.*

With the drawing up of the plans for Barbarossa, it was considered that more concentration camps would have to be built to cater for a vast influx of new inmates. Himmler decided that these should be built in Poland. The first to be completed, in March 1941, and the most sinister of all, was Auschwitz. Within a few months these extermination camps had begun work, but it quickly became clear that shooting prisoners was too slow a method of dispatching the unwanted.

Much experience had been gleaned from the activities of the Einsatzgruppen, which had been organized by Reinhard Heydrich, the head of the Reich Main Security Office (RSHA), which controlled the German police forces, including the Gestapo. The Einsatzgruppen had been sent into Russia with Heydrich's express orders to kill all agitators, Jews, and Communist Party officials, and were responsible more than any other group for turning the Russian population against the Germans. In every Russian town they came across, they headed for the Jewish quarter, turned out the inhabitants and shot them.

In September 1941, Cyclon B gas, originally manufactured to kill rats, was tried for the first time in Auschwitz on Russian prisoners of war. It proved highly effective and was quickly adopted on a wide scale. From now on Jews were rounded up in both Eastern and Western Europe and sent in cattle trucks to the concentration camps, the so-called convoys. On arrival they were inspected, and the fit put to slave labor until they were broken, which often did not take long. The rest were then driven into the gas chambers and killed. Once dead, everything of value was stripped from them before they were consigned to crematoriums.

LEFT: *Another ghetto scene. The children, of course, could not understand why such cruelty should be inflicted on them. Their faces almost reflect those of old people, and in their eyes there is hopelessness. They know that they have no future and that death is imminent.*

BELOW: *A Jewish transport. With the implementation of the Final Solution at the beginning of 1942, trains began to roll from all over Occupied Europe to the extermination camps of the east. Often 100 to 150 people were crammed to a single cattle wagon, with little food or water, and many died even before they reached the camps.*

Although this system was operational by the fall 1941, it was not until January 1942 that it was formally adopted. Heydrich, who had now been made Reich Protector of Bohemia and Moravia, convened a conference at Wannsee on the 20th in order to coordinate the efforts of relevant government and Party agencies in implementing what was euphemistically called the 'Final Solution of the European Jewish Question.' This confirmed the system that had already been set up.

The death camps themselves had a limit on the number which they could take at any one time, and the ghettoes continued to exist. The most infamous of these was that in Warsaw. Here some half a million Jews were confined in a small area of the city and kept on minimum rations. Many died of starvation. The most bizarre was Theresienstadt, which was a paradise compared with the other ghettoes and almost had a vacation atmosphere. Indeed, the German Ministry of Propaganda made a film of it in 1944 to allay rumors in neutral countries about the treatment of Jews in German-occupied territory. For the inmates, though, it was only a temporary reprieve.

Another aspect was the use of Jews and Russian prisoners of war for 'medical' experimentation. Sterilization, high altitude and extreme cold tests, supposedly to see how much the human body could withstand, were commonplace.

No exact figure of the number of Jews murdered by the Germans exists, but conservative estimates put it at at least four million, of which Auschwitz was responsible for almost half. While the camps in Germany itself were not specifically death camps, many people held within them died, usually of starvation or typhus. The Final Solution was undoubtedly the most inhuman aspect of the war, and those responsible for it were to be prime targets for Allied retribution at the end of hostilities.

ABOVE: *Concentration camps were initiated as soon as Hitler came into power in order to remove communists and other undesirables from circulation. Oranienburg outside* *Berlin was one of the earliest. The extermination camps had a different purpose to the normal concentration camp, where people died from indifference.*

BELOW: *Buchenwald within Germany itself was one of the more notorious concentration camps, which generally housed gentiles as opposed to Jews. Nonetheless, even though there* *was no active extermination policy, some 63,500 inmates had died before war's end and many would never recover from the dreadful treatment which they received.*

Burma 1943-1944

The failure of the British offensive in the Arakan at the beginning of 1943 showed, if nothing else, that the Allies were not yet ready to begin the reconquest of Burma. The Japanese were still their superiors at jungle warfare and the British logistic system was very inefficient, especially on the medical side. Indeed, much of the problem lay in the high incidence of malaria casualties. Stilwell was continuing to

experience intense frustration in his dealings with Chiang Kai-shek, and the British were having to grapple with a rising tide of Indian nationalism, which meant that many troops were kept tied to internal security duties. It was as well that the Japanese were, for the time being, content to remain on the defensive.

In mid-1942 a young British officer had approached Wavell with a

ABOVE: *Japanese infantry on the march in the Moulmein area, close to the border with Siam (Thailand). The Burmese in the foreground were at first not against the Japanese invasion and many believed that this was how they would gain their independence from the British. Japanese treatment of them, however, quickly led to disillusionment.*

BELOW: *Lord Louis Mountbatten, cousin to King George VI and Commander-in-Chief Southeast Asia Command (SEAC), addresses the men of No 1 Air Commando, the USAAF formation which supported the Chindits. Their youthful commander, Colonel Cochrane, leans against the jeep.*

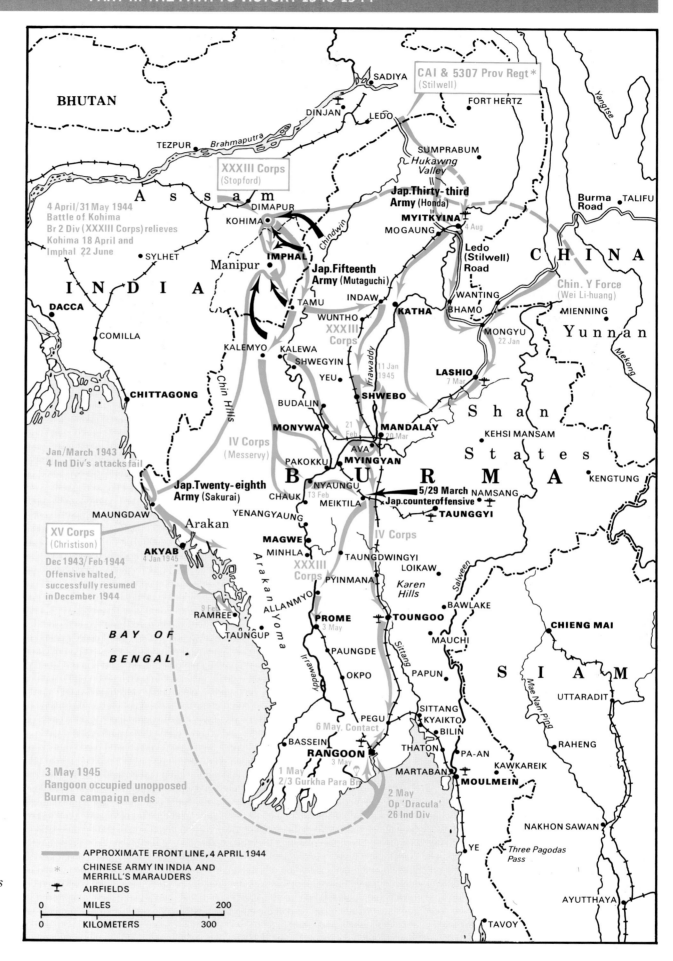

BHUTAN

A s s a m

4 April/31 May 1944
Battle of Kohima
Br 2 Div (XXXIII Corps) relieves
Kohima 18 April and
Imphal 22 June

XXXIII Corps
(Stopford)

CAI & 5307 Prov Regt *
(Stilwell)

FORT HERTZ

SUMPRABUM

*Hukawng
Valley*

Jap.Thirty-third
Army (Honda)

MYITKYINA

Burma TALIFU
Road

Ledo
(Stilwell)
Road

C H I N A

Chin. Y Force
(Wei Li-huang)

Y u n n a n

I N D I A

Manipur

IMPHAL

Jap.Fifteenth
Army (Mutaguchi)

XXXIII
Corps

S h a n

S t a t e s

IV Corps
(Messervy)

B U R M A

Jap.Twenty-eighth
Army (Sakurai)

XV Corps
(Christison)

Jan/March 1943
4 Ind Div's attacks fail

Dec 1943/Feb 1944
Offensive halted,
successfully resumed
in December 1944

Arakan

Arakan Yoma

B A Y   O F
B E N G A L

5/29 March
Jap.counteroffensive

IV Corps

XXXIII
Corps

S I A M

3 May 1945
Rangoon occupied unopposed
Burma campaign ends

6 May. Contact

RANGOON

1 May
2/3 Gurkha Para Bn

2 May
Op 'Dracula'
26 Ind Div

CHIENG MAI

Three Pagodas
Pass

APPROXIMATE FRONT LINE, 4 APRIL 1944
* CHINESE ARMY IN INDIA AND
   MERRILL'S MARAUDERS
✈ AIRFIELDS

0   MILES   200
0   KILOMETERS   300

RIGHT: *The course of the Burma
campaign, 1943-45. The Allied troops
fighting there considered it the
forgotten war as it received little
publicity at home compared with
other theaters.*

new concept for helping to defeat the Japanese. Orde Wingate had had
much experience of irregular warfare, both in Palestine before the war
and with the Abyssinian Patriots. His idea was to raise longrange
penetration groups which would infiltrate the Japanese lines and harry
their communications. Wavell authorized him to raise a bridgade for
this. Its badge was the mythical Burmese beast, the 'Chinthe,' and its
men became known as the Chindits. On 14 February 1943, Wingate
set out on his first expedition and spent the next six weeks blowing up
railroads, destroying bridges and carrying out ambushes. The
Japanese considered the threat so serious that they deployed two out
of their five divisions in Burma to tackle the Chindits, the survivors of
whom got back to India in mid-April. While the damage they had
caused was not strategically significant, important lessons were
learned from their experience. The first was that the Allied soldier

could operate in the jungle as well as the Japanese, and this caused a
sharp increase in morale. Just as important was that air resupply was
the answer to the logistic problem.

The success of the Chindits and the failure in the Arakan spurred
General Bill Slim, commanding the British Fourteenth Army, to further reforms. He had already begun jungle training schools the year
before, and now reformed their programs. He also insisted on aggres-
sive patrolling in the front line. He began to improve the road and rail
network leading up to the front, and reorganized the medical services.

It had been agreed at Casablanca that, after British and Chinese
offensives in northern Burma, Rangoon should be seized in an amphibious assault. The monsoon season prohibited major operations beginning until well into the fall, but also they could not take place without a
significant build up of air and naval power. In view of the demands for

LEFT: *Chinese coolies working to open up the Ledo Road. If Chiang Kai-shek was to cooperate effectively with his allies in the reconquest of Burma it was vital that he had land communications with them, especially for the passage of supplies. The photograph shows clearly what a mammoth engineering task this was.*

these elsewhere, Wavell convinced Churchill that a more indirect approach, namely an attack on Sumatra, stood a better chance of success. By this time the demands for landing craft in the Mediterranean and Pacific meant that there was little chance of sufficient landing craft being sent to Southeast Asia, besides which, the Americans were insistent that the reopening of the Burma road must be the immediate priority. Thus this plan was also shelved and attention concentrated on northern Burma.

At the end of August 1943, there was a major reorganization in the theater. A new unified command, Southeast Asia Command (SEAC) was set up, with Admiral Lord Louis Mountbatten as Supreme Commander and Stilwell as his deputy. An offensive in northern Burma by the British and Chinese was agreed, preceded by another limited attack in the Arakan and a diversion by Wingate's Chindits, now grown

to six brigades, in northern Burma. While naval assets remained small, there was a sizeable increase in air strength, a third of it American. But the Japanese too were planning an offensive, also in northern Burma, with preliminary attacks in the Arakan and Yunnan.

The British began their advance in the Arakan in December 1943. At first all went well, but then, at the beginning of February, the Japanese attacked. At first the British were driven back, but Slim then gave orders to stand fast and promised he would keep supplies coming by air. This proved effective and the Japanese eventually gave up their offensive. Wingate's second Chindit operation was launched on 5 March 1944, with the majority of his troops being inserted by glider. His task was to capture Indaw, which lay near the Irrawaddy some 150 miles north of Mandalay, between Stilwell's Chinese and the northern corps of Fourteenth Army, and to disrupt communications in the area.

LEFT: *American-built M4 General Shermans of the Chinese Army moving toward the front in northern Burma.*

RIGHT: *British troops in a Bren gun carrier moving up during the bitter fighting around Imphal and Kohima in spring 1944. It was these battles which proved the turning point of the war in Burma.*
BELOW: *The enigmatic Orde Wingate, founder and leader of the Chindits. His experience of irregular warfare was greater than any other British officer of his day.*
BELOW RIGHT: *General Sir William (Bill) Slim, the revered commander of the British Fourteenth Army. His warm personality and dogged determination inspired the soldiers of the many races that fought under his command.*

Wingate, himself, was unfortunately killed when his plane crashed in the jungle, but this did not deter his men, although Japanese reinforcements prevented them from capturing Indaw.

In the meantime Stilwell had been spurring the cautious Chinese on in the construction of an overland route from India to China, the Ledo Road, to replace the original Burma road. It was a slow business, but the Chinese, assisted by a group of United States Commandos modelled on Wingate's Chindits, the 5307th Provisional Regiment, but more aptly dubbed by the American media, Merrill's Marauders, had been making progress, and Stilwell planned to seize Myitkyina before the 1944 monsoon season started.

On 14 March 1944, however, the Japanese launched the main blow of their offensive in northern Burma. Their target was Kohima, the terminus of the main supply road from India. Once again, Slim, after allowing initial withdrawals, ordered his men to stand and fight, which they did at Kohima and Imphal. By now Allied air superiority in Burma was overwhelming and he was able to keep Imphal and Kohima resupplied by air. By early May, Slim was in a position to counterattack, driving the now exhausted Japanese back to the Chindwin. The monsoon coming in July stopped further progress. In the meantime Stilwell continued to progress, albeit slowly, assisted for a time by the Chindits before they were withdrawn to India, and he finally seized Myitkyina on 3 August. The way was now prepared for the final Allied offensive, which would begin once the monsoon was over.

Italy Changes Sides

With the overrunning of Sicily and the fact that the Italians were now suing for an armistice, on the surface prospects for the invasion of Italy looked bright in August 1943. Underneath, though, matters were a little more complicated. For a start, the agreement of unconditional surrender reached at Casablanca was not acceptable to the Italians, and Marshal Badoglio wanted better terms. He also found it difficult to establish contact with the Allies, and it was not until mid-August that he was able to send an envoy to Portugal to open negotiations. Hitler, on the other hand, had reacted very quickly; on 30 July he ordered Rommel, who had just been sent to Greece because of continuing concern over a possible Allied invasion, to seize the passes over the Alps. Matters did not stop here, and by early September there were eight German divisions in northern Italy.

Not until 3 September did the Italians and Allies sign a provisional armistice, and on that day Montgomery crossed the Straits of Messina and landed on the toe of Italy. In the early hours of the 9th, and a few hours after the armistice had been announced, General Mark Clark's United States Fifth Army landed at Salerno. On the same day, further elements of the British Eighth Army landed at Taranto.

Axis resistance in the very south of Italy was sparse, and Montgomery had little trouble in clearing it. Salerno was a different matter. The Germans reacted surprisingly quickly and were ready for the landings. Although both the American and British troops in Fifth Army managed to get ashore and establish beachheads, the Germans prevented any exploitation and, sending up reinforcements, began a series of fierce counterattacks. By the evening of the 13th, the picture was grim and serious thought was given to re-embarking part of the force. Next day, thanks to a massive naval bombardment and air effort, the Germans

ABOVE: *Part of the invasion fleet off Salerno, September 1943. While farther south the British Eighth Army faced just Italians, Mark Clark's forces had German opposition.*

BELOW: *Mussolini at the moment of his successful rescue by German glider troops from Gran Sasso in the Abruzzi mountains. This did not bring the Italians back to the fold.*

were halted. Although they renewed their efforts on the 16th, Albert Kesselring, the German commander-in-chief, realized that the chance to throw the Allies back into the sea had now passed, and ordered a withdrawal to the line of the River Volturno, 20 miles north of Naples. This withdrawal was skillfully conducted, and not until 1 October was Naples entered. In the meantime, on the night of 22/23 September, further Eighth Army troops were landed at Bari on the Adriatic coast, and a linkup achieved with Fifth Army on the 20th at Auletta. Finally, on 2 October, British Commandos took Termoli, also on the Adriatic coast.

Earlier, on 13 September 1943, in a dramatic glider *coup de main*, Mussolini was rescued from his incarceration in the Abruzzi mountains, and, by the end of the month, had declared a new Italian Socialist Republic. He was, however, to be no more than a puppet, entirely reliant on German arms to support him. At the same time, Churchill wanted to seize Rhodes, but the Americans, distrusting his motives, refused to allow him landing craft. Nevertheless British troops were put ashore on some of the other islands in the Dodecanese, but without any air support these were overrun before the end of November by German troops based in Greece.

ABOVE: *The heat of the Italian summer. A British 5.5in gun crew in action in southern Italy. The camouflage netting was vital to hide them from hostile aircraft.*
RIGHT: *German shells burst amid DUKW amphibious vehicles trying to land supplies in the Anzio bridgehead, early in 1944. Far from achieving the quick capture of Rome, the Allies were very nearly driven back into the sea.*

At the beginning of October 1943 heavy rains came in Italy which slowed down the Allied advance. Mark Clark closed up to the Volturno defenses, but the Germans successfully held these until the middle of the month, when once again they withdrew to their next line, which ran along the Garigliano and Rapido Rivers. This was the Gustav or Winter Line. In the east, Montgomery was beset by a series of river lines, and by the end of the year, having crossed the River Sangro, was also closed up to the Gustav Line.

By now Anglo-American attention had switched to preparations for the cross-Channel invasion, which was billed as the main event for 1944. This had its effect on the Italian front. Montgomery and three of his veteran divisions returned to Britain, his place in the Eighth Army being taken by General Oliver Leese. Nevertheless additional troops were sent to the theater, including Poles, French and even, later in 1944, the Brazilian Expeditionary Force. It was clear, however, that Italy was now a secondary theater and a means of keeping German troops, which could otherwise be used against Allied troops soon to be landing in France, tied down.

The first priority for 1944 was to prise the Germans out of the Gustav Line. The plan for this called for attacks on its western side combined with an amphibious landing at Anzio to distract the Germans and cut their lines of communication. The offensive opened on 17 January, and initially there was encouraging progress, until the Americans were halted in front of the formidable Monte Cassino position. The landings at Anzio took place on the 22nd, but soon ran into trouble. The American commander, General John P Lucas, had been given somewhat vague orders and, instead of taking advantage of initial surprise and driving inland, preferred to consolidate his beachhead.

ABOVE: *As a military policeman ducks from a nearby German shellburst, heavy equipment is unloaded at Salerno. The chicken wire was to prevent vehicles from becoming bogged. By this time, the Allies were becoming well experienced in amphibious landings.*
RIGHT: *Across the River Arno, south of Florence, August 1944. These are troops of the all-black 92nd US Infantry Division. It was not until the Korean War that blacks and whites were fully integrated in the US Army.*

This gave the Germans time to organize a counterblow, and for the next four weeks there was desperate fighting here. The Allies managed just to hang on, but for the next few months they were powerless to assist the main attacks to the south.

Operations now became concentrated around Monte Cassino, which became the graveyard of Allied troops of all nations. The German defense was resolute, and it was not until mid-May that it finally fell to the Poles and Free French. This was the signal for Kesselring finally to withdraw from the Gustav Line. Mark Clark's longheld desire to enter Rome was satisfied on 4 June, and the Allies made good progress all along the front.

Kesselring's plan was now to hold on to the Gothic Line, which ran north of Florence and made maximum use of the Apennines. By early August he was secure in this, and the Allies were faced with yet another problem of how to prise him out of it. It was not as great as it first appeared. While Fifth Army attacked across the River Arno, the main effort was made by Eighth Army in the east. Led by the Canadians, they broke through by mid-September, and the Germans withdrew, only to deny the Allies Bologna, which was the next objective. By now, the wintry weather and general exhaustion caused Alexander, now supreme commander, to put a halt to offensive operations until the following spring.

TOP LEFT: *B-25s of the Twelfth USAAF, on their way to bomb targets in the Monte Cassino area, pass an erupting Mount Vesuvius.*
TOP RIGHT: *The monastery of Monte Cassino shortly after its final capture in May 1944. This battle was the fiercest and most costly of the campaign in Italy.*
ABOVE: *Field Marshal Albert Kesselring, the German Commander-in-Chief in Italy, lives up to his nickname of 'Smiling Albert' as he visits some of his troops. He proved to be a shrewd and realistic commander.*
RIGHT: *Massed pipe bands of Scottish regiments serving in Italy celebrate the liberation of Rome, June 1944. Many of the pipe tunes they played were composed to commemorate recent battles in which these regiments took part.*

Preparations for D-Day

As early as April 1943 the Americans and British had set up a combined headquarters in England, under a Briton, General Frederick Morgan, to begin planning the cross-Channel invasion. It was a formidable undertaking in the extreme. The Germans had now held the Channel coasts for three years, they expected an invasion to come and were carrying out extensive fortification. Furthermore, the specter of the failure at Dieppe in August 1942 was there to haunt the planners and they knew that failure might prolong the war by years.

The first task was to decide where to land. One thing that Dieppe had shown was that to land around a port was to court disaster, since the defenses were likely to be heavier than elsewhere. The Pas de Calais was the most obvious option, since it is here that the English Channel is at its narrowest, but it would be where the Germans would most expect a landing and hence surprise would be lost. The beaches in Holland and Belgium were considered unsuitable for landing large bodies of troops, and the farther toward the coasts of north Germany the longer the lines of communication from Britain. Looking west of the Pas de Calais, the only other feasible option was Normandy, and it was this on which the planners lighted. Detailed planning of the operation could now begin.

BELOW: *Field Marshal Erwin Rommel inspects Channel defenses. The Germans knew that the Allies were going to invade France, but the debate lay in where this would be.*

RIGHT: *An invaluable vehicle when it came to amphibious landings, the US DUKW, known as a 'Duck.' The Americans also had amphibious tracked vehicles, the LVTPs Mks 1-4.*

The next task was to define precisely where in Normandy the landings should take place. This required very detailed intelligence. Here the French Resistance provided much help, but there were other sources. Extensive air photographic reconnaissance was carried out, and specially trained teams of divers made a detailed analysis of the beaches. Meteorological records were consulted and even people's prewar vacation snaps and postcards examined. Gradually the options were whittled down to the coast north of Caen, and, by the end of 1943, Morgan's team had produced a plan for a three division assault here, aimed at Caen. With this secured, there would be a drive into the Cotentin Peninsula to seize Cherbourg as a port, followed by a thrust on Paris. The next question was who was to take command.

ABOVE: *Eisenhower (second from right) and Montgomery (right) on a visit to men of the 3rd US Armored Division at Warminster, England, February 1944. This division was to distinguish itself in NW Europe, as part of Patton's Third Army.*

BELOW: *During spring 1944, constant rehearsals for D-Day were carried out on British beaches similar to their Normandy counterparts. On one such, on 28 April 1944, at Lyme Bay, Dorset, German E-boats caused a number of American casualties.*

Since the Americans were going to have the largest forces, the British agreed that they should appoint the supreme commander. The obvious choice was George C Marshall, who headed the United States Joint Chiefs of Staff and had been involved with Overlord, as the invasion was called, from its inception. He had no obvious successor,

ABOVE: *The final hours of waiting. GIs pass the time in a constructive way. The storms of 5 June would cause severe discomfort and seasickness for the troops on their way to France.*

LEFT: *Men of the British 13th/18th Hussars wait for the armada to set sail. The tank is a Sherman Firefly equipped with a 17-pounder gun, the only armament really effective against the German Tigers and Panthers.*

RIGHT: *Royal Army Medical Corps personnel attached to 51st Highland Division, one of the British divisions which assaulted on D-Day. They are clearly delighted that the long months of training are now at an end.*

though, and after much debate, Roosevelt decided at the beginning of December 1943 on Eisenhower, now well experienced in handling Allied forces. In order to provide balance, Montgomery was selected to command the actual landings. The two men arrived in England in January 1944, and Montgomery's first step was to change Morgan's plan radically. He considered that the beachhead was too small and vulnerable to German counterattack, and instead proposed additional landings by two divisions at the base of the Cotentin Peninsula. To this Eisenhower agreed. The final plan was for the initial landings to be carried out in the west by Omar Bradley's United States First Army and north of Caen by General Miles Dempsey's British Second Army, under the overall command of Montgomery's 21st Army Group.

Much else, however, had to be done. Large numbers of landing craft had to be gathered in the ports of southern England. Because it was likely to be some time before a fully functioning port would be available to the Allies, two artificial ports were built, codenamed Mulberry, which would be towed in sections across the Channel and anchored off the invasion beaches. All supplies, apart from fuel would flow through these. Fuel would be transported through specially laid pipelines, Pluto (Pipeline Under The Ocean). The British also devised a number of special armored vehicles, such as flamethrower and bridgelaying tanks and tanks armed with special guns for demolishing strongpoints.

There was much debate on how best to harness Anglo-American strategic airpower to the needs of Overlord. Experience in Italy suggested that the best targets were the enemy's road and rail communications, thus preventing the deployment of reserves. Both Spaatz and Harris, however, were unwilling to call off their offensive on Germany, the former because he thought oil a more effective target, and the latter because he was still convinced that area bombing could make the invasion a mere 'constabulary' action. Eisenhower overrode both, and transportation targets, particularly in France, became the main priority, together with the wearing down of the German fighter strength. Finally, on 14 April 1944, the strategic

bombing forces were placed under his command so that they could provide direct support for Overlord.

Perhaps the greatest problem was how best to achieve surprise and prevent the Germans deducing that the invasion would be in Normandy. The accumulation of equipment in southern England made it impossible to hide the preparations, but what the Allies could do was to disguise their intentions. Under the overall codename of Fortitude, a number of elaborate deception plans were put in train. One was to maintain a feigned interest in Norway and force the Germans to keep a large garrison there. Another involved General Patton, who had been under a cloud since slapping a battle-fatigued soldier's face in Sicily. He had been appointed to command one of the follow-up armies in Normandy, Third United States, but for German ears it was put about that he was commanding an army group in southeast England, close to the Pas de Calais. Skeleton headquarters were set up, which passed mythical radio traffic to one another.

Fortitude was very effective in fooling the Germans. Von Rundstedt, who had overall command in the West, remained convinced that the Pas de Calais was the main target and that any landings elsewhere would merely be a diversion. However, Rommel, who as commander Army Group B had actually to conduct the defense of the French coasts, was certain that it was Normandy. Hitler eventually sided with von Rundstedt and decreed that the German armor reserve, crucial for driving the Allies back into the sea, was to be held back and centrally. It was not allowed to be deployed forward without his express permission.

Studies of the weather and tides gave 5 June as the most favorable date for D-Day, but during the days immediately before this the weather forecast became increasingly hostile. At the eleventh hour, therefore, Eisenhower was forced to make a 24-hour postponement. It could be no longer than this since the tides would not be suitable for a landing for another three weeks. This was perhaps the hardest decision of his life.

Normandy

Preceded by airborne landings, the Allies stormed ashore on 6 June on five beaches – operations Gold, Juno and Sword for the British and Canadians, and Omaha and Utah for the Americans. The Germans were taken by surprise, with many commanders, including Rommel, absent from their headquarters. The low-grade troops defending the coast soon disintegrated in the face of the massive Allied naval and air bombardment, and the beachheads were quickly secured. While there were casualties on all beaches, only on Omaha was there any real problem. Here, steep cliffs and units landing in the wrong place caused initial difficulties and heavier casualties, and Bradley was, at one point, tempted to abort the landing. However, as further reinforcements arrived, the problems were overcome and by nightfall the Americans were firm. In the east Montgomery had hoped to reach Caen by the end of the first day, but the one Panzer division deployed forward stopped him.

Hitler was convinced that the landings were a feint and that the main effort would come in the Pas de Calais area. He therefore only gradually and grudgingly released the Panzer divisions that Rommel so badly needed. Even then, the Allied air attacks on transportation targets and further attacks as they moved made their journeys to the front immensely difficult. But, feint or not, Hitler was determined that the Allies should be contained in Normandy.

In spite of the overwhelming Allied superiority both in the air and on the ground, the Germans did enjoy one or two advantages. Firstly, their tanks and anti-armor weapons were generally much more powerful than those of the Allies and the rate of destruction of Allied tanks

was high. Secondly, the bocage terrain in Normandy – small fields with high earth banks topped with thick hedges – favored the defense, and it was not something that the Allies had really prepared for. Finally, the German soldier was generally better trained, especially in his ability to take over command if his superior became a casualty, and the Waffen-SS troops, many of whom fought in Normandy, had a fanaticism which was alien to the North Americans and British.

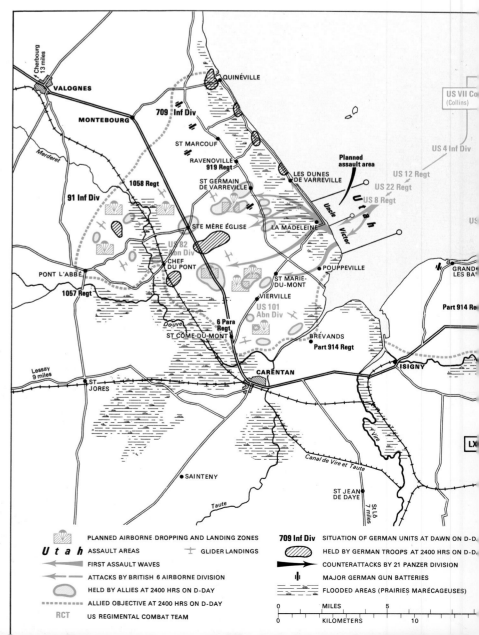

RIGHT: *The Overlord high command. Sitting (left to right): Tedder (Deputy Supreme Commander), Eisenhower (Supreme Commander), Montgomery (land commander). Standing: Bradley (First US Army), Ramsay (naval commander), Leigh-Mallory (air commander), Bedell Smith (Chief of Staff).*
LEFT: *Old Glory flies above Omaha Beach late on 6 June 1944. A significant factor in the success of the landings was that the Luftwaffe had been cleared from the skies.*
BELOW LEFT: *The sight that met the follow-up waves as they came ashore at Utah Beach. These GIs are luckier than some in that they are able to get ashore with only their feet wet.*
BELOW: *The organization and progress of the D-Day landings, 6 June 1944.*

In the west, the Americans concentrated on clearing the Cotentin Peninsula, taking Cherbourg on 27 June. Unfortunately, the Germans had left the port installations in ruins and it would be some time before the port could function again. Fierce storms in mid-June also caused much damage to the Mulberry harbors anchored off Omaha and Gold beaches, which slowed down the rate of supply for a period. In the center, Bradley's troops reached Caumont by 18 June, but Caen, defended by the Waffen-SS, withstood frontal attacks by the Canadians. At the end of the month Montgomery tried to outflank it from the west, but this attack was also repulsed, again by Waffen-SS Panzer divisions.

Although the Germans were holding up well, von Rundstedt and Rommel soon became convinced that Hitler's policy of stand and fight in Normandy would merely lead to the destruction of the German

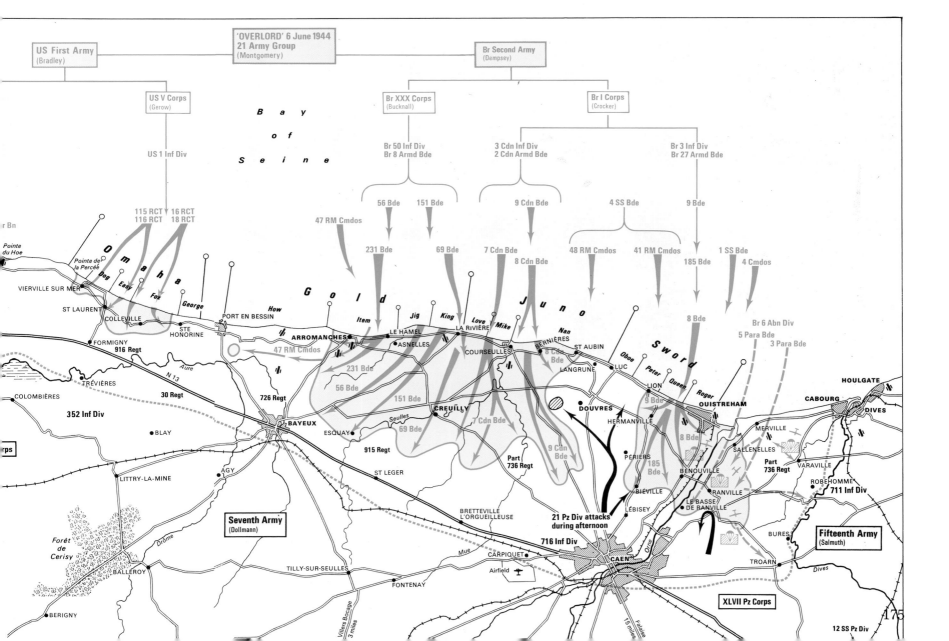

RIGHT: *Canadian troops pick their way through the ruins of Caen. The city was a D-Day objective, but desperate resistance by Waffen-SS troops, notably of the Hitler Jugend Division, meant that it was almost two months before Caen was finally secured.*

BELOW RIGHT: *Exhausted British infantry snatch a quick rest in a Normandy hedgerow. The fighting in Normandy was prolonged, tough and nervewracking.*

ABOVE: *Gliders fly over the hardpressed US troops on Omaha Beach on 6 June 1944. This was the toughest of the six landings because of the cliffs which covered much of the beach.*

RIGHT: *Some of the first German prisoners captured by US troops. The German coastal divisions were generally low grade and many were filled with other than ethnic Germans. The fighting became very much tougher with the arrival of Waffen-SS reinforcements.*

armies there. They pleaded with him for permission to withdraw, but he replied by sacking von Rundstedt and replacing him with von Kluge, but he too quickly became caught up in the general pessimism. As for Rommel, he was badly wounded on 17 July after his car was strafed by Allied fighter-bombers, and he left the stage.

This was on the eve of the most controversial Allied operation of the campaign, Goodwood. This was a thrust by three British armored divisions on a narrow front east of Caen. The debate, which lasts to this day, is whether Montgomery intended it as a breakout operation or, as he argued, merely a means of drawing the German armor to the east to make the planned American breakout in the west easier. In the event, the thrust did not get very far, with heavy tank casualties being suffered. Yet it did draw the Panzers to the Second Army front.

During the latter part of July, Patton's Third Army, which was to execute the breakout, arrived in Normandy. Until this time he had continued to masquerade as commander of the notional 1st Army Group in order to make the Germans remain worried about the Pas de Calais. The preliminary stage of the breakout was an operation mounted west of St Lô on 25 July, aimed at gaining a springboard from which to clear Brittany. Before they attacked southward Bradley's troops were preceded by a massive air bombardment, as had become commonplace with the Allied attacks, but badly aimed bombs killed a number of Americans including General Lesley J McNair, responsible for organizing the US Army for war. On the 31st the advance secured Avranches and then immediately turned to the west, quickly clearing Brittany.

By this stage, because of the buildup of Allied troops, there was a reorganization. Bradley was now promoted to command 12th Army Group consisting of First United States Army, now under Courtney Hodges, and Patton's Third Army, while Montgomery's 21st Army Group had the British Second and Canadian First Armies, the latter commanded by General Henry Crerar. Patton's Third Army now swept south and east toward Le Mans, while 21st Army Group and the remainder of First United States Army began to squeeze the remaining German forces into a pocket around Falaise. In a last desperate

effort, Hitler, against the advice of his generals, ordered a counterattack on the flank of First United States Army. This was launched at Mortain on 7 August, but was repulsed, airpower playing a dominant role.

The Germans made desperate efforts to keep the pocket around Falaise open so that their troops could escape, but on 18 August the Canadians and Americans joined hands and the pocket was finally closed. By this time Hitler had replaced von Kluge with Model. The former was ordered back to Germany to explain his failures, and, on the 19th, took a cyanide pill while on his way back. He left Model trying desperately to get the remnants of Army Group B back across the River Seine. The Allies could now really savor the fruits of victory.

Resistance to Hitler and the July 1944 Bomb Plot

On 20 July 1944 a bomb exploded in the conference room of Hitler's eastern headquarters at Rastenburg in East Prussia while a briefing for the Führer was taking place. Hitler himself escaped with minor injuries, although some were killed and others of those present seriously injured. It was not the first, but it was certainly the last attempt to assassinate Hitler.

From the mid-1930s, there had been a number of covert groups opposed to the totalitarian nature and the growing excesses of Hitler's regime, but there was little or no cohesion among them since they had widely differing views on what they wanted in its place. What all had in common was the realization that unless they had a significant part of the Wehrmacht on their side any coup would fail, but, except for a few, the generals were not prepared to commit themselves, mainly because Hitler had given back to the generals what they wanted, a large army.

After the victory in Poland and the decision to turn against the West, some generals, horrified at the prospect of another major war, did attempt to organize a plot, but it quickly caved in. Then, on 8 November 1939, a bomb exploded in a Munich beerhall where the Nazi

hierarchy had met to celebrate the anniversary of the 1923 putsch. Hitler had already left when it went off and a communist was arrested as the perpetrator.

The heady victories of 1940-41 curbed the activities of the conspirators, but once the Germans found themselves bogged down in the East and doubts grew over Germany's ability to win the war, so the view grew in some quarters that the war must be stopped. This could only be done by removing Hitler. During 1943, there were a number of bungled attempts on Hitler's life, but with the Allied invasion of Normandy determination grew.

The plan of the July 1944 Bomb Plot was for a staff officer, Colonel Claus von Stauffenberg, to plant the bomb. Once it had exploded, troops of the Berlin garrison would secure the capital, and there would be a similar action in Paris, whose military governor, Heinrich von Stülpnagel, was also implicated in the plot. A government, headed by two longtime anti-Hitler plotters, General Ludwig Beck and Karl Gördeler, onetime Mayor of Leipzig, would then be formed and negotiations opened with the Allies.

LEFT: *Hitler with Mussolini, who was scheduled to visit Hitler's headquarters, the Wolf's Lair, on 20 July 1944, discussing the bomb with members of Hitler's staff. On the left, Göring (white uniform) and Martin Bormann, Hitler's closest aide.*
RIGHT: *The wreckage in the conference room. Hitler might have been killed if an officer had not inadvertently shifted the briefcase to behind a table leg with his foot.*
BELOW: *Field Marshal von Witzleben, one of the plotters, on trial. He suffers the indignity of being forced to keep his trousers up with his hands.*

In the event von Stauffenberg flew back to Berlin, convinced that Hitler was dead. Himmler, in the meantime, arranged for the news of Hitler's escape to be broadcast, and this threw the conspirators in Berlin into confusion. Troops loyal to the regime then arrested them. Some were shot out of hand, but Beck himself committed suicide. The remainder were held to stand trial. In Paris, the story was much the same. Although many SS and Gestapo men were arrested, the plotters were forced to release them.

Those held for the plot were tortured and then arraigned before a People's Court. Here they suffered untold indignities, before being found guilty and brutally executed. Their families also suffered. Rommel, still recovering from his wounds, was one who became enmeshed in the ever widening net cast by Himmler and his men, and was forced to commit suicide. In all, some 5000 people lost their lives in the aftermath, and Hitler's distrust of his generals grew more and more obsessional.

The Soviet Advance on Warsaw

The Russian strategy for 1944 was to continue the policy of concurrent offensives all along the front. There would be no halt for winter, and this was helped by the fact that the winter of 1943-44 was exceptionally mild. A further advantage was that their numerical superiority over the Germans was growing all the time. The Germans, on the other hand, suffered a grave disadvantage in that, as they withdrew westward, the front did not become any shorter, and the result was that their defenses became ever thinner.

While an attack in January 1943 had succeeded in establishing a narrow corridor between Leningrad and the main Russian front, the city was still, to all intents and purposes, under siege a year later. In mid-January 1944, however, Russia launched a double-enveloping offensive designed to trap the German forces in front of Leningrad. Although the Germans managed to escape, the siege was lifted and the vital Leningrad-Moscow railroad secured. Just as important, Finland was now isolated, and in mid-February began armistice negotiations with the Russians. The latter's terms were reasonable, but the Finns balked at the demand that they disarm the German forces in their country, and the talks were broken off. The offensive meanwhile finally ran out of steam at the beginning of March on the borders with Estonia and Latvia.

South of Kiev, the Russians continued their efforts to eradicate the large German salient with Zaporozhye just beyond its eastern tip. Von Manstein and von Kleist dearly wanted to withdraw to the line of the Dniestr in order to shorten their front, but Hitler refused to countenance this. The result was inevitable. The First Ukrainian Front, attacking west from Kiev on Christmas Eve 1943, forced von

Manstein back and quickly reached the old frontier with Poland, and by early February had penetrated 100 miles beyond this. Farther south, at the end of January, a complete Panzer army was cut off between Kiev and Cherkassy, although a rescue operation did succeed in extricating a portion of it. Simultaneously, the point of this huge salient came under pressure from Malinovsky's Third Ukrainian Front, and by early April von Kleist was back behind the Dniestr. The German Seventeenth Army in the Crimea was left to its fate and finally overrun in early May. In March, meanwhile, a furious Hitler had sacked both von Manstein and von Kleist.

The spring thaw brought about a temporary pause and gave the Germans the chance to draw a little breath, but in June the Russians renewed their attacks. First came a thrust north into Finland, which caused the Finns once more to seek terms, but Stalin now demanded surrender. With the Russian advance losing impetus, and the Germans promising to send reinforcements, the Finns decided to fight on. This would not be for long, however, and on 19 September they did finally sign a peace treaty. With this, the Russians now turned their attention to clearing northern Norway of German troops.

Next, the Russians struck between the Baltic and Pripet marshes, breaking through Army Group Center, which had, as a result of the attacks earlier in the year, a long exposed right flank. In spite of some desperate German counterattacks, there was no stemming the tide, and by the end of August, the Russians had entered East Prussia. This totally isolated the remnants of Army Group North in the Courland Peninsula. A further lightning thrust in mid-July resulted in the Germans forces still in the Ukraine, being driven back, in the south, to the

Carpathian Mountains, and, farther north, to the Vistula and beyond. Between here and Army Group Center lay Warsaw and by the end of July it seemed that its liberation by the advancing Russian army could be only weeks away.

In Warsaw itself the Poles had a large underground army, the Polish Home Army under General Tadeusz Bor-Komorowski. On the instructions of the Polish Government-in-Exile in London, this army rose against the German garrison on 1 August 1944. The rising was not so much to assist the Russian capture of the city, but more to demonstrate that Poland was still a nation in being. By the end of the month, the Russians were on the Vistula facing Warsaw, but here they halted. Meanwhile the Poles fought on with growing desperation. In the end, with still no signs of a move forward by the Russians, the remnants of the Home Army, now reduced to operating from the sewers, were forced to surrender on 2 October.

The Russian reason for halting was that they had outrun their supplies and that there was a danger that if they crossed the Vistula at this juncture they would be flung back into the river by four Panzer divisions which they mistakenly believed to be in the neighborhood. Yet they refused to allow British and US aircraft to support the Poles from Russian bases, and it is difficult not to believe that Stalin had a political motive. Determined that Poland should be firmly in the

Russian sphere of influence after the war, he could not risk the setting up of any form of independent Polish government. As it was, it would not be until the new year that the Russians would make any further move forward in this area.

Instead, Russian attention now switched to the south. Toward the end of August 1944, Russian troops broke through into Rumania, and immediately brought about her surrender. Bulgaria fell next, and on 8 September changed sides, declaring war against Germany. The Russians now turned toward Hungary and Yugoslavia. In conjunction with Tito's Partisans, who were coming up from the south, they struck at Belgrade toward the end of September, hoping to trap the German Army Groups E and F, which were now withdrawing northward through the Balkans. This they failed to do, although Belgrade was liberated on 19 October. German resistance in Hungary was much tougher, and only at the end of the year was Budapest reached.

With the evacuation of Greece by the Germans, the communist partisans saw their chance to seize power in the country, and civil war erupted. They hoped to have Russian support, but this was not forthcoming as Stalin had agreed that Greece lay within the sphere of influence of the Western Allies. Meanwhile the British sent troops into the country, and these became embroiled in the civil war, fighting against the communists.

FAR LEFT: *Marshal Georgi Zhukov photographed postwar in full dress uniform. Many of his decorations and orders were awarded to him by the Western Allies for his part in the defeat of Germany.*
ABOVE LEFT: *The liberation of the Polish city of Lvov by the First Belorussian Front, July 1944.*
ABOVE: *A Russian infantry battalion deploys for a quick attack during the advance into Poland. By this time the Red Army was becoming a well-oiled machine.*
RIGHT: *One of the periodic roundups of Jews in the Warsaw Ghetto.*

On to the Philippines

By early 1944, the main Japanese base of Rabaul in the southwest Pacific had been isolated. It was now neutralized by constant attacks from the air, and MacArthur moved on to tackle Dutch New Guinea, thus taking one step farther toward his main immediate objective of the Philippines. In the central Pacific, Nimitz, after securing the Gilberts and Marshalls, now looked 1000 miles west to his next target, the Marianas. Between here and the Marshalls, however, lay Truk, the Rabaul of the central Pacific. Like MacArthur, rather than attempt to capture it, Nimitz used his growing airpower instead. During 17 and 18 February, American bombers dropped so much explosive as to render it unusable and it ceased to play a part in the war.

The Marianas, besides being a useful stepping stone, also had the attraction of being within bombing range of Japan. There were three main islands in the group, Saipan, Tinian, and Guam, and it was known that they were heavily defended. Accordingly, Nimitz gathered together the largest force yet seen in the Pacific, 127,000 troops and 530 ships. These set sail from the Marshalls in early June, and the first landings were made on Saipan on the 15th. Once again Japanese resistance was fanatical and it was not until 9 July that it ended. Two weeks later, the United States Marines landed on Tinian, Saipan's southern neighbor, and cleared this in a week. Simultaneously, Guam was tackled and the main fighting here ended on 10 August, but mopping-up operations continued for some months to come. Indeed, the last Japanese soldier did not surrender until 1960!

ABOVE: *US naval pilots being briefed on board their carrier prior to attacking Roi Island in the Marshalls, January 1944. It was a time for forced humor.*

BELOW: *A flight deck crewman, showing great courage, scrambles up to the cockpit of this Grumman F6F Hellcat, in order to rescue the pilot. Casualties from misjudged deck landings were common when tired pilots returned from missions.*

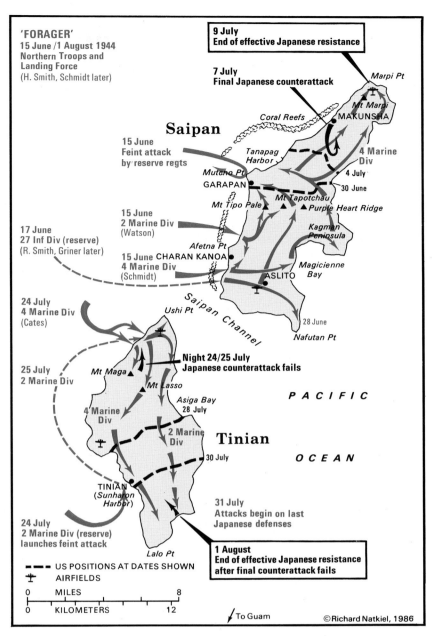

The Japanese, however, were not prepared to stand by idly and allow the Americans to take the Marianas without outside interference. Indeed, the loss of the Marianas would mean that their empire was virtually cut in half. Accordingly they concentrated two fleets, determined to destroy the United States Task Force commanded by Admiral Marc Mitscher, which was supporting the landings. United States submarines warned Mitscher of the Japanese approach and he decided to divide his force into five groups, four built round his seven heavy and eight light carriers, and the fifth his seven battleships. In contrast, the Japanese had two groups, with three light carriers and escorts steaming ahead of the main body, which had a further light and five heavy carriers, together with battleships and heavy cruisers.

On 19 June, Japanese reconnaissanace aircraft sighted the US ships and air strikes were immediately ordered. The Japanese fighters were picked up on Mitscher's radar and he ordered his own aircraft into the air to intercept them. The result was some 200 Japanese aircraft shot down for the loss of only 23 American. In the meantime, American submarines located the Japanese main force and sank two aircraft carriers. A further Japanese air strike mistakenly flew toward Guam

ABOVE LEFT: *Another Japanese aircraft is destroyed. This is a 'Kate' torpedo bomber, which has just been shot down by a carrier's guns.*
ABOVE: *The capture of Tinian and Saipan.*
LEFT: *Awaiting the order 'Ramps down!' US Marines approach their landing beach at Kwajalein Atoll in the Marshalls, 2 February 1944. The Atoll was secured by 4 February.*

183

instead of the US fleet, but was also intercepted and largely destroyed. Next day Mitscher set off in pursuit of the now withdrawing Japanese, and sank another carrier and two oilers. Mitscher now turned back to cover the Marianas, while the Japanese continued their withdrawal to

Okinawa. Thus ended the Battle of the Philippine Sea, or, as it is more familiarly called, 'The Great Marianas Turkey Shoot.' This was apt. Some 300 Japanese naval aircraft had been lost, reducing the Japanese task force to only 35 operational aircraft.

ABOVE: *US troops come ashore at Saipan, 17 June 1944. This was two days after the initial landings. The 'veterans' on the right look on.*
LEFT: *So often clearing islands in the Pacific was a matter of digging the Japanese out of their bunkers. Usually the flame thrower was the only way to achieve this.*
RIGHT: *Grumman TBF Avenger torpedo bombers and Curtiss SB2C Helldivers on their way to attack the Japanese fleet during the Battle of the Philippine Sea.*

It was at this stage that a debate took place as to what the next objective should be. A school of thought questioned whether the Philippines were the right stepping stone to the Japanese mainland. Rather, they argued, Formosa was better since it meant that not only could a heavier bombload be flown against Japan, but also an air route could be opened up to China. Another view believed in an invasion of the southernmost Japanese island of Kyushu. Neither course of action found favor with MacArthur or Nimitz, since both believed that they would unnecessarily overextend the Allied forces in the Pacific. Also, MacArthur was very conscious of the vow he had made to the Filipinos on his departure in early 1942 that he would return. Eventually this argument won the day, although to begin with the planners in Washington would only concede the capture of the southernmost islands of the Philippines.

It was logical, not just for emotional reasons, that the liberation of

the Philippines should fall to MacArthur. He was closer than Nimitz and his forces were fresher. It was also agreed that MacArthur could bypass the Japanese forces in the Dutch East Indies, Borneo and the Celebes, since these would merely be a distraction from the main objective. His original plan had been to seize a number of small stepping stones, but probing of Filipino waters by Halsey's ships in September 1944 established that the Japanese coastal defenses were weak. Most of these intermediate targets were therefore dropped, except for two where preparations were too far advanced. Thus, on 15 September, MacArthur's troops landed on Morotai Island, north of New Guinea, and on the same day Halsey invaded the Paulau Islands, which lay west of Truk. This was especially significant since these lay only 500 miles from the Marianas, and meant that the two main thrusts in the Pacific had almost converged. The stage was now set for tackling the Philippines themselves.

Leyte Gulf

The Japanese, conscious of their lack of naval airpower, as a result of the Battle of the Philippine Sea, saw the American attack on the Philippines as an opportunity to neutralize both American land and naval power in the Pacific. To defend the islands themselves, the army commander, General Tomoyuki Yamashita, had sizeable forces, equivalent to some 15 divisions. While these pinned down the American landings, the Japanese naval commander, Soemu Toyoda, would play the decisive role. Using his remaining carriers as a lure, he planned to draw the American fleet northward and trap it between two battleship task groups.

MacArthur's own plan was to make his initial landing on Leyte, one of the smaller islands, and in the center of the Philippines. In this way, he hoped to be able to split the Japanese defenses and make reinforcement between the northern and southern islands impossible. The landings would be carried out by Walter Krueger's United States Sixth Army, supported by Halsey's Third and Kinkaid's United States Seventh Fleets.

During the ten days before the landings, United States Navy aircraft had struck at targets in Formosa, Okinawa and Luzon, partly as a deception, but also further to reduce Japanese airpower. Indeed, they destroyed some 500 aircraft for the loss of only 80 of their own. Then, on 20 October 1944, four divisions of Krueger's troops began to come ashore on Leyte. It was time for the Japanese to set their maritime plan in action.

BELOW: *General MacArthur fulfils his vow made in Australia in March 1942. On 20 October 1944 he waded ashore at Leyte. The liberation of the Philippines would, however, take some months.*

RIGHT: *Admiral 'Bull' Halsey, the victor at Leyte Gulf. His impetuosity, however, almost resulted in the destruction of the task force supporting the landings on Leyte.*

The bait was the four surviving carriers proper and two converted battleships, but among them there were only some 100 serviceable planes. The main fleet, under Admiral Takeo Kurita, had to come up from the Dutch East Indies, where it was based, to be close to its sources of oil. American submarines intercepted it en route, sinking two cruisers, including Kurita's, although Kurita himself was rescued, and crippling a third. The carrier bait now came down from the north, but, in spite of every effort, including the transmission of uncoded messages, could not attract Halsey's attention. Beating off attacks from landbased aircraft, although these did destroy the carrier *Princeton*, Halsey's eyes were fixed on Kurita. Halsey's aircraft sank the mighty battleship *Musashi* and disabled a heavy cruiser. This was too much for Kurita, who now withdrew westward. It was, however, only a temporary measure, for, once darkness fell, he turned about. Halsey, meanwhile, had now finally become aware of the Japanese carriers and sailed north to deal with them.

ABOVE: *Admiral Takijiro Ohnishi, founder of the Kamikaze Special Attack Force. 'Divine Wind' represented the typhoon which had blown back Kublai Khan's invasion fleet on its way to Japan in the 14th century.*

ABOVE RIGHT: *A kamikaze aircraft streaks across the flight deck of an Allied carrier. These aircraft proved by far the greatest threat to Allied naval power in the Pacific during the last year of the war.*

RIGHT: *Kamikaze pilots, dressed in their symbolic white scarves, receive their final orders prior to an attack on Allied shipping. To die for their emperor was their goal.*

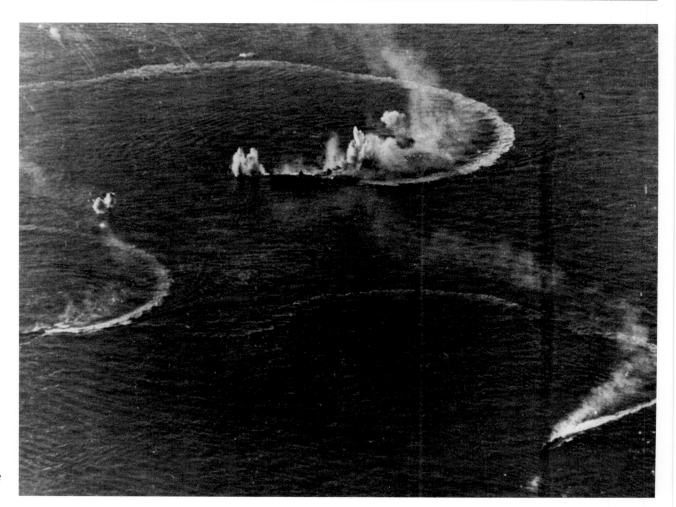

RIGHT: *Japanese ships under attack during the Battle of the Philippine Sea, June 1944.*
BELOW: *Filipino guerrillas meet with US soldiers. By 1944-45 there were substantial resistance forces opposing the Japanese on many of the Philippine islands.*

LEFT: *A dramatic photograph of a Japanese bomber plunging to its death after trying to attack a carrier task force.*

Near midnight that same night, 24/25 October, American planes spotted Kurita once more, a bare 40 miles from the San Bernardino Strait, which ran north of Samar, the island immediately north of Leyte. Halsey believed that Kurita was merely on a suicide mission and that Kinkaid could deal with him, while he tackled the carriers. In fact, Kurita had split his force into two, one group continuing through the San Bernardino Strait and the other passing south of Leyte. Kinkaid ignored the northern group and sent the bulk of his fleet against the other thrust. This, thanks largely to radar, was utterly destroyed, including two battleships. No sooner had this been achieved than Kinkaid received news that the other arm of the Japanese fleet was threatening the small part of his fleet which he had left to cover the landings. This now came under fire and fled southward, but the gallantry of the escort destroyers and naval aircraft on the six escort carriers present enabled the ships to get away with one carrier and three destroyers sunk.

Kurita now turned north once more to deal with the unprotected transports and landing craft. Halsey had so far ignored Kinkaid's calls for help, so intent was he on destroying the carriers – not for nothing did he have the nickname 'Bull.' He had by now severely battered them with his aircraft and was about to finish them off with his battleships. Finally, in view of the clearly critical situation to the south, he did break off, but was too far north to be able to affect the issue.

It seemed that nothing could save the American transports, but now the 'fog of war' came to the rescue. From intercepted radio messages, Kurita became convinced that Halsey was farther south than he really was, and that landbased aircraft were about to attack him. Fearing for his withdrawal route through the San Bernardino Strait, he turned north, and late that night, the 25th/26th, finding the Strait empty, slipped back through it.

Kurita's forces may have escaped, but the Battle of Leyte Gulf was decisive, more so than the Americans realized at the time. The American carriers, which Halsey had left when he turned south, had succeeded in sinking all four of their opposite numbers, leaving the Japanese with none. Without carriers, as the Pacific war had proved so often, the Japanese fleet was crippled. Yet this did not mean that the threat no longer existed. In the closing stages of the battle the Japanese introduced a new weapon, *Kamikaze*, or divine wind. These were aircraft packed with explosives, whose pilots dived them onto the decks of enemy ships. Although a clear indication of growing Japanese desperation, kamikaze would continue to give the Allies cause for concern during the remainder of the Pacific war.

With the Japanese naval threat removed, MacArthur could continue his land operations without outside interference. It was not until Christmas Day 1944, however, that Leyte was finally secured. In the meantime landings were made on 15 December on Mindoro, off the south coast of Luzon. Opposition here, however, was light, and MacArthur could now turn to the liberation of Luzon itself.

Liberation!

The concept of Anvil had been the cause of much debate between the British and Americans. It was an American plan, which had been agreed in principle at the Teheran Conference in November 1943, but during the early months of 1944 the British had increasing reservations over it. The troops to be used for it would have to come from Italy, which would mean that chances of success here would be reduced even further and thus fewer German troops would be tied down. The American argument, which eventually won the day, was that France was the decisive theater, and that, anyway, given the Italian terrain, progress here would inevitably be slow. Thus, on 15 August 1944, troops of General Alexander Patch's United States Seventh Army came ashore on the Riviera west of Cannes in a virtually unopposed landing. Followed up by the French Corps of four divisions under Alphonse Juin, which had also been fighting in Italy, this force drove quickly northward, linking up with Patton's Third Army on 12 September north of Dijon.

Patton himself was now in his element and demonstrating to all how armor should be handled. Charging across France, with only scattered German opposition, he had reached the Seine at Fontainebleau on 20 August. Establishing a bridgehead here, he had carried on eastward, through the American battlefields of the First World War, such as Château-Thierry and St Mihiel, and into Lorraine.

To the north, Hodges, too, had been having his successes. It had been Eisenhower's intention (he had now arrived in France to take

With the breakout from Normandy and the disintegration of the German forces there, the liberation of Western Europe could really begin. At the same time as the drive across northern and central France, however, the Allies had also made additional landings in the south of France, under the code name of Anvil.

over the conduct of the land battle from Montgomery) to bypass Paris in order to get to the German frontier as quickly as possible. The French Resistance and de Gaulle were not, however, happy about this. Indeed de Gaulle had word that communist elements were plan-

ning an early uprising in order to seize the reins of power. Consequently Hodges detached General Jacques Leclerc's 2nd French Armored Division, which was under his command, and this entered Paris on 24 August, accepting the surrender of the German garrison which had

ABOVE LEFT: *British M4 General Shermans await the order to break out in Normandy. Although good tanks, their tendency to burn when hit gave them the nickname 'Ronson lighters.' (From the advertising slogan 'They always light first time').*
LEFT: *US M10 tank destroyers cross the River Seine, 24 August 1944. Tank destroyers were designed for defense, but were increasingly misused during the campaign.*
ABOVE: *US paratroopers cautiously approach the bodies of Germans whom they have just shot.*
RIGHT: *A moment of triumph for Charles de Gaulle as he greets the inhabitants of recently liberated Bayeux. For him it had been a long road since the disasters of 1940.*

refused to obey Hitler's order to raze the city to the ground. Next day de Gaulle entered Paris in triumph and was installed as President of the Committee of National Liberation, the provisional government of France. Hodges now pressed on, his forces penetrating into Luxembourg and reaching the German border at Aachen on 12 September.

The British and Canadians had also not been idle. Dempsey's troops had liberated Amiens on 31 August and Brussels on 3 September. They also reached Antwerp on the 4th. The Canadians had a rather less glamorous task, having been ordered to clear the Channel ports. Hitler had ordered these to be turned into fortresses and defended to the last man. They therefore took time to reduce, and, once captured, it would take some time to make them operational.

It seemed during those last days of August and early September 1944 that nothing could stop the Allies and that Germany would be defeated before the year was out. A dark cloud was, however, quickly

looming over the horizon. It concerned the problem of ports.

The Allies were still dependent on the Mulberry harbors and Pluto for resupply, and the farther east they advanced, the more stretched their supply lines became. Hitler's order that the Channel ports must be defended to the last was not just the ravings of a man living increasingly in a fantasy world, but made sound military sense. The capture of Antwerp would have done much to solve the problem, but, because of misunderstandings among the British commanders, it was not realized that the dock installations were some way from the city, and the Germans were able to deny to the Allies these and both sides of the Scheldt, which was the approach to Antwerp. Indeed, it would not be until the end of November, after a fiercely contested amphibious landing on the island of Walcheren in the mouth of the Scheldt, that the port would be finally opened.

In the meantime, in spite of the efforts of the American 'Cannonball

ABOVE: *The US 28th Infantry Division parades on the Champs Elysées in Paris to celebrate its liberation. No sooner had the parade finished than the division was back in action with no chance to sample the delights of the capital.*

LEFT: *Although the Germans chose not to defend Paris, in spite of Hitler's demand that it be razed to the ground, some fanatical elements were determined to fight on. Here French Resistance members battle with snipers during the liberation celebrations.*

ABOVE RIGHT: *The battle for the Brittany port of St Malo, which fell on 16 August 1944.*

ABOVE, FAR RIGHT: *The penalty of collaboration – a French girl accused of being too friendly to the Germans has her hair shorn.*

RIGHT: *The liberation of Brussels, 3 September 1944.*

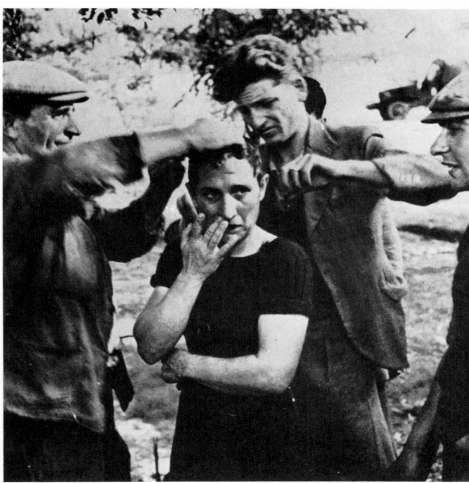

Express' – an endless conveyor belt of trucks running from Normandy to the front – gas tanks began to run dry and the advance slowed almost to a halt. This gave the Germans a valuable breathing space, and they were once again able to restore some cohesion to their defense. For the Allies this development provoked a bitter argument over strategy.

Eisenhower, who was as much a diplomat – some would argue even more so – as he was a soldier, firmly believed that for the sake of Allied unity, an advance on a broad front was the only answer. To allow merely one ally to reap all the military glory would create jealousy and

discord, not just in the theater of operations, but at home as well. In contrast, Montgomery, who had much greater military experience, and was no diplomat, was convinced that the war in Europe could only be won in 1944 if a narrow front strategy was adopted. This meant diverting the bulk of the available supplies either to him or to Bradley. Only in this way could the momentum of the advance, which was now dying on its feet, be maintained. There was a good case to be made for both arguments, but in early September Montgomery came up with a plan for breaking the growing deadlock, and Eisenhower agreed that it should be put into operation.

Market Garden and After

Throughout the summer of 1944 the First Allied Airborne Army commanded by General Lewis H Brereton USAAF had waited in Britain. It consisted of two US and two British airborne divisions, and a Polish parachute brigade, together with transport aircraft. Since the breakout it had had a frustrating time. Several ideas had been put forward for using it to speed up the Allied advance, but each plan had come to naught, usually because the success on the ground had made it superfluous before it could be put into action. It was this formation which Montgomery now wanted to use.

He believed that the German flank in the Netherlands could be turned, and that this would open the way into Germany. Southern Holland is, however, bounded by three east-west river lines, the Maas, Waal and Lower Rhine, and, below the Maas, by two canals. Bridges over these would have to be quickly secured for the plan to work. This was an ideal task for airborne forces.

The plan, as it eventually evolved, called for the use of three of the airborne divisions and the Poles. The United States 101st Airborne Division was to drop north of Eindhoven to deal with the canals, and the United States 82nd Airborne near Nijmegen to secure the Maas and Waal bridges. The farthest target – the bridge at Arnhem over the Lower Rhine – was given to the British 1st Airborne Division, which would be reinforced by the Polish Parachute Brigade. The whole operation would be commanded by General Frederick Browning's I Airborne Corps. Simultaneously, Dempsey would send his XXX British Corps, under General Brian Horrocks, and drive northward to link up with the airborne formations in turn. Market was the codename given to the airborne side of the operation, and Garden the codename of the XXX Corps aspect.

The operation was launched on 17 September 1944. The American landings took place as planned and they soon secured their bridges. At Arnhem, however, there were soon problems. The RAF, concerned

ABOVE LEFT: *Douglas DC-3 Dakotas dropping British paratroopers over Arnhem.*
BELOW LEFT: *British paratroopers patrol ruined houses on the outskirts of Arnhem.*
RIGHT: *Having landed by glider, these British troops move toward the center of Arnhem. The seeming peace is illusory.*
BELOW: *A US paratrooper under fire sprints for cover.*

about the air defenses around the town, had insisted on a dropping zone well away from it. Consequently, the airborne troops had a long march to their objective. At the same time, a fact that had not been recognized by Allied intelligence, there were two SS Panzer divisions in the area, refitting after the fighting in Normandy. The British paratroopers were soon embroiled in heavy fighting and were pinned down in the suburbs of the town, apart from one battalion, which did

manage to get through to the bridge. The arrival of the Poles was not sufficient to alter the situation.

In the meantime, the ground advance had also begun to have difficulties. They reached Nijmegen without too many problems, but from here northward, the troops were confined to a single road, with low marshy ground on either side. It thus required little effort on the Germans' part to slow the advance right down. In Arnhem, the

paratroops fought and died and, after a week's intense combat, they were forced to concede defeat, and the survivors crossed the Lower Rhine into the arms of XXX Corps which had just arrived there.

Market Garden had been an imaginative gamble, which had just failed, but it meant that the war would not end in 1944. From now on, with winter coming on, the Allied troops would be condemned to a slow slog toward Germany and the Rhine. The Narrow Front option was no longer relevant.

The Allies were now committed to a frontal assault against the Siegfried Line, the German equivalent of the Maginot Line. Almost all the Allied armies became bogged down in step-by-step slogging matches. Leaving the Canadians to complete the clearance of the Scheldt and cover the northern flank, the British Second Army became embroiled in the Reichswald, an area of dense woodland at the northern end of the Siegfried Line. To its south, the US Ninth and First Armies fought a bloody battle for control of the Aachen Gap through

ABOVE: *British paratroopers en route to the dropping zone. They are checking their equipment. The next order will be to stand up and hook up their lines. Then, once the green light comes on, they will jump.*
LEFT: *Still defiant, British paratroopers are marched into captivity at the end of the battle for the bridge at Arnhem. Only 20 percent of the British 1st Airborne Division managed to get back across the Rhine.*

RIGHT: *The results of a V-bomb landing in the center of the Belgian city of Antwerp. Hitler's 'miracle weapon' arrived too late to halt the Allied drive, but caused many casualties both in Belgium and in London during the late summer and fall of 1944.*
BELOW: *The liberation of Eindhoven by the British, 18 September 1944. On the same day British troops achieved a linkup with the US 101st Airborne Division. Two days later they reached 82nd Airborne Division, but Arnhem was the bridge just too far.*

the Siegfried Line. Progress was slow and casualties heavy, especially in the Huertgen Forest, which gained an infamous reputation with American troops. South of here was the Ardennes, where the Americans were content to sit facing the Siegfried Line, using the sector as somewhere to rest tired divisions from the north and blood others fresh from Stateside.

Below the Ardennes, Patton had become very entangled in trying to prise the Germans out of the ancient French fortress of Metz. Not until toward the end of November was he able to secure it completely and advance on into the Saarland. Here he found himself tackling the Maginot Line. The Germans, however, had done little to it, and it proved less of an obstacle than it might have been. Patton soon closed

up to the Siegfried Line. Finally, in the very south, Patch's United States Seventh Army and the French First Army, commanded by Jean de Lattre de Tassigny, liberated Lorraine and secured the west bank of the Rhine. With the Siegfried Line and the Black Forest facing them on the other side, a crossing of the river would have made little tactical sense.

By mid-December 1944 the Allies were most concerned over how to break through to the Rhine in the north of Germany, cross it, seize the Ruhr, advance into the German heartland and achieve final victory. There was still much to be done, but the one consolation was that the Germans were strictly on the defensive and that the time for counter-attacks had long past, or so they thought.

The Ardennes Counteroffensive

Hitler had first decided on a counteroffensive in the West as early as 16 September 1944. With his enemies closing in on every front, there was an urgent need to buy time. The Eastern Front was too vast and the Russians too superior in numbers for such an operation to have much effect. In the West there was more chance. Besides, if he could inflict a bloody nose on the British and Americans there was that much more chance that they might see sense and join him in the 'crusade' to stem the communist onrush in the East.

He laid down Antwerp as the objective, partly because of its value to the Allies as a port, but also because it would split the Americans from the British. The attack itself was to be through the Ardennes in hopes that the success of May 1940 there could be repeated. During the fall, his battered Panzer divisions which had been in France were re-equipped and refurbished. All this was done in the utmost secrecy, and not until toward the end of October was anyone outside Hitler's immediate military circle informed of the plan. Von Rundstedt, now restored as Commander-in-Chief West, was to have overall responsibility for the conduct of the offensive, and the armies involved were Fifth Panzer Army, commanded by Hasso von Manteuffel, Sixth Panzer Army, under the leading light of the Waffen-SS, Sepp Dietrich, and consisting mainly of SS formations, and Erich Brandenberger's Seventh Army.

The German generals were aghast at Hitler's plan, which they thought much too ambitious. Instead, they proposed a more limited operation, designed to encircle and destroy the American forces in the Aachen area. This became known as the Small Solution, as opposed to Hitler's Big Solution. Hitler rejected this out of hand, and the only concession he made was to postpone the attack from 25 November to 10 December. The key role was given to Sepp Dietrich, whose army was to seize crossings over the Meuse, south of Liège, and then drive on to Antwerp. Von Manteuffel was to guard Dietrich's left flank and aim for Brussels, while Brandenberger would follow in his wake.

ABOVE: *Bewildered American prisoners during the first days of the Battle of the Bulge. The Germans achieved surprise to a large measure, but the plan was too ambitious.*
RIGHT: *Two noncoms from the crack 1st SS Panzer Division, the Leibstandarte Adolf Hitler, during a pause in the advance to Malmédy. They are part of a battle group following up in the wake of Joachim Peiper's battlegroup.*

LEFT: *103rd Tank Destroyer Battalion from the US 82nd Airborne Division moves up to stem the German advance.*
BELOW: *Oberfahnrich Günther Billing, a member of one of the German Brandenburger commando teams sent behind the lines in Allied uniforms to create alarm and confusion, is prepared for summary execution by firing squad.*

Eventually, after further protests, Hitler allowed the attack to be put back further to 16 December.

Although a veil of secrecy covered the German preparations right up to the launching of the attack, the Allies had received a number of intelligence indicators, all of which pointed toward a German attack. For a start, there was the evidence produced by Ultra, and this was supported by reports from Belgian civilians and German prisoners. Yet with a few exceptions, Allied intelligence refused to believe that the Germans were capable of mounting a large-scale offensive at this stage in the war, and no attempt was made to reinforce the Ardennes sector or implement increased alert measures.

Before dawn on 16 December, the German barrage opened and soon afterward, the German infantry, who were to carry out the initial break-in operation, advanced. Although the Americans were taken totally by surprise, they fought well, and it was not until late that evening that the Panzers could begin their dash to the Meuse. It was now, once the German armor had begun to penetrate, that confusion began to take hold, and this was encouraged by the infiltration of Germans dressed in American uniforms.

Nevertheless, where American units stood and fought, they did much to blunt the German thrusts. The Germans were also not helped by the wintry conditions and the Ardennes terrain, which made movement difficult off the roads, which themselves were mainly narrow and very windy. The Ardennes in December was very different to May. One of Dietrich's SS Panzer groups, commanded by Joachim Peiper, did have more success than the others and was soon deep into the American lines. By the afternoon of the 17th, he was near the village of Malmédy, where he intercepted a convoy carrying an American observation battery, part of 7th Armored Division, which was being switched from the north to help stem the tide. Opening fire on it, he forced the Americans to surrender. Shortly afterward the surviving Americans were mowed down by machine-gun fire, but some managed to escape and regain their own lines. This was the first time that American troops had definitely been victims of German war atrocities, and American public opinion immediately demanded that the culprits be brought to book. The eventual result was that all commanders, and those directly concerned with this and other atrocities that Peiper's men were alleged to have committed, from Dietrich downward, stood trial in 1946, in what became one of the most controversial of the war crimes cases.

Peiper's dash to the Meuse was eventually brought to a halt, and by the 19th it became clear to the German High Command that von Manteuffel was making better progress than Dietrich, and hence the

latter was gradually ordered to pass most of his Panzer formations across to the Fifth Panzer Army.

On Christmas Day 1944, von Manteuffel's leading elements were at a point four miles short of the Meuse at Dinant. It was to be the German highwater mark. The fog, which had largely protected the Germans from the might of Allied airpower during the opening days of the offensive, had now largely dispersed and Allied aircraft were able to hammer the German lines of communication. Von Manteuffel, too, had been held up by United States 7th Armored Division at St Vith, which had done much to make him fall behind his timetable. More important, a thorn remained in his rear. The town of Bastogne was a key communications center, and the defense of it had been entrusted to 101st Airborne Division, under the temporary command of Briga- dier General Anthony C McAuliffe. He refused to give in, replying 'Nuts!' to demands for surrender, and was thus able to throttle von Manteuffel's lines of communication to a considerable degree.

By this stage Eisenhower had agreed that Montgomery should take control of the northern part of the salient, and British troops were sent down to hold the Meuse bridges south of Dinant. In the meantime Patton had been ordered to switch his army through 90 degrees and attack northward into the southern flank of the German salient. This he did, relieving Bastogne on 26 December and continuing northward to meet eventually with Hodges' First United States Army on 16 January, but it had become clear to the Germans well before this that they had shot their bolt.

While the Battle of the Bulge would impose a six weeks' delay on the Allies closing up to the Rhine, this was all that Hitler had achieved with his grandiose and unrealistic plan. Germany could not afford the losses in men and equipment which resulted from the attack, and these losses would merely make the task of the Russians and Western Allies easier in the final battles for Germany.

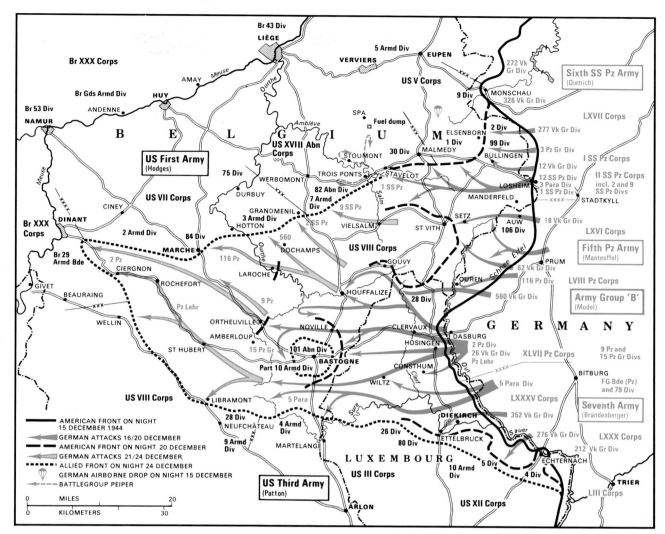

LEFT: *Bradley, Eisenhower and Patton survey combat-scarred Bastogne, the defense of which was the greatest epic of the battle.*

BELOW LEFT: *German prisoners make their way to the rear. The one on the left appears very underage, but by this stage the Germans were forced to rely increasingly on boys and old men for the final defense of Germany.*

RIGHT: *Only at one point did the Germans come anywhere close to the Meuse.*

BELOW: *Graves of sacrificial victims of Hitler's last gamble in the West at Forge-à-la-Plez.*

1945

The War is Won

Chronology 1945

January 17	Warsaw liberated
February 4-11	Yalta Conference – Roosevelt, Stalin, Churchill
February 13	Budapest falls to the Russians
February 13-14	Bombing of Dresden
February 19	US landings on Iwo Jima
March 3	Manila, Philippines secured
March 7	US troops seize Remagen bridge over Rhine
March 9-10	US fire raids on Tokyo
April 1	US landings on Okinawa
April 1	Final Allied offensive begins in Italy
April 12	President Roosevelt dies
April 25	US and Russian troops meet on the Elbe
April 28	Mussolini killed by partisans
April 29	German forces in Italy sign armistice
April 30	Hitler commits suicide
May 1	The Russians secure Berlin
May 3	Rangoon recaptured by the British
May 7	Germany's formal surrender
June 21	Okinawa finally secured
July 16	First atomic bomb test is successful
July 16–August 2	Allied conference at Potsdam, Germany
July 26	Attlee succeeds Churchill as British Prime Minister
August 6	Atomic bomb dropped on Hiroshima
August 8	Russia declares war on Japan
August 9	Atomic bomb dropped on Nagasaki
September 2	Japan formally surrenders

'Home at last.' A British soldier back from the war. He now faces the struggle to pick up the threads of civilian life.

Outline of Events

In spite of the delay imposed on the British and Americans in the Ardennes, it was clear that the war in Europe could not last many more months. This was reinforced when the Russians resumed their offensive against Germany from the east, an operation which would hardly halt until they reached the center of Berlin. With this in mind, the Big Three – Roosevelt, Churchill and Stalin – met once more, in February, this time at Yalta on the Black Sea.

Roosevelt's priorities were to bring Russia into the war against Japan as soon as Germany had been defeated, and also, with the stability of the postwar world in mind, to get Stalin to agree to join the United Nations. He was, or so it seemed at the time, successful in both. In return, Roosevelt confirmed the agreements reached at Teheran, that Stalin should have a free hand in Eastern Europe, with the exception of Greece, but that he would recognize an independent postwar Poland.

Roosevelt, by now a very sick man, returned home, believing that the post-1945 world would be a much safer place. His labors completed, he died amid much sadness around the world on 12 April 1945. His vice-president, Harry S Truman, immediately took over the reins of power. It would not be long, either, before Churchill, albeit temporarily, left the world scene. In a British general election held in July 1945, he was decisively defeated by the Labour Party under the leadership of Clement Attlee.

In the meantime the Russian steamroller kept driving west remorselessly. Warsaw was quickly liberated, East Prussia isolated, and the Germans driven back to the Rivers Oder and Neisse. Here, by rushing in reinforcements from the West, the Germans managed to hold the Russians for a short time before they entered Germany proper. To the south, Budapest finally surrendered in mid-February, and Czechoslovakia was entered. The transfer of German troops to the East helped the British and Americans to reach the Rhine, which they crossed toward the end of March. They then sealed the Ruhr, and moved eastward to join hands with the Russians.

By now Hitler had taken up permanent residence with his immediate entourage in his bunker in Berlin and became more and more divorced from reality. Eventually, on 30 April, he took his own life as Russian troops entered the center of Berlin. His fellow dictator, Mussolini, lost his life two days earlier at the hands of Italian partisans, but by this time the fighting in Italy was virtually over. The final Allied offensive, launched earlier in the month, swept all before it, and the German forces had sued for an armistice.

RIGHT: *Churchill, Truman and Stalin at Potsdam, 15 July 1945. The main task of the Western Allies was to push Stalin into declaring war against Japan, but by this time the atomic bomb was now fact.*
ABOVE RIGHT: *The ruins of Dresden. The Allied bombing raids on Dresden on the night 13/14 February 1945 and the subsequent two days mark the most controversial strategic conventional bombing operation of the war. The town had many historical buildings and was crowded with civilian refugees but it was also an important communications center for the German forces on the Eastern Front.*

On 8 May 1945 Victory in Europe was formally declared, although it was not until early on the 9th that the fighting finally ceased, since Stalin was determined to liberate Prague before the end of hostilities. The only vestige of the Third Reich left was in Schleswig-Holstein, to which Dönitz, whom Hitler had appointed as his successor, had fled. Dönitz was, however, only allowed to retain any trappings of power for as long as it took to recall all the U-boats still at sea.

There remained only Japan, and the Western Allies began to trans-fer forces from Europe to the Pacific for the final blow against her. By this stage of the war she was in a desperate state. The United States Navy had her under total blockade, a prolonged American bombing offensive was, as the Allies had done to Germany, reducing her cities to ruins, and everywhere her forces were in retreat. Rangoon, capital of Burma, fell in May, and after mopping up, the British prepared the liberation of Malaya. While the fighting in the Philippines would continue until the end of the Pacific war, the American forces had landed

ABOVE: *Celebrating VE Day in Trafalgar Square, London. The euphoria was not, however, quite the same as it had been in 1918. The war had gone on too long, Japan was still to be defeated and the British people were exhausted.*
RIGHT: *How New York newspapers carried the news of the German surrender. It would, however, be some time yet before Uncle Sam's boys came home.*

RIGHT: *The crew of* U.858 *surrender to the Allies. Getting the U-boats still on the high seas back to port took some days to achieve after the German surrender.*
BELOW: *Japanese pilots give a ceremonial bow to their US captors. They surrendered only because their emperor had given them a direct public order to do so.*

on Iwo Jima in mid-February, aiming to use the island as another base from which to launch air attacks on Japan. Deciding to bypass Formosa in favor of Okinawa, which was much closer to the Japanese mainland, US forces landed there on 1 April 1945. Such was the fanatical resistance of the Japanese, that it took three months to clear the island. How many troops, and at what cost, would it take to subdue Japan itself, wondered the American planners?

It was against this background that the last of the Allied war conferences took place, at Potsdam in Germany in mid-July. Stalin had still not entered the war against Japan, but this was not the setback that it had been. For the Americans had just perfected a new and devastating weapon, the atomic bomb. Truman intimated this to Stalin, but there were considerable doubts among the US planners that it would have to be used. The Japanese had been putting out peace feelers, and there

was a belief that the current conventional destruction of Japan would be sufficient.

At Postdam, however, it was decided that unconditional surrender must apply to Japan as it had to Germany, and this resulted in Japanese hesitation when they were informed of it. Furthermore it was known that there was still a sizeable militarist element in the government, which could well overrule the peace faction. As a result, the Western Allies decided that if no positive response to the unconditional surrender demand from the Japanese was forthcoming, the A-bomb would have to be used. Although the Japanese Ambassador to Moscow did

approach Soviet Foreign Minister Vyacheslav Molotov, the latter refused to see him.

Consequently, on 6 August, the first atomic bomb was dropped on Hiroshima and, when still no positive response was forthcoming, the second on Nagasaki, three days later. In the meantime, on 8 August, the Russians finally declared war on Japan, launching a blitzkrieg style of attack on Manchuria. On 14 August the Japanese finally accepted the Allied terms of unconditional surrender. The formal surrender was signed aboard the USS *Missouri* in Tokyo Bay on 2 September 1945. World War II was finally over.

Christmas together . . . Have a Coca-Cola

. . . welcoming a fighting man home from the wars

The Soviet Offensive

On 12 January 1945, after having been static on the Vistula since the previous August, the Russians launched a fresh offensive, liberating Warsaw in five days. In just three weeks, western Poland had been overrun, East Prussia isolated and the German border crossed, the advance being temporarily halted on the River Oder, just 50 miles from Berlin. Now the German people began to experience at first hand the Russian hatred. The Russian troops, as they liberated their own country, had seen the desolation caused by the Germans and vowed to return it in kind. Rape and pillage of the local population in the eastern part of Germany was widespread, and, as stories of these atrocities spread westward, it seemed that darkness was engulfing Germany.

The Western Allies, recovering from the Ardennes fighting, were still in no position to advance, but, in order to support the Russians and demonstrate to Hitler that they and the Russians were as one, they agreed to bomb the German cities of the east. This was in response to a Russian request at Yalta. At the time, Spaatz and, to a lesser extent, Harris, were concentrating on oil targets, but on the night of 13/14 February they selected Dresden as their target. The city contained few military targets and was filled with refugees from the east. It was virtually destroyed in two concurrent attacks, the RAF by night and the USAAF the next day, in what has since been regarded as the most controversial bombing raid of the war. Other cities, including Berlin, were subsequently attacked before the end of the month.

In the center, attacking from southern Poland, the Russians also closed up to the River Neisse during February, but in western Hungary they met unexpected resistance. Although surrounded, the Hungarian and German garrison in Budapest refused to surrender and the Germans even attempted a relief operation in January, but it met with no success. In mid-February, the garrison then tried to break through to the German lines, but few were successful, and Budapest finally fell. No sooner had this happened than the Russians were faced

ABOVE: *Russian armor rolls westward through Mülhausen in East Prussia with scarcely a glance at its dead defenders.*
RIGHT: *Russian infantry enter the port of Danzig, 30 March 1945. It was Hitler's demand to control the port and his claim on Poland for land to provide access to it which had been the immediate cause of the war.*
FAR RIGHT, ABOVE: *A Siberian, a Georgian, a Muscovite and a native of Stalingrad meet in downtown Vienna after its capture.*
FAR RIGHT, BELOW: *Haggard German prisoners of the Russians. Note how elderly some of them are.*

with a further problem. Hitler became obsessed with retaining the oilfields around Lake Balaton, some 60 miles southwest of Budapest. Two German armies, including Sepp Dietrich's Sixth Panzer Army, launched desperate counterattacks here and penetrated to a depth of 20 miles before they were brought to a halt. The Russians now flung them back, to the fury of Hitler, who believed that his men had not fought hard enough. As the Russian attacks gathered momentum, Army Group South, now commanded by Otto Wöhler, was forced back into Austria, and then northwest toward Vienna, which Hitler ordered was to be defended to the last. By early April it was under attack, East Prussia had been overrun, and Zhukov was poised to mount his final attack, the objective Berlin.

The Rhine Crossings

The Americans and British resumed their advance toward the Rhine in early February. Although they now broke through the Siegfried Line with comparative ease, they still faced some tough resistance, especially since the Germans were now fighting on their own territory. This was particularly so in the north where Montgomery, now with General William Simpson's Ninth United States Army under command – which did not please some of his fellow American commanders who were upset at the way that he claimed to have pulled their chestnuts out of the fire in the Ardennes – closed up to the river west and north of the Ruhr. Nevertheless before mid-March the Allied armies were firm on the west bank down as far as Koblenz, and could now set about tackling the Rhine itself.

The operations which followed are classic examples of the three types of river crossing practiced in war – opportune, hasty and deliberate. The first crossing was carried out by a small armored spearhead of the United States First Army as early as 7 March. It took the Germans guarding the bridge in the small town of Remagen by surprise and they were only able to blow it partially. Quickly establishing a bridgehead on the other side, Bradley now wanted to exploit it as soon as possible, but was refused permission by Eisenhower since this did not fit into the overall plan of overrunning the Ruhr first. First Montgomery would need to make a crossing and this was not due to take place for another two weeks. For the same reason, Montgomery had refused to allow Simpson to cross by Düsseldorf which he had managed to reach on the 3rd

While Montgomery could be accused of being unnecessarily cautious, he did have some sound arguments on his side. His experience of the past few weeks had shown him that the Germans were still defending tenaciously, and a crossing without adequate preparation might well result in disaster. Also, once across the Rhine it was vital not to allow the enemy any pause for breath. Exploitation must be immediate, which meant ensuring that the forces for this were in the right position to cross the river quickly.

ABOVE: *Denazification begins immediately. The GI is removing this street sign for obvious reasons. The German people were generally past caring what happened to them.*
LEFT: *US troops cross the Ludendorff Bridge at Remagen on 7 March 1945 under heavy fire. The failure of the German officer in charge of the bridge to ensure that it was successfully demolished resulted in a field court-martial and death.*
RIGHT: *The closing up to and crossing of the Rhine. The next stage would be the encirclement and overrunning of the Ruhr, or what remained of it after the Allied bombing of the previous five years.*

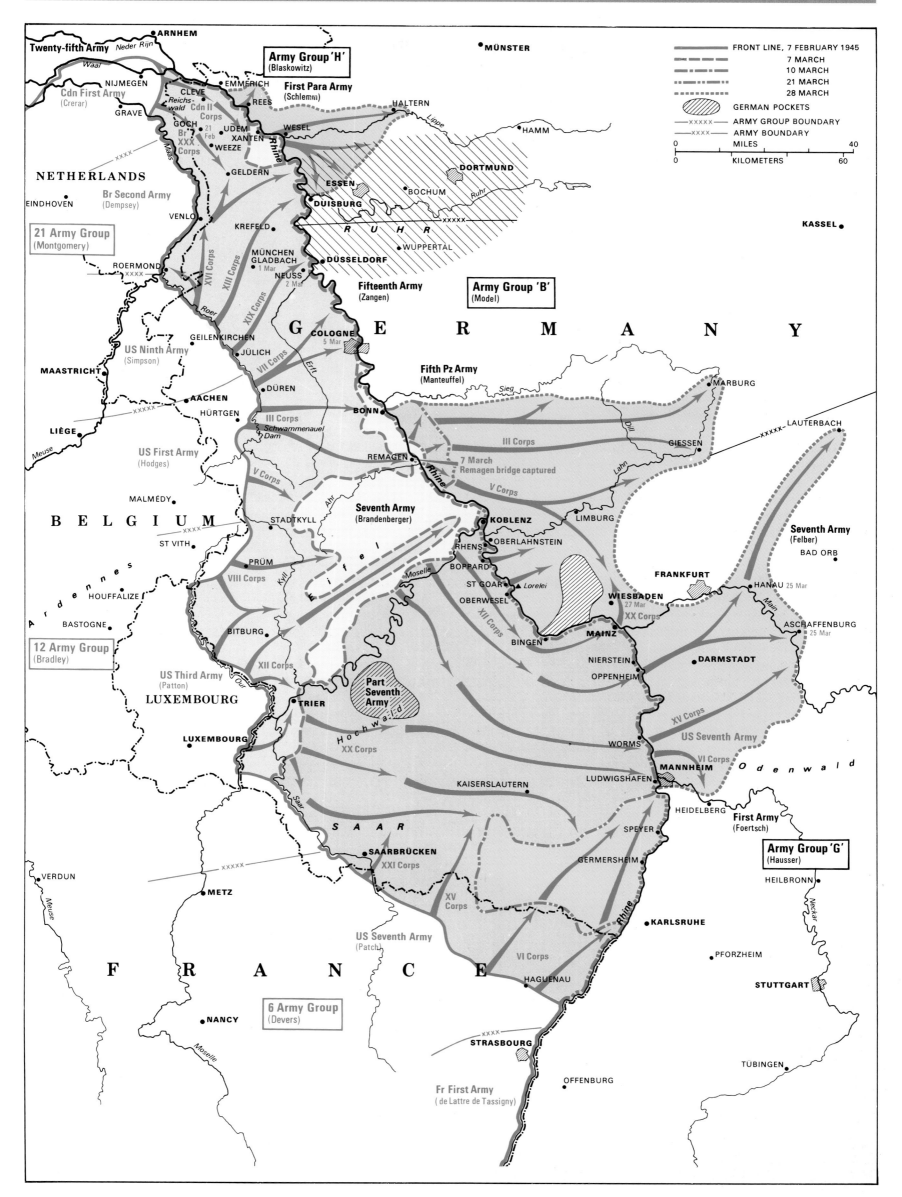

ARNHEM
Twenty-fifth Army
Neder Rijn
MÜNSTER

Waal
NIJMEGEN
Army Group 'H'
(Blaskowitz)
Cdn First Army
(Crerar)
CLEVE
Reichs-
wald
Cdn II
Corps
EMMERICH
First Para Army
(Schlemm)
REES
HALTERN
Lippe
GRAVE
GOCH
21
Feb
UDEM
XANTEN
WEEZE
Br
XXX
Corps
WESEL
HAMM

NETHERLANDS
GELDERN
ESSEN
BOCHUM
DORTMUND

EINDHOVEN
Br Second Army
(Dempsey)
VENLO
KREFELD
DUISBURG
Ruhr
R U H R
KASSEL

21 Army Group
(Montgomery)
ROERMOND
MÜNCHEN
GLADBACH
1 Mar
NEUSS
2 Mar
DÜSSELDORF
WUPPERTAL

XVI Corps
XIII Corps
Fifteenth Army
(Zangen)
Army Group 'B'
(Model)

Roer
GEILENKIRCHEN
G E R
COLOGNE
5 Mar
M A N Y

US Ninth Army
(Simpson)
JÜLICH
XIX Corps
Erft
Sieg
MARBURG

MAASTRICHT
VII Corps
DÜREN
III Corps
Fifth Pz Army
(Manteuffel)
Dill
GIESSEN
LAUTERBACH

AACHEN
HÜRTGEN
III Corps
Schwammenauel
Dam
BONN
7 March
Remagen bridge captured
Lahn
LIMBURG

LIÈGE
REMAGEN
V Corps
Rhine

Meuse
US First Army
(Hodges)
Ahr
V Corps
Seventh Army
(Brandenberger)
KOBLENZ
OBERLAHNSTEIN
Seventh Army
(Felber)
BAD ORB

MALMÉDY
STADTKYLL
RHENS
BOPPARD
Moselle
ST GOAR
Lorelei
OBERWESEL
FRANKFURT
HANAU 25 Mar

B E L G I U M
ST VITH
E i f e l
Kyll
XII Corps
WIESBADEN
27 Mar
XX Corps
ASCHAFFENBURG
25 Mar

Ardennes
HOUFFALIZE
PRÜM
VIII Corps
BITBURG
BINGEN
MAINZ
DARMSTADT

BASTOGNE
XII Corps
NIERSTEIN
OPPENHEIM

12 Army Group
(Bradley)
Our
US Third Army
(Patton)
Part
Seventh
Army
Hochwald
XV Corps
US Seventh Army

LUXEMBOURG
TRIER
Saar
WORMS
Odenwald

LUXEMBOURG
XX Corps
VI Corps
LUDWIGSHAFEN
MANNHEIM

KAISERSLAUTERN
HEIDELBERG
First Army
(Foertsch)

VERDUN
S A A R
SPEYER
Army Group 'G'
(Hausser)

METZ
SAARBRÜCKEN
XXI Corps
GERMERSHEIM
HEILBRONN

XV Corps
Rhine
KARLSRUHE

US Seventh Army
(Patch)
VI Corps
PFORZHEIM

F R A N C E
HAGUENAU
STUTTGART

NANCY
6 Army Group
(Devers)
STRASBOURG
TÜBINGEN

Moselle
Fr First Army
(de Lattre de Tassigny)
OFFENBURG

FRONT LINE, 7 FEBRUARY 1945
7 MARCH
10 MARCH
21 MARCH
28 MARCH
GERMAN POCKETS
XXXXX ARMY GROUP BOUNDARY
XXXX ARMY BOUNDARY

MILES 0 40
KILOMETERS 0 60

LEFT: *Having secured bridgeheads on the east bank of the Rhine, the next stage was to build pontoon bridges so that the flow of supplies could be maintained.*
BELOW LEFT: *US infantry pass through the Siegfried Line and on into Germany.*
BELOW RIGHT: *US armor rolls through downtown Munich, which appears surprisingly unscathed. Note the German reactions.*
RIGHT: *'All is lost.'*

The next to cross the river was Patton. Having broken through the German defenses in the Eifel during the first week of March, he now cleared the area north of the Moselle, and then swung southeast, cutting off the Germans still west of the Rhine between Koblenz and Mainz. All the bridges had, of course, been blown, but he achieved a virtually unopposed bounce crossing at Oppenheim, south of Mainz, on the night of 22/23 March.

Finally came Montgomery's crossing, which was in the Wesel area north of the Ruhr. Preceded by a massive air and artillery bombardment, and the dropping of a British and an American airborne division beyond Wesel, his troops crossed early on the 24th. By the end of the month he had built up a massive force of 21 divisions and 1500 tanks in the bridgehead and was ready for the next phase.

There now followed another major disagreement over strategy. As far as Eisenhower was concerned, and he had the support of the dying Roosevelt in this, Berlin was to be left to the Russians. Yet they were still temporarily stalled on the Oder, while the Americans and British, having broken the back of the German resistance in the West, stood a good chance of getting to the capital first. Montgomery, supported by Churchill, who wanted to keep the Russians as far east as possible in terms of the postwar map of Europe, argued for Berlin as the primary objective. Eisenhower refused to agree. Likewise Patton, who now had his whip out once more, wanted to seize as much of Czechoslovakia as possible, but, again, it had been agreed that this was to be a

Russian responsibility. Also, Eisenhower had become mesmerized by the idea of a Nazi redoubt being built up in the Alps, from which a dramatic last stand would be conducted, and hence ordered his forces in the south to advance southeast rather than east. True, Hitler did set up a headquarters here, but only because of the now very real danger of the ever-shrinking Third Reich being split laterally, and the idea of an Alpine Little Big Horn was nothing but a myth.

During the first week of April, the Ruhr was surrounded, and Model's Army Group ceased to exist, he himself preferring suicide to captivity. The British and Americans now advanced on a broad front. Montgomery was given the task of clearing northern Germany and securing the North Sea ports, while Bradley, with Simpson now back under his command, cleared the center, his objective being the Elbe, but no farther. In the south the task of preempting the Nazi redoubt and overrunning southern Germany lay with Jacob Devers's United States 6th Army Group.

Resistance was scattered, but there were still SS elements about, mainly from training schools, and these were prepared to fight to the death. The ordinary German soldier, finally realizing that Hitler's promises of new wonder weapons which would dramatically turn the tide were now totally empty, was happy enough to surrender rather than lay down his life at the eleventh hour. What was now uppermost in the minds of the soldiers, American, British, Canadian and French, was what would happen when they met their Russian allies.

The End in Italy

In Italy during the winter of 1944-45, the Allies had paused to regain their strength after the exhausting battles of the summer and fall. For their final offensive, General Mark Clark, now commanding 15th Army Group, proposed to Alexander, the theater Supreme Allied Commander, a two-phased double blow. First, the British Eighth Army, now commanded by General Dick McCreery, was to seize the Argenta Gap, lying between Lake Commacchio and the marshlands east of Bologna, and then he would advance on Ferrara. After a few days General Lucien Truscott's United States Fifth Army would attack and seize Bologna. Both armies would then move north and enter Austria. The reason for separate attacks was so that each army could have maximum use of the available airpower in the initial stages of its attack. This plan was accepted by Alexander.

On 9 April 1945, Eighth Army launched its attack. Given the difficult state of the low ground, boggy and intersected by numerous canals, McCreery had hit upon the original idea of turning the German flank with an ambitious amphibious assault across Lake Commacchio. This was carried out by British Commandos, and achieved its aim. With more conventional forces thrusting up the Ravenna-Ferrara highway, the Argenta Gap was forced on the 18th, and the German forces withdrew to the Po Valley.

On the 14th came Truscott's attack. He, too, had problems with the terrain, but, in contrast to McCreery, he had to break out of the mountains, and the first four days of the attack were hard going, until the United States 10th Mountain Division achieved the necessary breakthrough, and on the 21st Bologna was entered. The German commander, Count von Vietinghoff, had, as early as the 14th, pleaded with Hitler to be allowed to break away and withdraw behind the Po, but in vain. Finally, on the 20th, he had taken the law into his own hands, but it was too late. The two Allied armies had linked up behind him, and too few of the Vietinghoff's troops escaped to establish any form of cohesive defense behind the Po.

The Allied advance now became little more than a rout. Quickly crossing the Po themselves, they speedily secured the cities of northern Italy, and before the month was through the two armies had

ABOVE: *A typical Italian partisan. They did much to hamper the Germans and tie down their forces.*
LEFT: *An Italian 105mm artillery piece, now with the Allies, in action during the final weeks of the campaign.*

RIGHT: *Field Marshal Sir Henry Wilson, known as 'Jumbo,' Supreme Allied Commander Mediterranean Theater 1944. His car hood carries the US, British and Polish flags.*
FAR RIGHT: *Troops of the British Eighth Army enter Austria in May 1945.*

LEFT: *British Commandos attacking at Lake Commacchio, April 1945. The photograph was taken by a fellow Commando.*
BELOW: *The end of a dictator. The corpses of Mussolini and his mistress. Since 1943 he had ruled northern Italy only in name.*

reached the Alps. In the meantime there had been a wholesale rising among the Italian partisans. Not only did they catch Mussolini and his mistress, Claretta Petacci, in the Lake Como area and literally string them up by their heels, but they also blocked the Alpine passes, thus allowing the Germans no escape. Yet the Germans themselves had seen the writing on the wall long before this.

As early as February 1945, they had opened secret negotiations with the Americans over the surrender of the German forces in Italy. The American representative was the head OSS man in Switzerland, Allen Dulles. On the German side, and very unofficially, the key figure was SS General Karl Wolff, the German military governor of northern Italy and plenipotentiary to Mussolini. He was realistic enough to understand that the Germans had no hope of victory in Italy, or anywhere else, but he also hoped that an early surrender might increase the chances of the Western powers joining Germany in the fight against Russia. Indeed, the Russians were understandably suspicious of the negotiations, which was one reason why they did not get anywhere before the final Allied offensive was launched. Another was that, in early April, Himmler got wind of what was afoot and forbade Wolff to take the negotiations any farther.

By 23 April, however, the situation was clearly so hopeless that von Vietinghoff and Wolff decided to approach Dulles again. The result was that, without permission from Berlin, they signed an unconditional surrender agreement on the 29th, to come into effect on 2 May. In truth there was little further fighting after the 29th. The British then dashed up through the Alps, getting as far as the Brenner Pass, the main entrance to Austria, by 6 May. While the Americans secured Milan and Turin in the west, the British in the east occupied Trieste, where they found themselves confronting not Nazis, but Tito's Yugoslavs, keen to renew a territorial dispute which had its origins in the Treaty of Versailles of 1919.

For the Allies and the Germans too, Italy had been rather like a backwater. Yet it had kept some 25 German divisions tied down and given Hitler a third front to worry about. The terrain, so favoring the defender, meant that it would never be the decisive theater in Europe, but without it, the war would have been further prolonged.

The End of the Third Reich

The Russian assault on Berlin was conducted by Zhukov's First Belorussian Front and Koniev's First Ukrainian Front. Both were to attack westward initially, and then Koniev would swing north toward the city. Farther to the north, Rokossovsky with his Second Belorussian Front was to clear the remainder of the Baltic coast. Facing them were the remnants of Siegfried Heinrici's Army Group Vistula and Ferdinand Schörner's Army Group Center.

The offensive began on 16 April, but it took two days' bitter fighting to get crossings over the Oder and Neisse. Between here and Berlin

itself, the Germans had constructed a number of defense lines in which they continued to offer stiff resistance, which slowed Zhukov down considerably. Part of this reflected sheer desperation on the part of the defenders, but it was also because just behind the front line, squads of SS men roamed with orders to shoot anyone seen retreating. Eventually, however, the Soviet armor was able to break through and split the German armies from one another, and by 20 April, Hitler's birthday, the fate of the city was sealed.

Hitler himself, secure in his bunker under the Chancellery building, was living in a fantasy world, refusing to accept that the Third Reich's last hour had arrived. His birthday marked the last gathering of the Nazi inner circle, all of whom tried to persuade him to leave Berlin for the Bavarian Alps. Next day he ordered a massive counterattack against the approaching Russians, but the means were no longer available to do this. It was then that he made the irrevocable decision to remain in Berlin to the last. Göring, whom Hitler had appointed as his successor by a June 1941 decree, had arrived in Bavaria and proposed that he should now take over the reins of power since Hitler could no longer exercise them in besieged Berlin. Hitler regarded this as betrayal and promptly stripped Göring of all his offices, not that this meant much any more.

In the meantime Koniev's tanks had successfully carried out their swing northward and had now entered the suburbs of Berlin, and Zhukov's troops followed shortly. Away to the south, the Russians had secured Vienna by 13 April, but now turned their attention to Czechoslovakia. Here part of the Army Group Center was still holding out in front of Prague, trying desperately to hold on to Germany's last significant industrial region. This at least kept the Russians out of the rest of Austria, but it could only be a temporary reprieve.

In the west, the first Allied elements, units of Hodges's United States First Army, had reached the Elbe near Magdeburg as early as

ABOVE LEFT: *Hitler's last appearance in public, 20 March 1945. He decorates members of the Hitler Youth for bravery under Russian fire.*
LEFT: *Germany is cut in half. GIs and Russians meet at Torgau on the River Elbe, 25 April 1945.*
ABOVE RIGHT: *As GIs pass through a destroyed German town an old woman gazes in disbelief at what has happened to her fatherland.*
RIGHT: *Russian T-34s await the next move forward during the battle for Berlin.*

12 April, but had been ordered to halt here. During the next two weeks the other Allied armies also closed up to the river, but the first meeting between the Allies was not until 25 April, at Torgau on the Elbe south of Berlin, where some of Hodges's and Koniev's troops met. After some initial hesitation, there was much jubilation, and this was repeated elsewhere along the Elbe during the next few days. What, however, the Torgau meeting immediately achieved was the cutting of Germany into two parts.

In Berlin the battle raged nearer and nearer the Chancellery, and by the end of the 29th the city had been cut up into three parts. Hitler himself was now resigned to his fate. The day before, it had come to his ears, through a report by Reuters, that Himmler had been trying to negotiate peace terms with the Allies, using the Swedish Count Bernadotte as an intermediary. Like his leader, Himmler had also lost all sense of reality and seemed to believe that the Allies would accept him as the leader of a reconstituted Germany. This was, in Hitler's eyes, the final betrayal. In the early hours of 30 April, he went through a form of marriage with his longtime mistress, Eva Braun, and then dictated his last will and testament to the German people, appointing Dönitz as his successor. A few hours later, he and Eva took their own lives, to be followed a day later by the faithful Goebbels and his family, who had remained with Hitler until the last. The others in the bunker then tried to make good their escape. Outside, after desperate fighting around the Reichstag, the fighting in Berlin ceased on 2 May.

For the German troops still fighting on in Germany, the main concern now was to hold the ring against the Russians for as long as they could so that as many as possible could surrender to the Western Allies. In the north there was concern that the Russians might not halt on the Elbe and be tempted to dash into Schleswig-Holstein. To forestall this, Montgomery ordered his troops into the peninsula, securing Hamburg, Lübeck and Kiel and eventually arriving at Flensburg by the Danish border, where Dönitz had set up his headquarters. In the south, in order to speed things up, with Russian assent Eisenhower allowed Patton to enter Czechoslovakia. By 7 May Patton had reached as far east as Pilsen. His troops also entered northern Austria. By this time, the only significant fighting taking place was around Prague.

Dönitz had realized as soon as he found himself pitchforked into power that he would have to surrender. His only question was how rigid the Allied insistence on unconditional surrender was. On 3 May he sent a deputation to Montgomery's headquarters. This tried to get Montgomery to accept the surrender of merely the German forces in

LEFT: *Victory! The Red Flag is hoisted above the ruins of the Reichstag in Berlin.*
BELOW LEFT: *Hitler's Chancellery lies destroyed.*
RIGHT: *The scene of Hitler's suicide, the bunker entrance with the jerricans for the fuel used to burn the bodies.*
BELOW: *Captured Nazi paraphernalia is paraded by the Russians.*

the West, allowing those in the East to fight on against the Russians. Montgomery, however, insisted that it was a question of all or nothing, and the deputation signed a surrender document to this effect on the evening of 4 May. The surrender, however, could not become fact until it had been approved by Eisenhower and the Russians. Accordingly, next day the deputation set off for Eisenhower's headquarters at Rheims. Here again they tried to achieve a surrender of merely the troops facing the Western Allies, but with no success, and were eventually forced to sign the main surrender document in the early hours of 7 May. The Russians also insisted on a signing ceremony in their sector, which was carried out early the next day. Orders had meanwhile been sent out to all German units ordering them to lay down their arms, but there was concern that the SS units might ignore it and hence it was repeated specifically to them. Not until the morning of the 9th, however, did the guns in Europe finally cease to fire, and then, after a last massive bombardment, with the entry of Russian troops into Prague. The war against Hitler's Germany was finally over, but Japan was still fighting on.

The End in Burma

The final offensive in Burma began in November 1944, after the end of the monsoon season. On the 19th, Slim's troops crossed the River Chindwin. By this stage the Japanese position was becoming increasingly serious. Because of the landings in the Philippines, the Japanese commander, Hyotaro Kimura, had been told that he could expect no more reinforcements, and he was left with little more than 10 weak divisions with which to hold the whole of the country. He believed that the decisive battle would be fought on the Irrawaddy, south of Mandalay, and deployed his forces accordingly. Slim's plan, on the other hand, was to approach Mandalay from two directions, northwest and southwest.

Farther north, as 1944 had worn on, Stilwell had suffered increasing frustration in his dealings with the Chinese leadership. One major irritation was Chiang Kai-shek's refusal to have anything to do with Mao Tse-tung's communists. Indeed, a significant proportion of his forces were held back to contain Mao. In the late summer the Americans, wondering whether it would not be better to give support to Mao, sent a delegation to visit him, which came back with favorable reports. Matters were aggravated, also, by a Japanese offensive in southern China, which denied the USAAF use of bases there from which to bomb Japan. Eventually, in desperation, the Americans proposed to Chiang Kai-shek that he should make Stilwell generalissimo of his forces in order to ensure that they made more of a contribution to the Allied war effort. This was too much for the Chinese leader and Stilwell was sacked in October 1944 and replaced by General Daniel Sultan. This, and the replacement, in August 1944, of the exhausted Chindits by a fresh British division, improved matters and by December the Chinese in northern Burma were on the move once more, pressing the Japanese back toward Mandalay.

The seizure of the airfields off the Arakan coast was still considered important as this was the only way in which Allied air cover could be extended to cover Rangoon. Therefore, in mid-December 1944, Slim launched another attack here, which quickly secured the islands of Akyab and Ramree, and drove back the Japanese 28th Army.

By the beginning of March 1945, Slim had closed up to Mandalay. At the same time he sent a division to seize Meiktila, a vital railroad junction to the south. This threatened the withdrawal route of the Japanese in the Mandalay area, and so they gathered all available

ABOVE LEFT: *Used to carrying heavy loads in his native Nepal, this cheerful Gurkha now crosses the Irrawaddy. Included in his burden is a two-inch mortar.*
LEFT: *Chinese M3 General Stuarts, with men on foot in front to check for mines, advance toward Lashio, March 1945, during the final Allied offensive in Burma.*

LEFT: *Pegu, only fifty miles from Rangoon, is liberated. The monsoon, however, is on the verge of breaking. It will not stop Slim from recapturing Burma's capital.*
BELOW: *After a Gurkha parachute battalion has secured Elephant Point, which dominates the mouth of the estuary leading to Rangoon, troops are landed in the area and will now go on to liberate the city.*

forces to retake it. Meiktila held, however, and the weakening of the Mandalay garrison enabled Slim to break in and, after some heavy fighting, it fell on 20 March. Kimura was now forced to withdraw south toward Rangoon.

In the meantime the Chinese had removed the Japanese presence from Yunnan, had linked up with the forces advancing east along the Ledo Road, and had then advanced southward down the Burma Road, reaching well south of Lashio by the end of March.

For Slim it was now a race to get to Rangoon before the monsoon broke, although he was prepared to continue his attacks through it if necessary. In a lightning advance his forces drove down the main highway from Meiktila, reaching Pegu, less than 50 miles from Rangoon, on 29 April. A subsidiary thrust was also directed on Prome, which fell on 2 May, in order to prevent the Japanese forces withdrawing from the Arakan, which would interfere with the thrust on Rangoon. On the day that Prome fell, the monsoon arrived, but Slim also had another string to his bow. First, on 1 May a Gurkha battalion parachuted on to Elephant Point, at the mouth of the estuary that led to

the port of Rangoon. Then, Slim brought an Indian division round by sea to land south of Rangoon on the 2nd. The Japanese now evacuated the city. The Indians entered it on the 3rd, and then advanced north to link up on the 6th with the main thrust from the north.

The capture of Rangoon marked the final decisive defeat of the Japanese in Burma. Yet Slim had left some 60,000 Japanese troops in western Burma and it was important to prevent them from escaping east into Thailand. He therefore set up two lines, one on the Irrawaddy and the other on the Sittang. During May the Japanese forces made determined efforts to get across the Irrawaddy. Most were unsuccessful, but some 17,000 did get to the Sittang. Here they tried to split into small parties to slip past the defense, but the mesh was too narrow. Only some 6000 actually reached the far bank and they no longer had any combat power.

Meanwhile British attention turned to the liberation of Malaya and Singapore. A vast airborne and amphibious operation was planned, and the amphibious forces had already set sail when news of the final Japanese surrender came.

Iwo Jima and Okinawa

On 9 January 1945, MacArthur's troops landed on the main island in the Philippines, Luzon. The landings themselves took place in the Lingayen Gulf, some 100 miles northwest of Manila. Part of the force held off the Japanese in the north of the island, while the other advanced on Manila. It reached the suburbs in early February, but it took a complete month of bitter fighting before the capital was finally liberated. Corregidor and the Bataan Peninsula were then retaken, and landings made on the other islands. Eventually the Japanese were holed up in mountainous northern Luzon and the central region of Mindanao and fighting in both these areas would continue until the end of the war.

Rather than wait for the Philippines to be totally cleared of Japanese, the Americans wanted to push on toward Japan itself. They now identified two final stepping stones which were needed to achieve this. The first was the tiny volcanic island of Iwo Jima, which lies midway between Saipan and Tokyo and is one of the Bonin Islands. The Americans wanted this as an emergency landing ground for the B-29 Superfortresses which were now bombing the Japanese mainland, and also as a base for fighters escorting them, the bases in the Marianas being beyond their range.

Admiral Raymond Spruance, who had taken over from 'Bull' Halsey at the end of January 1945, and his United States Fifth Fleet were given the task of capturing the island, which had been subjected to continuous air strikes since early December. Yet when the United States Marines landed on 19 February, they were met by intense fire from heavily fortified and well-emplaced Japanese defenses. It was some time before they were even able to get off the beaches, and from then on it became a step-by-step process, with heavy casualties on both sides. It was undoubtedly the toughest fighting that the Americans had experienced in the Pacific thus far and boded ill for the operations to come. Not until 26 March was the island secured, and even then it took another two months to reduce the remaining Japanese pockets. It cost the United States Marines about 7000 dead and many wounded. About 23,000 Japanese died and some 1000 were

ABOVE LEFT: *A Curtiss SC-1 plane from USS* Alaska, *having completed a reconnaissance, now lands by the ship. It will be recovered by crane.*
LEFT: *US Marines are pinned down on the beach at Iwo Jima, the toughest battle of the Pacific campaign.*
ABOVE RIGHT: *Perhaps the most famous and symbolic photograph of the war in the Pacific: US Marines raise Old Glory on Iwo Jima.*
RIGHT: *US gunners on board the battleship* Missouri *desperately try to fend off an attacking kamikaze aircraft.*

taken prisoner. Even so, as early as the end of March there were three operational airfields there.

The other vital stepping stone was Okinawa, many times the size of Iwo Jima and held by almost 100,000 men of the Japanese 32nd Army. Furthermore, in their determination not to allow the island to be overrun, the Japanese had assembled some 2000 aircraft in Formosa and Japan, and intended to use kamikaze tactics on a wider scale than ever before.

The Americans were well aware that Okinawa presented a formidable task. In order to ensure numerical superiority for the landings, no less than 10 United States Army and Marine divisions were to be employed, all under General Simon Buckner's newly formed United States Tenth Army. In terms of seapower, the United States Pacific Fleet had now been swelled by the arrival of the British Pacific Fleet, which, among other units, brought an additional two battleships and four carriers. All naval elements were placed under the command of Admiral Kelly Turner USN. In order to reduce the air threat, Mitscher's fast carrier force carried out raids on Japan during the third week of March, destroying a large number of Japanese aircraft, but three of its carriers were damaged severely by kamikaze attacks. Also, there were B-29 strikes on airfields in Kyushu, the southern of the two main Japanese islands.

The landings themselves took place on 1 April, near the center of Okinawa and and close by two of the three airfields there. This time, the Japanese had more room and, instead of trying to hold the beaches and be subjected to the supporting naval bombardment, they preferred to remain inland. Hence there was little initial opposition and the two airfields were quickly captured. Only when the Americans turned south and came up against the Shuri Line did the fighting become intense, and not until the end of May did they break through.

LEFT: *Men of the 5th US Marines repel a counterattack on Okinawa, the last bastion before mainland Japan.* BELOW: *This photograph illustrates almost the entire paraphernalia involved in an amphibious landing operation, in this case Okinawa. The leading waves are already inland, but amphibious fighting vehicles are deployed to give them fire support. On the beach itself supplies and heavier equipment are beginning to arrive.*

At sea, Japanese aircraft were active from the start and a number of Allied ships fell victim to kamikaze attacks. Indeed, during the campaign no less than 34 were sunk and 368 damaged. The most dramatic event came, however, early on, on 6 April, when the pride of the Japanese Navy, the superbattleship *Yamato*, was sent on a suicide mission with insufficient fuel to return to base and no air cover, to disrupt the Allied shipping off the beaches. She was quickly spotted and at midday on the 7th was sunk by some of Mitscher's carrier aircraft. With her died the Imperial Japanese Navy, whose life, from victory over the Chinese Fleet at Port Arthur in July 1894, could be said to have lasted a bare 50 years.

On 17 June 1945, the battle for Okinawa finally came to an end. It had cost the Japanese some 100,000 killed and the Americans 12,500 killed and 36,500 wounded. Only Japan itself now lay ahead. But if the Japanese had put so much into defending Iwo Jima and Okinawa, how much more would they put into defending their homeland?

LEFT: *Many Japanese, especially officers, preferred to commit hari-kari or suicide rather than surrender. They usually did this by disemboweling themselves with their swords.*
BELOW: *US Marines on Okinawa being moved up to the front line after a spell of rest. This was in the later stages of the battle, during the mopping-up operations.*

Fortress Japan

The American planners had recognized long before the war that Japan was heavily dependent on overseas trade, especially in obtaining the vital raw materials which she herself lacked. Consequently from very

early on, United States submarines began to prey on Japanese shipping routes. At the outbreak the United States Navy had only some 50 submarines, but by August 1944 this number had trebled. As the navy's strength rose, so did the number of sinkings, until mid-1944 when some 50 Japanese ships per month were being sent to the bottom of the ocean. In terms of mercantile tonnage, what this meant was that the six million tons which the Japanese had available in December 1941 had dropped to less than half by the end of 1944, and by war's end this had been halved yet again. At the same time, the Japanese never exploited their own submarine fleet as they should have done. Indeed, it never rose much above 60 submarines during the whole war.

By early 1945, however, it was not just the supply of raw materials which had been reduced to a trickle. The Japanese were becoming very short of food. While they had always had to import 20 percent of their rice requirements, a disastrous 1945 harvest aggravated the problem. Also, such was the dominance of American submarines in Japanese coastal waters by this stage that the Japanese fishing fleets hardly dared venture out, thereby depriving the people of another of their staple foods. Indeed, in early June 1945, the Army Deputy Chief of Staff declared that the war could not be prolonged beyond spring 1946 because the country would run out of food. Thus, the United States submarine force, although no more than two percent of the United States Fleet, played a very major part in the final defeat of Japan, and achieved what Hitler's U-boats had failed to do to Britain.

ABOVE: *B-29 Superfortresses in the skies above Japan, spring 1945. Their effect on Japanese industry and cities was devastating.*
RIGHT: *Final check for the crew of Easy's Aces for this their 16th operation along 'Hirohito's Highway,' as the air route from the Marianas to Japan was called.*
FAR RIGHT, ABOVE: *Incendiary bombs rain on the docks at Kobe, Japan's sixth largest city.*
FAR RIGHT, BELOW: *The air raid siren sounds and these Japanese schoolchildren run to their shelter.*

The rapidly weakening economy was not, however, the only thing which the Japanese had to worry about at the beginning of 1945. Apart from the worsening military situation and the fact that the Allies were creeping ever nearer the mainland, the Japanese people themselves were now feeling the weight of American airpower. On 15 June 1944 American aircraft based in southern China raided a steelworks at Yawata on Kyushu, the first raid on mainland Japan since the epic Doolittle operation of April 1942. The reason that the USAAF was able to resume attacks on Japan was the introduction into service of the massive B-29 Superfortress which could carry 10,000 pounds of bombs over 3000 miles. This offensive lasted only a short time, because the American bases in south China came under threat from the Japanese attacks there later in the summer. Once, however, the Marianas had been secured in August 1944 and suitable airfields had been built, the bombing offensive could be resumed, with greater bombloads being carried.

On 24 November 1944 no less than 111 B-29s took off from the Marianas to attack an aircraft factory in Tokyo, the first time that the capital had been attacked since the Doolittle raid. This was the start of an all-out offensive against Japanese industry. The Germans had been forced to disperse their industries around the countryside to try to minimize losses and the Japanese were compelled to do the same.

In early 1945 General Curtis LeMay was appointed to command 21st Bomber Command based in the Marianas and thus became responsible for the bombing campaign against Japan. He was not impressed by the accuracy of the daylight high-level bombing, and at the beginning of March he switched his aircraft to low-level bombing by night. More significantly, he ordered that the bombloads should be made up of incendiaries, rather than high explosive.

On the night of 9/10 March over 300 bombers took off and for three hours dropped incendiaries on Tokyo. Most Japanese houses were built of wood and the result was devastating. No less than 10 square miles of the city were completely destroyed and the official death toll

was put at 130,000. The damage was far greater than any raid against Germany had achieved, and during the next 10 days similar attacks were carried out on the cities of Kobe, Nagoya, and Osaka. The USAAF then ran out of incendiaries and there was a pause. There was a massive Japanese exodus from the cities and industrial production plummeted to an all-time low.

All too soon the offensive was resumed, with the bombload ever increasing. It soon became clear to the Japanese people that, faced with this level of destruction, the war could not be prolonged much longer. But what was the view of the leadership?

In spring 1945 Japanese Prime Minister Admiral Kantaro Suzuki commissioned a wide-ranging study into Japan's capacity to continue to

wage war. The conclusions were grim and for the first time peace was discussed openly in the Japanese cabinet. An approach was made to the Russian Ambassador to Tokyo with a view to using Russia as a go-between for negotiating a peace with the Western Allies and China. The Japanese military, however, who still held much influence over the government, reaffirmed their determination to fight on until the end, and the approaches to the Russians were temporarily ended. The peace party in the government was, however, undeterred and managed to obtain the Emperor's approval for negotiations with the Russians to be reopened. Moscow, however, did not respond to these overtures and by now it was mid-July and the Allied leaders were meeting at Potsdam with Truman, in the knowledge that he now possessed an untried but potentially devastating weapon which could quickly bring about Japan's surrender.

LEFT: *All that was left of downtown Tokyo after the US incendiary raids. It is as though the city had been hit by an atomic bomb.*
ABOVE: *The remnants of the Japanese midget submarine fleet in the destroyed dry dock at Kure. One of the mysteries of the war was why the Japanese did not make much effort to expand their submarine force.*
RIGHT: *Preparing themselves for the Allied invasion of their homeland, these soldiers sing a traditional song to the sea.*

The Ultimate Weapon

The technology that lay behind the development of the atomic bomb had its origins in the discovery of radioactivity by the Frenchman Henri Becquerel in 1895. During the next 35 years it was established that enormous energy could be generated from the nucleus of an atom when it was bombarded with particles. The leaders in this were two German scientists, Hahn and Strassman, and a Hungarian, Leo Szilard, who had settled in the United States. By 1939, teams in the States and several European countries were working on nuclear fission and it seemed that the concept of a nuclear bomb was at least feasible, but there were many major technical obstacles that had to be overcome.

With the outbreak of war the pace quickened. The British and French pooled their resources, and it looked like a race between them and the Germans over who could produce a bomb first. When Britain stood alone and began to look to the United States for help, she was prepared to give her knowledge to the Americans. Once the United States entered the war it soon became clear that only she had the resources to bring the project to fruition and in June 1942 Roosevelt and Churchill formally agreed that she should take the lead in what became known as the Manhattan Project.

There were constant fears that the Germans were ahead in the race, and Allied attention in 1942 concentrated on the heavy water plant at Rjukan in central Norway. After one disastrous attempt in October 1942, Norwegian saboteurs carried out a successful operation against the plant the following February, which put the Germans behind. They managed to restore production, and another successful mission was carried out against the plant in February 1944. The other bonus the Allies had at this time was that the leading nuclear physicist of the time, Niels Bohr, had managed to escape from his native Denmark and settle in Britain. During 1943 the first nuclear reactor was constructed at Oak Ridge, Tennessee. The center of Project Manhattan then moved west to Los Alamos, in California, where gradually the first bombs were constructed.

Such were the technical problems that had to be overcome that it was not until July 1945 that the scientists actually had a bomb with which to carry out a test. On 15 July, at 0530 hours local time, the first nuclear device was successfully detonated, and the news was immediately transmitted to President Truman, then in conference with the other Allied leaders at Potsdam.

The decision to use the atomic bomb against Japan was, however, not one which was lightly taken. Almost all Truman's military advisers did not consider it necessary, arguing that the maritime strangulation and conventional bombing campaigns were sufficient to bring Japan to her knees in a very short time, even without an invasion. It was now known that Japan was putting out peace feelers, and the only sticking point appeared to be unconditional surrender, which the Potsdam Conference had reaffirmed. Yet, it was known that there was still a sizeable militarist element, determined to fight on to the bitter end, in the Japanese government. If this gained the upper hand, invasion would become inevitable and it would, given recent experience in the Pacific, be very costly in Allied lives. Furthermore, there was a suspicion in Western circles that Stalin, now ready to enter the war against Japan, was only interested in making territorial gains. The longer the war dragged on with the Russians involved, the higher Stalin's demands would be.

On 26 July 1945 Truman, Churchill and Chiang Kai-shek issued a final ultimatum to Japan. There was no immediate response, but on 2 August the Japanese Ambassador to Moscow made an approach to Molotov, who refused to see him until the 8th. That same day, the 2nd, was the deadline which the Western Allies had agreed for a Japanese response. Truman therefore ordered that the atomic bomb be used.

On 6 August, a B-29 called *Enola Gay* took off from Tinian and at 0815 hours local time dropped an atomic bomb on the city of Hiroshima. The resultant detonation killed some 80,000 people outright, seriously injured another 37,000, and literally devastated four square miles of the city. Debate between the peace and war factions within the Japanese government became intense, the only agreement being that the institution of the Emperor must be maintained at all costs. There was no response to the Allies, and so Truman ordered a second,

LEFT: *The crew of the* Enola Gay, *who dropped the atomic bomb on Hiroshima.*
BELOW LEFT: *The mushroom cloud which marked the atomic detonation on Nagasaki.*
RIGHT: *'Little Boy,' the bomb that was dropped on Hiroshima. It was 10ft long and had an explosive equivalent of 20,000 tons of TNT.*
BELOW: *The Hiroshima Fire Department's base, 4000ft from ground zero.*

and only remaining operational bomb, to be dropped. This took place on the 9th, the victim this time being the city of Nagasaki. The day before, the Russian government had informed the Japanese Ambassador to Moscow that they were declaring war, and on the 9th they launched a lightning thrust into Manchuria.

It was now that the Japanese finally gave a positive reaction, but in an unprecedented way. The Emperor, who was deified as a god, and who never spoke in public, realized that only he could now break the deadlock and save his people further suffering. At a cabinet meeting on the 10th, Hirohito spoke for the first time. He sided with the peace faction and ordered that a message be sent to the Allies expressing his country's willingness to surrender unconditionally. The Allied response was that the Emperor would be 'subject to' the Supreme Commander for the Allied Powers and that the people of Japan must be given the democratic right to decide what form of government they wanted in the future. This caused another debate within the Japanese cabinet, which was again only resolved by the intercession of Emperor Hirohito on the 14th. Some fanatical officers tried to overthrow the government, believing that it had misled the Emperor, but widescale unrest was prevented by another unprecedented step on the part of Hirohito. He broadcast to his people on the radio.

Because of the vast distances involved, it took time to arrange the formal surrender. Finally, on 2 September 1945, on board the battleship USS *Missouri*, the Japanese delegates signed the surrender in the presence of General Douglas MacArthur. World War II, the most devastating conflict in history, had finally ended.

The Cost

For the victorious Allies, World War II had achieved its aim of ridding the world of fascism, both Western and Oriental. The cost, however, had been enormous. During the six years that the war lasted no less than 50 million human lives were lost. Yet, of these, less than one fifth were combatants. It had been truly total war, with civilians as much as armed forces being in the firing line.

In terms of the losses suffered by each country, the Russians had the highest, with 20 million killed, while the lowest of the major combatant powers was the United States, with 300,000, but these last were almost entirely military. Yet in terms of proportion, Poland, where the war had started in 1939, came off worst, with 22 percent of her prewar population being killed in one way or another.

The vast loss of human life was but one factor. Whole regions of the world had been devastated. Japan and Germany were in ruins, as was much of western Russia. Britain bore the scars of the Blitz and her European allies those of the fighting on land which had taken place in their countries. Elsewhere, too, in China, Burma and the Pacific, much physical damage had been wrought. In many countries industry had been destroyed. This and the sheer cost of waging war meant that national economies were at rock bottom. The only exception to this was the United States which had not been physically attacked. Her 'arsenal of democracy' policy meant that not only was her industry flourishing as never before, but all those countries which had fought on the Allied side were in her financial debt, debts which they could not hope to repay for a very long time.

Furthermore, the peoples of Europe and elsewhere were physically and mentally exhausted. Restricted food supplies, long working hours, and the general discomforts of wartime life had sapped their energy. Many, too, bore physical and psychological scars, some of which would be with them for the rest of their lives. There were those who had been wounded in battle, those who had lost loved ones, the survivors of the concentration camps and Japanese prisoner-of-war

camps, and the fire and radiation victims of Hiroshima and Nagasaki. There were those who had lost their homes and others who had lost their countries.

Much needed to be done to make good the damage that had been inflicted. For a start, the world had to be made a more peaceful place and steps taken to ensure that such a conflict as had just occurred would never happen again. The ideals that had been laid down in the August 1941 Atlantic Charter had been pursued further while the war

ABOVE: *'Man's inhumanity to man.' A barely alive concentration camp inmate discovered by US forces at Nordhausen, Germany. Liberation has probably come too late to save this victim.*
LEFT: *French recognition for an American soldier's sacrifice, Normandy, June 1944.*

was still being fought. From this arose the concept of the United Nations, which it was hoped would be more effective in keeping world peace than its predecessor, the League of Nations. The detailed structure for it had been worked out at a two-stage conference held at Dumbarton Oaks, Washington DC in late summer 1944. The United Nations Charter itself was produced at the San Francisco Conference attended by 50 nations in the spring and early summer of 1945, and the Charter came into force on 24 October 1945.

As for the more immediate problems, the Allies now found themselves saddled with having to look after the populations of Japan and Germany. They had to be fed and, in many cases, housed, as well as governed. Much needed to be done before they could attain a reasonable degree of self-sufficiency once more. Furthermore, people had to be re-educated, especially in Germany, and those who had been responsible for the horrific crimes committed had to be brought to justice. There were, too, many people in Europe who for one reason

ABOVE: *The suffering that was Russia's. Russian peasant women mourn their dead in a newly liberated village.*
RIGHT: *In stark contrast, US troops returning home are reunited with their wives. Others, though, suffered break up to their marriages because they had been gone too long.*

or another had nowhere to go, the so-called Displaced Persons, and they, too, had to be looked after.

It was essential that national economies be restored to a peacetime footing. It soon became clear, however, that many European nations could not do this on their own, and eventually the United States came to the rescue with the Marshall Plan, named for its originator, General George C Marshall.

There were, however, many problems which were not immediately apparent at the end of the war, and which were, in years to come, to provoke much tension. It had been the hope in the West that, as fellow victors, they would be able to live amicably with communist Russia, but this soon proved not to be so. Stalin became increasingly suspicious of Western intentions. At the same time, determined that his country should never suffer as she had during the years 1941-45, he resolved to make a buffer of Eastern Europe and gradually installed communist governments there. This was not through democratic elections, as had been agreed by him with the other wartime leaders, and neither was his gradual sealing off of the Russian zone of occupation in Germany from the remainder of the country in line with wartime agreements. In addition, it seemed that he was bent on exporting communism abroad. A resurgence of civil war in Greece, his support for Mao Tse-tung in China, and communist-inspired unrest in Southeast Asia, all seemed to point to this. Tensions between East and West would increase still further once Russia successfully exploded her first nuclear device in 1949, and the world took on the appearance of two armed camps.

Another problem was one that affected the British. There had been agitation by Indians for self-government long before the war started. The early reverses suffered by the British in the Far East had demonstrated that they were not infallible, and served to increase political

LEFT: *Berlin women begin to repair the ravages to their city.*
BELOW LEFT: *For these concentration camp inmates liberation has come in time and they will survive, but many others will be left with no home or country to go back to.*
RIGHT: *The pity of war.*
BELOW: *The perpetrators are finally brought to justice, Nuremberg, 1946.*

agitation, not only in India, but elsewhere, especially in countries which had suffered Japanese occupation. There was also a feeling that Indians had contributed to Britain's war effort and deserved to be given the right of self-determination as a reward. This created unrest which taxed Britain's already severely strained resources.

Many European Jews, those who had survived the barbarities inflicted on them during the past few years, wanted to start a fresh life elsewhere, and looked to Palestine. But this was shared with the Arabs, and as the influx of Jews from Europe increased in spite of efforts made to control it, so the Arabs became more resentful.

None of these problems was going to go away in a hurry, and many remain with us today, the legacy of 1939-45.

Picture Credits

The publisher would like to thank Martin Bristow, who designed this book; Wendy Sacks, the editor; Melanie Earnshaw and Mandy Little, the picture researchers; and Ron Watson, the indexer. We would also like to thank all the picture agencies and individuals listed below and, particularly, The Imperial War Museum, London, who supplied all the illustrations except for the following (B = bottom, C = center, L = left, R = right and T = top):
Archiv Gerstenberg: pages 21T, 24B, 30R, 52T, 57BR, 68B, 73T, 74B, 80T, 83T, 101B, 102T, 118B, 135B, 166B, 178, 179(both), 193TR, 206T, 210T, 217CR, 218B, 221T, 230; Australian War Memorial: page 186B; BBC Hulton Picture Library: pages 48B, 82T, 150T; BBC Hulton/Bettmann Archive: pages 16B, 78T, 91B, 99(both), 126B, 130, 136B, 144T, 146T, 184T, 187TR, 200T, 206B, 209T, 212B, 227T, 232(both), 235B; Bison Picture Library: pages 1, 6B, 11, 14B, 22TL, 23, 31T, 32T, 33T, 34(both), 35T, 36B, 37T, 38T, 39, 40B, 46, 48T, 53(all 3), 54T, 59B, 64, 65T, 70R, 79(both), 84, 85B, 87T, 88, 89T, 93TL, 95TR, 96B, 97, 101L, 120T, 145T, 149B, 161T, 162T, 174B, 180R, 194B, 198(both), 200B, 212T, 215, 219B, 220(both), 221B, 229B, 231(both), 235T; ECP Armées: page 113T; John Frost Newspapers: page 41(T inset); Robert Hunt Library: pages 2-3, 6T, 12T, 13(both), 14T, 15, 16T, 20T, 21B, 25T, 29(both), 30L, 31B, 32T, 36T, 37B, 40T, 45T, 56T, 57BL, 58B, 63, 67T, 68T, 69T, 70L, 71, 72, 73B, 74T, 78B, 91T, 93B, 95TL, 96T, 100, 102B, 104T, 106B, 107T, 108T, 109B, 112T, 114B, 115(both), 116(both), 117T, 118T, 126T,
137, 138B, 139(both), 140(both), 144B, 145B, 149T, 152(both), 154(both), 156T, 158R, 159(both), 160(both), 161B, 165(all 3), 169C&B, 170(both), 172T, 174T, 175, 176B, 177T, 180L, 181T, 186T, 188T 189, 191B, 193L, 196B, 197T, 199B, 207B, 208B, 209B, 214T, 218T, 219T, 223B, 225B, 226(both), 228B; The Mansell Collection: page 26L; Collection of Charles Messenger: pages 142T, 151B; Peter Newark's Western Americana: pages 7, 42T, 55; Novosti Press Agency: pages 75(both), 76(top 2), 120B, 121(both), 132T, 133TR&B, 134, 135T, 156-7; Pictorial Press: pages 22TR, 26R, 51, 66B, 67B, 76B, 119T, 155, 157, 210B, 211(both); Royal Marines Museum: page 110; TPS/Central Press: pages 4-5, 17B, 28B, 41T, 44B, 45B, 49B, 82B, 98B, 119B, 158L, 237B; TPS/Fox Photos: pages 25B, 42B, 50TL&B, 85TR, 103T, 129T; TPS/Keystone: pages 27BL, 47B, 56B, 69B, 77, 103B, 110T, 114T, 125, 127B, 138T, 164(both), 173, 177B, 181B, 185B, 188B, 190B, 192B, 195B, 201, 214BL&R, 216B, 222(both), 223T, 225T; TPS/Three Lions: pages 19B, 24T, 27T&R, 92L, 101R, 131; TRH: pages 150B, 176T, 187L&B; US Air Force: pages 98T, 153T, 162B, 169TL, 228T, 233B; US Army: pages 92R, 108B, 113B, 136T, 143T, 168B, 171(both), 191T, 192T, 224B; US Defense Department/Marine Corps: page 117B; US Marine Corps: pages 183B, 227B; US National Archives: pages 90, 111B, 166T, 167B, 183T, 208T, 224T; US Naval Historical Center: pages 94T, 106T, 107B; US Navy: pages 104B, 105(both), 168T, 182(both), 185; US Signal Corps: page 199T.

SELECT BIBLIOGRAPHY

Allen, Louis Burma: The Longest War, 1941-45 (London: J M Dent, 1984)
Blumenson, Martin The Patton Papers: 1940-1945 (Boston: Houghton Mifflin, 1972)
Brett-Smith, Richard Hitler's Generals (London: Osprey, 1976)
Cooper, Matthew The German Air Force 1933-1945: An Anatomy of Failure (London: Jane's, 1981)
Foot, MRD SOE: The Special Operations Executive 1940-46 (London: BBC, 1984)
Graham, Dominick & Bidwell, Shelford Tug of War: The Battle for Italy, 1943-45 (London: Hodder & Stoughton, 1986)
Horne, Alistair To Lose a Battle: France 1940 (London & New York: Macmillan, 1969)
Lewin, Ronald Ultra Goes to War: The Secret Story (London: Hutchinson, 1978)
Lewin, Ronald The Other Ultra: Codes, Ciphers and the Defeat of Japan (London: Hutchinson, 1982)
Liddell Hart, B H History of the Second World War (New York & London: Putnam & Cassell, 1970)
MacIntyre, Donald The Naval War Against Hitler (London: Batsford, 1971)
Messenger, Charles 'Bomber' Harris and the Strategic Bombing Offensive, 1939-1945 (London: Arms & Armour & New York: St Martins, 1984)
Morison, Samuel Eliot The Two Ocean War (New York: Little, Brown, 1963)
Office of the Chief of Military History, Department of the Army Command Decisions (New York: Harcourt Brace, 1959 & London: Methuen, 1960)
Russell of Liverpool, Lord The Scourge of the Swastika: A Short History of Nazi War Crimes (London: Cassell, 1954)
Russell of Liverpool, Lord The Knights of the Bushido: A Short History of Japanese War Crimes (London: Cassell, 1958)
Seaton, Albert The Russo-German War 1941-45 (New York: Praeger, 1981)
Shirer, William L The Rise and Fall of the Third Reich: A History of Nazi Germany (London: Secker & Warburg, 1960)
Smith, R Harris OSS: The Secret History of America's First Central Intelligence Agency (University of California Press, 1972)
Strawson, John The Battle for North Africa (New York: Scribner, 1969)
Toland, John The Rising Sun: The Decline and Fall of the Japanese Empire 1936-1945 (New York: Random House, 1970)
Tuchman, Barbara W Stilwell and the American Experience in China, 1911-1945 (New York: Macmillan, 1971)
Warner, Philip The Secret Forces of World War II (London: Granada, 1985)
Weighley, Russell Eisenhower's Lieutenants: The Campaigns of France and Germany 1944-1945 (Indiana University Press & London: Sidgwick & Jackson, 1981)
Winton, John War in the Pacific: Pearl Harbor to Tokyo Bay (London: Sidgwick & Jackson, 1978)